MW00990351

Isherwood on Writing

....

Books by Christopher Isherwood
Published by the University of Minnesota Press

Christopher and His Kind

The Condor and the Cows: A South American Travel Diary

Down There on a Visit

Kathleen and Christopher: Christopher Isherwood's Letters to His Mother

Lions and Shadows: An Education in the Twenties

A Meeting by the River

The Memorial

My Guru and His Disciple

Prater Violet

A Single Man

Where Joy Resides: A Christopher Isherwood Reader

The World in the Evening

Isherwood on Writing

Christopher Isherwood

Edited by James J. Berg

Foreword by Claude J. Summers

MINNESOTA

University of Minnesota Press

Minneapolis • London

Published by the University of Minnesota Press
111 Third Avenue South, Suite 290
Minneapolis, MN 55401-2520
http://www.upress.umn.edu

Library of Congress Cataloging-in-Publication Data

Isherwood, Christopher, 1904–1986.
Isherwood on writing / Christopher Isherwood ; edited by James J. Berg ; foreword by Claude J. Summers.
p. cm.
Includes bibliographical references and index.
ISBN: 978-0-8166-4693-7 (alk. paper)
ISBN-10: 0-8166-4693-7 (alk. paper)
1. Isherwood, Christopher, 1904–1986. 2. Fiction—Authorship. 3. Authorship. I. Berg, James J. II. Title.
PR6017.S5Z46 2007
823'.912—dc22

2007031467

Printed in the United States of America on acid-free paper

The University of Minnesota is an equal-opportunity educator and employer.

14 13 12 11 10 09 08 07 10 9 8 7 6 5 4 3 2 1

Contents

Foreword

Claude J. Summers

The lectures that Christopher Isherwood delivered at California universities in the late 1950s and early 1960s are fascinating on a number of levels. Reading them fifty years after they were originally delivered is to observe an accomplished and versatile artist in the process of evolving. It is also to feel acutely—through their reticences and euphemisms—the constraints he felt then at speaking openly about homosexuality even at liberal universities before congenial audiences. The lectures offer us a valuable glimpse into a thoughtful writer's literary strategies and theories at a pivotal moment in his life, a time when he is redirecting his career. They also capture the legendary charm of a practiced public performer.

But most important, the lectures show Isherwood struggling toward an apologia that can account not only for the work that would have been best known to his audience at the time (the novels of the 1930s) but also for the work that he was contemplating at some degree of consciousness, the writing of the remarkable period of productivity that would yield *Down There on a Visit* (1962), *An Approach to Vedanta* (1963), *A Single Man* (1964), *Ramakrishna and His Disciples* (1965), *A Meeting by the River* (1967), *Kathleen and Frank* (1971), *Christopher and His Kind* (1976), and *My Guru and His Disciple* (1980). The lectures look both backward and forward, explaining what he had already written and adumbrating the books that were to follow.

Isherwood's lectures bear some resemblance to E. M. Forster's *Aspects of the Novel* (1927), which originated as the Clark Lectures at Trinity College, Cambridge. The two sets of lectures share a colloquial style and the mask of a "ramshackle course" (as Forster phrased it) that disguise their ambition. Both writers eschew critical systems and technical rigor in favor of a relaxed and intensely personal approach. For all their unpretentiousness and apparent modesty, however, the lectures are ideological documents that reveal and implicitly defend each author's practice. More particularly, both sets of lectures betray a yearning for ontological completeness that transcends merely technical aspects of plot, pattern, and characterization and that, in effect, defines the distinctive artistic credo of each writer.

Although both writers speak insightfully about problems of technique, they always connect the technical to larger issues. At the heart of Forster's book is his discussion of prophecy and fantasy, which implicitly defends his own work and reflects the romantic ideology that informs both his theory and practice of fiction. At the heart of Isherwood's lectures is the similar but more specifically religious vision that had already been expressed, albeit obliquely, in *Prater Violet* (1945) and *The World in the Evening* (1954), and which would become even more central in his subsequent writing. The foundation of Isherwood's later work is an awareness of "the pain of hunger beneath everything," as he phrased it in *Prater Violet,* an awareness that helped create what Alan Wilde some years ago described in his biography of Isherwood as the novelist's "double vision of man seen through his own eyes and, as it were, through those of God."

In the lectures Isherwood offers a wealth of interesting material about his books, describes his influences, discusses techniques of composition and characterization, considers the problems of narrating in the first person, expounds on the difference between writing for the stage and the cinema, expresses his admiration for outsiders and his belief in individualism, contends that he writes "in order to find out what my life means and who I am," explains the crucial concepts of the anti-heroic hero and the Truly Weak Man, delineates his and Auden's contributions to the plays and travel book on which they collaborated, usefully distinguishes between his novels that are "real constructed, contrived" works and those that are extended portraits, and in passing makes intriguing comments about other writers (especially

Melville, Tolstoy, Forster, and D. H. Lawrence)—but the "nerve of interest" of the lectures is spirituality. The informing idea of Isherwood's theory and practice of fiction is that "the novelist works simultaneously in a novel on two levels," the level of the human and the level of the divine, depicting the circumstances of everyday life but also looking down on his creation with "the eye of eternity."

The highest achievements in art, Isherwood insists, convey "a kind of super joy, a joy in experience, which contains both the ordinary concept of pleasure and happiness and also the ordinary concept of sorrow." This kind of joy that accepts the whole of human experience expresses a "transcendental vitality" and a love of the Creation that is called *agape* by Christians but that Isherwood designates as "compassion." Although the writer must be passionately engaged in the action—delineating the characters, describing the scene, breathing life into the story, and so on—"another part of the writer must look down on the action with what—for want of a better word—one could call compassion."

Isherwood derived his spiritual approach to the works of his American period from his immersion in Hinduism, and he freely acknowledges this debt in the lectures, but he quite deliberately illustrates the presence of the "super joy" that is the necessary condition of great art not by reference to Eastern religious works but by citing a variety of Western authors, including some whose work is not usually regarded as religious at all. Although his spiritual awareness is rooted in Vedantic ideas, he is by no means parochial, recognizing as he does that other traditions reach similar conclusions and communicating an attitude of tolerant ecumenism.

Tellingly, in his most explicit moment of "moralizing" in the lectures, Isherwood boldly distinguishes his beliefs from those of Christianity by dismissing the central Christian concept of sin, remarking that he finds it psychologically difficult to believe "that certain actions offend a supreme Being; and that we should feel guilty because that Being has been offended by our actions." In Hinduism, he continues, "I found a concept which to me was much more helpful, and might be more helpful to some of you, and that was to regard the sins not as sins in this sense, but as obstacles."

The influence of Hinduism in the later novels tends to be expressed subtly and unobtrusively, enriching but not burdening the works. In the novels, Isherwood most often translates Vedantic concepts into the familiar language of Western religion and psychology. In *The World in the Evening,* for example, Quaker spirituality serves as a vehicle for communicating Eastern ideas. Only in *A Meeting by the River,* which is set in a Hindu monastery on the banks of the Ganges near Calcutta, does Isherwood explicitly evoke Vedantism, and even there the religious view can plausibly be interpreted in psychological terms.

In his greatest novel, *A Single Man,* Isherwood never mentions Hinduism or Vedantism, or even evokes Christianity directly, yet he manages to write a great religious novel, according to the criteria outlined in the lectures, depicting his Everyman hero in the ordinary circumstances of his life while also observing him through the eye of eternity. The religious texture of the novel is established through an elaborate and carefully orchestrated series of allusions to Western and Eastern spiritual concepts and texts. Concerned though it is with death and decay and grief and the disparity between body and spirit, *A Single Man* is nevertheless a sacred comedy, brilliantly conveying the "super joy" the author identifies as the necessary condition of great art. Surely, as Isherwood prepared these lectures, he was grappling with particular problems that he knew he would face in the novels that he hoped to write in the future. One of the pleasures of reading the lectures is to observe how the ideas expressed in them bear fruit in the works to come.

The lectures confront directly the question of depicting spirituality in the novel, which was to be one of Isherwood's two major preoccupations in the later work, but they resolutely avoid any extended engagement with the other, namely, the presentation of homosexuality. Because we so often look back on Isherwood from the perspective of the end of his life, when he became closely identified with the movement for homosexual rights that developed in the late 1960s and the 1970s and in speeches and interviews talked freely about homosexual oppression and the aspirations of gay men and lesbians, we sometimes forget the difficulties the movement faced, not least from the unspoken assumption in the early 1960s that homosexuality was not a topic to be mentioned in polite society.

Although Isherwood would not come out in print as a homosexual until the publication of *Kathleen and Frank* in 1971, his homosexuality was an open secret in the literary world in the early 1960s, and many people who attended the lectures would have been aware of it. Indeed, he had already become a cult figure among literate homosexuals, so it is likely that many members of the audience for these lectures were homosexual. Certainly, homosexuality's major influence on Isherwood's art would have been obvious to some of his auditors. After all, his interest in certain psychological predicaments and in recurring character types and themes, especially such mythopoeic types as the Truly Weak Man, the Truly Strong Man, and the Evil Mother, and such obsessions as war, The Test, the struggle toward maturity, and the search for a father, may all be directly or indirectly related to his homosexuality. His fascination with the anti-heroic hero, his rebellion against bourgeois respectability, his empathy for the alienated and the excluded, and his ironic perspective were all intertwined with his awareness of himself as a homosexual, as he would later make clear in *Christopher and His Kind.* Yet in the lectures, while Isherwood mentions these interests and influences, he pointedly (and understandably) fails to connect them with his sexuality, which is never mentioned.

Many who attended the lectures would certainly have known that homosexuality features in the early novels in many guises, from the repressed passions of *All the Conspirators* (1928) to the fuller depictions of homosexual characters and situations in *The Memorial* (1932); and from the coyly comic portrait of Baron Kuno von Pregnitz, whose secret fantasies revolve around English schoolboy adventure stories, in *The Last of Mr. Norris* (1935), to the spoiled homosexual idyll of Peter Wilkinson and Otto Nowak in *Goodbye to Berlin* (1939). Moreover, the references in the beautifully written penultimate passage of *Prater Violet* to the narrator's lovers—designated by letters of the alphabet—were widely interpreted as covert allusions to the author's own homosexual liaisons. And in *The World in the Evening,* Isherwood not only presented a famous articulation of a homosexual aesthetic, "High and Low Camp," but he also created, in the character of Bob Wood, one of the earliest sympathetic portraits of a gay activist. Isherwood's presentation of homosexuality unapologetically and without the self-consciousness and melodrama that marked contemporaneous treatments of the subject had earned him a reputation as a writer particularly associated with homosexuality.

Homosexuality, therefore, was a topic that Isherwood's readers might well have expected him to confront in these lectures. Yet, except for a brief discussion of the problem of depicting the bisexual Stephen Monk in *The World in the Evening* and some comments on the "Ambrose" section of *Down There on a Visit* in "The Autobiography of My Books," where the subject could hardly be evaded entirely, Isherwood fails to broach the topic directly. He does mention that one of the themes of *The Memorial* is homosexuality, but then abruptly changes the subject.

This absence of homosexuality in the lectures is itself a kind of presence, for one of their most interesting aspects is how the topic of homosexuality is constantly in the background, alluded to in various guises and euphemisms, yet never brought to the fore. It is the elephant in the lecture hall that the lecturer refuses to address directly but which stubbornly makes its presence felt.

Homosexuality appears in the first of the lectures, "Influences," when Isherwood remarks that "my life as a writer has been mainly occupied in writing about people who don't fit into the social pattern," an observation that leads him to consider the "outsider, the constitutionally born member of a minority," and finally to declare that "the outsider is, should be, really, one of the most socially valuable people in the whole community." In a subsequent lecture, he defines the outsider as "somebody who realizes consciously that he belongs to a minority," adding that "every one of us does in one way or another." This is a rather unusual definition, and however well or ill it fits other groups it seems designed specifically to include homosexuals.

Isherwood's point that everyone is a member of one kind of minority or another is also made in *A Single Man.* In the novel, the author makes an important political point by presenting homosexuals as simply another tribe in a nation composed of many different tribes. In so doing, Isherwood is able to lessen the stigma against homosexuality by depicting homosexuals as a legitimate minority group with legitimate grievances against the oppressive majority, a depiction that was by no means widely shared in 1964 though it undoubtedly owes something to Donald Webster Cory's pioneering *The Homosexual in America* (1951). Whereas the minority consciousness of homosexuals and their oppression are crucial themes of *A Single Man,* balanced and qualified by a transcendent religious vision, in the lectures the references to the outsider and the "constitutionally born member of a minority" function as euphemisms or, viewed more positively, as coded allusions.

Similarly, in "The Autobiography of My Books," when Isherwood discusses *The Dog Beneath the Skin* (1936), he refers to the "Freudian heresy" that "we should all try to conform to a norm." He explains that this idea is a heresy because "it was not held by Freud but is held by many analysts who, whether they admit it or not, secretly want to make everybody the same as everybody else, which is disastrous and quite contrary to the truths promulgated by Freud, who wanted people to adjust to their situation, which is something very different again." Clearly, the real subject here is not conformity but the abandonment of Freud's tolerance toward homosexuality by his disciples; while Freud was skeptical of any attempt to "cure" homosexuality, many of his followers in the 1950s and early 1960s, such as Edmund Bergler, Charles W. Socarides, and Irving Bieber, became advocates of "aversion therapy" and other psychoanalytic attempts to change homosexuals into heterosexuals. But rather than address the subject directly, Isherwood in the lectures felt constrained to generalize about the dangers of conformity.

Precisely because Isherwood did not feel that he could discuss homosexuality openly, even before a sophisticated audience, his generalizations about individualism and dissent also turn out to be coded statements that at once evade the subject and allude to it. For example, in "A Last Lecture," he confronts his own reticence: "Now, not to be mealymouthed, I shall be expected to tell you at this point just in what ways I do, in fact, dissent from what can be called the majority opinion." What follows is not, as one might expect, a bold declaration of his belief in sexual freedom, but a generalized paean to individualism that seems wrested from him: "To me the individual is the paramount fact. To me the State exists for the individual and not vice versa."

Such a statement would hardly stir much opposition, except perhaps from Communists or Nazis, neither of which were likely to be in the audience, but Isherwood uses it as a cover to express highly generalized support for libertarian attitudes toward sexuality, which are presented as more daring than they really were. "I am opposed to the interference of the law in the life of the private adult individual," Isherwood declares. "I do not believe that the law should interfere in his life while he is harming no one other than himself, which is always a matter of argument, and I, therefore, am opposed to those laws which interfere with his sexual life, with the life and occupations that he chooses to lead in private, and with the kind of books he chooses to read." Many members of the audience would, no doubt, have recognized this libertarian credo as a coded defense of homosexuality, especially since it echoes the language of the Wolfenden Report, the British government study that in 1957 unexpectedly recommended the decriminalization of homosexual activity among consenting adults in private. (The Wolfenden Committee declared, "It is not, in our view, the function of the law to intervene in the private life of citizens, or to seek to enforce any particular pattern of behaviour." The recommendations that homosexuality be decriminalized were not adopted into law until 1967, and then only for certain portions of Great Britain.)

It is important to emphasize that Isherwood's reticence in discussing homosexuality openly in the lectures is not a sign of his timidity but of the pervasive homophobia that gripped the United States in the early 1960s and that effectively silenced the nascent movement for equality, especially in public gatherings. In light of such pressures, Isherwood's daring in alluding to homosexuality in the lectures, and in developing homosexual themes and characters in his books, is all the more stunning.

The California lectures are an altogether welcome addition to Isherwood's published work. As James J. Berg observes in his admirably comprehensive introduction, the lectures "are crucial to understanding his later work and establishing the American Isherwood." They announce the spirituality to which his late art aspired and they complexly foreshadow the role he would assume as courage-teacher and liberationist.

Editor's Acknowledgments

This project was inspired by Christopher Isherwood's brief mention, in *Kathleen and Frank,* of lectures he gave in the early 1960s. I marked that paragraph in my copy of the book long before I wrote a word about Isherwood. Years later, when the Huntington Library acquired the Isherwood papers, I was one of the lucky first scholars to review what was in the collection. I was very pleased to see transcripts and cassette recordings of some of the lectures. This collection is the result of my initial curiosity and the early and constant support from the Christopher Isherwood Foundation and estate, the Huntington Library, the University of Minnesota Press, and the Minnesota Humanities Commission.

Don Bachardy deserves praise and thanks everlasting for supporting the work of scholars at the Huntington and elsewhere. He is assisted in this by James White, director of the Christopher Isherwood Foundation. Without their support, personal as well as financial, this book could not have happened.

Major assistance was granted by the Huntington Library, which awarded me the first Christopher Isherwood Foundation Fellowship to pursue this project. I was in residence at the library and completed much of this work from November 2002 to January 2003. I was invited back in September 2004 to deliver the first Christopher Isherwood lecture at the library, and that talk included an early version of the introduction to this volume. My thanks go to the big four at the Huntington, who will no doubt shepherd many more publications from that rich archive: Robert C. Ritchie, director of research; David Zeidberg, director of the library; Sue Hodson, curator of manuscripts; and Romaine Alstrom, director of readers' services.

This project was made possible in part with funding from the

Minnesota Humanities Commission in cooperation with the National Endowment for the Humanities and the Minnesota State Legislature. President Stanley Romanstein and vice president Jane Cunningham are to be commended for the scholar works-in-progress grant program. The Friends of the Minneapolis Public Library and the Schochet Center for GLBT Studies at the University of Minnesota cosponsored a public program, "Isherwood in America," in May 2003 in partial fulfillment of the grant obligations. My thanks to Colin Hamilton, president of the Friends; Rachel Fulkerson, program director; Kit Hadley, director of the Minneapolis Public Library; Linnea Stenson, then director of the Schochet Center (and now a fellow dean); and my panelists, Chris Freeman, Barrie Jean Borich, and Patrick Scully.

Many professional colleagues contributed insight, editorial comments, and support. Chris Freeman is that rare associate who shows interest, reviews drafts, and asks serious questions. Carola M. Kaplan is a frequent correspondent on Isherwood matters and enthusiastically read an early draft of the introduction. Lisa Colletta is a supportive voice from either coast. Several people, including Catherine Stimpson, Louis Crompton, Claude Summers, David Bergman, and the late Carolyn Heilbrun, helped track down information on various talks given by Isherwood. Mary Franson was an excellent transcriber. Colleagues at Lake Superior College kindly listened to a run-through of my Huntington talk and gave good feedback. Thanks also go to Gary Schiff, Greta Gaard, John McFarland, and Dan Luckenbill for their support and wisdom.

Introduction

The American Isherwood

James J. Berg

> I'll start off with a reassurance: in order to follow my remarks it's quite unnecessary to have read any of my books. Furthermore, the whole question as to whether these books have any literary merit or not is entirely academic as far as this discussion is concerned. What I am going to talk to you about is simply this: as a child of my time, I have been concerned with certain themes which are typical themes of the different periods of my life and I have written about them. And by describing these themes, and so by indirection the books that I wrote with these themes, I shall in fact be referring to other books with the same themes and to many things in your own reading experience, I hope. So let's rather forget my personal involvement in this and just follow the productions of this writer, this alleged writer, Isherwood, and see where we get.

So begins a lecture Christopher Isherwood gave at the University of California, Berkeley, in April 1963. In addition to describing his intentions and methods for the lectures, his statement reveals more than public modesty. He is excusing the members of his audience from having read many of his works, as any author might do in such circumstances, but his broad disclaimer also suggests that his standing in the academic community, invited lecturer or not, was in question. In talking at a university in 1963, Isherwood could not be assured that his audience had even heard of his work, much less read it. Certainly they could not be expected to have read anything other than *The Berlin Stories.* While this was a frustration for the author, it was a situation he understood and, as his introduction shows, accepted to a point.

The Berkeley lectures in 1963 were not Isherwood's first talks to California college audiences, although they were perhaps the most succinct. Previous lectures were given in 1960 at the University of California, Santa Barbara, and subsequently at the University of California, Los Angeles. This book collects for the first time transcripts, edited and annotated, from all three of these UC lecture series, and this introduction explores the issues I encountered working on Isherwood as his centenary approached and passed.

Among these issues are readership and literary reputation. Christopher Isherwood is chiefly known as a British Writer of the 1930s (the phrase seems to need capitalization) and as the author of the works that inspired *Cabaret.* His American work is less read and not much discussed in academic circles. Oddly, I find that this situation has little to do with whether Isherwood's books have any literary merit or not, as he said. For while sympathetic scholars and critics have been bemoaning Isherwood's neglect, none has identified the roots of that neglect. I suggest that the roots are British resentment and anti-Americanism, American East Coast snobbery, and general homophobia. And so, in addition to introducing Isherwood's lectures in California, my aim here is to examine his reputation and to focus on what I have come to call the "American Isherwood." I wish to lay out a new version of Isherwood, an American Isherwood on equal footing with the English or European Isherwood.

Christopher Isherwood built his European reputation as a writer on his early modernist novels, *All the Conspirators* (1928) and *The Memorial* (1932). These were critical if not commercial successes, and *The Memorial* was praised by E. M. Forster. Isherwood achieved commercial success and a measure of fame for his subsequent novels about Weimar Germany and the rise of the Nazis, *Mr Norris Changes Trains* (1935) and *Goodbye to Berlin* (1939). Later published in one volume as *The Berlin Stories* (1945), the novels developed Isherwood's style of semiautobiographical, even documentary-like, fiction and introduced his trademark eponymous narrator (William Bradshaw in the first, Christopher Isherwood in the second). He collaborated with W. H. Auden on three stage plays and a book about the war between Japan and China, *Journey to a War* (1939). He also wrote a fictionalized memoir, *Lions and Shadows* (1938). When Isherwood and Auden came to the United States in 1939, they were, together and separately, established literary figures.

The American period of Isherwood's life is well documented in his diaries, but there are still many misconceptions about his work and experiences in the United States. The diaries for the years 1945 to 1951 were published under the title *Lost Years,* which unfortunately supports the characterization of this period as one of dissipation and aimlessness.[1] On the contrary, the diary shows that Isherwood was continuing his attempt at "intentional living," working frequently if unhappily on the novel *The World in the Evening* (1954) and continuing to be engaged in the social and intellectual life of Los Angeles and the United States. He traveled to South America with his then-companion William Caskey and published an account of that journey in one of his lesser-known works, *The Condor and the Cows* (1949). These years also saw the first adaptation of Isherwood's *Goodbye to Berlin* in John van Druten's play *I Am a Camera,* produced in New York in 1951. The former Christopher William Bradshaw Isherwood became a citizen of the United States, Christopher Isherwood, in 1946.

Isherwood scholar Chris Freeman has suggested that these years comprise a critical, transitional period.[2] The transition from the Isherwood of London and Berlin to the American Isherwood may not have been smooth, but to call the years "lost" is to apply a moralistic judgment to a period of spiritual and artistic struggle. Once he had finally submitted *The World in the Evening* to his publisher in November 1953, Isherwood felt himself back into the business of writing. Throughout the rest of the decade he continued his creative activity, and then the 1960s included some of his most productive years in the United States, as well as his first substantial academic appointment.

In the 1960s, Isherwood produced his three final works of fiction, each of which shows a command of his craft and a clear artistic and social vision; *Down There on a Visit* (1962), *A Single Man* (1964), and *A Meeting by the River* (1967) are as good as anything Isherwood wrote in the 1930s. Indeed, these novels are much more mature and self-assured than the earlier writing. They are also more frank about sexuality than the often coy and self-consciously transgressive Berlin novels. Isherwood was a pioneer in writing about gay and bisexual characters, introducing them openly for the first time in *The World in the Evening,* in which he also posed the first written definition of camp as performance and an extended discussion of gays in the military. After 1964, with the success of *A Single Man,* a matter-of-fact portrayal of a gay college professor, Isherwood became more and more outspoken about his own homosexuality, finally coming out in print in *Kathleen and Frank,* his biography of his parents, and writing explicitly about his homosexuality in *Christopher and His Kind.*

Lectures as Self-Definition and Rediscovery

In the midst of this creative stage of the 1960s, Isherwood finally yielded to his mother's wishes and became a college professor. He was named visiting professor for the academic year 1959–60 at Los Angeles State College (now California State University, Los Angeles), where he taught courses on the modern novel. Like many writers, he seems to have done this partly for the money. Early in his first semester, he was dissatisfied with his courses, which he felt "lacked direction" (*Diaries* 1: 827). Yet before his term was over, he was asked by the University of California, Santa Barbara to be a visiting professor in the fall of 1960. More a celebrity guest speaker than a guest teacher, his appointment was connected to a series of public lectures titled "A Writer and His World."[3] Christopher Isherwood's lectures in California provide valuable new evidence of an American Isherwood: they reveal contexts, motivations, and origins for his novels, plays, screenplays, and other writings.

They also reveal Isherwood's views on his own work, something he did not write about in his diaries. For example, in discussing the gestation of his first novel, *All the Conspirators,* Isherwood relates his reaction to first learning about Sigmund Freud:

> I was writing fundamentally about the Freudian revolution which had just hit England with tremendous force. It was, of course, the greatest literary event of my time—and has been, I guess, in all countries where the Freudian ideas have had any acceptance whatsoever. For those of you who are younger, it's almost impossible to imagine the excitement with which we received the news that our parents were responsible for absolutely everything. It was all their fault, and we would never, never forgive. And what's more, all of the things that they said about morality and life were wrong and exploded and out of date.

Scholars have recognized the influence of Freud on Isherwood's early novels, of course. But Isherwood's recollections of the "Freudian revolution" have an immediacy and impact even in 1963. He does show an understanding that he may have overreacted, creating demon mothers and hero fathers.

The lectures also disclose Isherwood's ideas on writing and his views on other writers. In his notes for "A Last Lecture," he states concisely one of his central beliefs as a writer:

> I believe that the function of a writer is to be, first and foremost, an individual. He writes, ultimately, out of his experience. And he should think of himself as addressing a number of other individuals—not a mass.

Isherwood approached these lectures as a writer, and they came at a significant time for his work. His whole approach to narrative was changing in the late 1950s and early 1960s, as he was moving away from autobiographical fiction, away from the narrator called "Christopher Isherwood." His last use of "Christopher

Isherwood," the central consciousness in a third-person narrative, was in *Down There on a Visit.* This book was followed by a very tight third-person focus on George in *A Single Man* and an epistolary form (essentially, alternating first-person narrators) in *A Meeting by the River.* As the decade of the 1960s closed, Isherwood moved toward biography, writing about his parents and himself in *Kathleen and Frank,* and memoir, in the classic *Christopher and His Kind.*

His lectures not only facilitated his shift toward autobiography; they may, in fact, have instigated that move. In *Kathleen and Frank,* Isherwood indicates precisely how the book came about. Writing about himself in the third person, he says:

> About 1960, Christopher began to consider a project which he called The Autobiography of My Books; it was to be a discussion, as objective as possible, of the relation between his own life and the subject-matter of his books. . . . Before starting to write this Autobiography, Christopher tried thinking aloud about it by giving a series of lectures. But the lectures showed him he didn't know his subject sufficiently well. He needed to study his Family and his own childhood in depth.[4]

Eventually, Isherwood lectured at several universities in California for a decade before ever starting his final autobiographical works. He seems to have taken more care in preparing for a visiting post the next year at the University of California at Santa Barbara than he did for the previous courses at Los Angeles State College. The lectures in Santa Barbara helped Isherwood formulate his approach to autobiography. As he told an interviewer in 1965, the lectures "made me see the possibility of writing a slightly different kind of autobiography."[5] The first lecture illustrates this point: what was initially a one-hour talk became the five-hundred-page book *Kathleen and Frank.* The lectures reveal Isherwood's "thinking out loud" about his "subject"—his life and work.

When Christopher Isherwood lectured in California, he did

so not as an authority on literature, and certainly not as the brilliant lay critic he saw in Auden, but as a practitioner in the field of twentieth-century fiction and later as an openly gay author. One of his students at UCLA in 1965, Dan Luckenbill, has written about those sessions: "Isherwood did not lecture in the strict sense, and there were no examinations or papers. It would take me some years to realize that these sessions stemmed from fertile 'table talk' and interview talk. The range of topics was probably staggering for almost anyone attending, let alone those of us who were young students."[6] Luckenbill remarks that several of the anecdotes Isherwood tells in the lectures may also be found in published interviews.

When he began lecturing publicly, Isherwood was not shy about proclaiming his personal views. He spoke out against loyalty oaths in Santa Barbara in 1960 (see "A Last Lecture"), although his employment the previous year was predicated on his signing a loyalty oath for L.A. State College. Those looking for a coming-out statement in the lectures of the 1960s will be disappointed, as Isherwood steers clear of his own sexuality. The closest he would come to a public statement about his own sexuality would be to proclaim his allegiance to the American Civil Liberties Union and to protest laws restricting sexual behavior in private. This may be the greatest weakness of these lectures: the man who seemed to reveal so much of himself in his fiction held back in his public appearances. In fact, an article in the *UCLAN Review Magazine,* a UCLA publication, from summer 1959, begins: "Christopher Isherwood lives alone on a quiet suburban street that winds its way through Santa Monica."[7] Still, the lectures stand as products of a period in our cultural history; they were delivered while Isherwood was out of the closet in his private life but before he came out in print. Luckenbill's notes and recollections are supported by the transcripts from UCLA: "He did mention homosexuality when discussing the bisexuality of characters in *The World in the Evening*. . . . Isherwood did not reveal facts about his past love life, so when someone asked if Waldemar [in *Down There on a Visit*] were the same character as Otto [Nowak in *Goodbye to Berlin*], his reply was brief: 'He's a combination of a certain type of Berlin street boy'" (33). The lectures are an example of a man, comfortable in his own sexuality and self, trying to talk about himself and his own life in a society that is not yet ready to hear the whole story.

Careful, and even casual, readers of his work would not be surprised by the author's homosexuality, but his most clearly gay novel came after the Santa Barbara and Berkeley lectures. In *A Single Man,* the character George enacts the open secret of the closet as he shares clandestine looks with a gay student, whom he thinks of as his "little minority-sister." Later, with the ostensibly straight student Kenny, George chafes when he is referred to as "cagey."[8] Perhaps Isherwood felt himself to be cagey in his on-campus demeanor, aligned with the newly vocal gay minority by dint of his often-expressed liberalism but not yet publicly identified as a member of the minority. As Luckenbill recalls, "It was tempting to project pieces of George in *A Single Man* onto Isherwood, but none of them fit precisely. George's lover Jim was dead. Isherwood's was not, but it was not to be spoken of in public in that class at UCLA in the spring of 1965" (33). As the transcripts show, homosexuality was a "theme" to be discussed in Isherwood's work, not a personal issue to bring into the lecture hall.

Isherwood's reticence in the lectures may have led him toward a greater openness in his autobiographies, saying things in the 1970s that he chose not to say in the 1960s. He announced his homosexuality matter-of-factly in *Kathleen and Frank* in 1972 (1971 in Britain). Few transcripts exist of his talks after this period, when one might have expected him to self-identify as gay, or when he might have been invited specifically because he was an openly gay author. A version of his "Last Lecture" at the honors convocation at the University of Southern California in 1974 was recorded, and he was then ready and able to declare his membership not only in the ACLU but in the "homosexual minority."

In an interview in 1973, he explained his reasons, literary as well as personal, for keeping the sexual identity of his "Christopher Isherwood" narrator out of the early novels:

> I'm often asked if I regret that I didn't say outright in *The Berlin Stories* that I was homosexual. Yes, I wish I had. But I should have had to say it very casually, if I had said it; otherwise, I would have made the Christopher character too odd, too remarkable, and that would have upset the balance between him and the other characters. Christopher is the narrator, so he mustn't stand out too prominently. To have made him a homosexual, in those days, would have been to feature him as someone eccentric. I would have made a star out of a supporting actor. That's a valid literary reason. But I must also frankly say that I would have been embarrassed, then, to create a homosexual character and give him my own name.[9]

Isherwood saw himself as an advocate rather than an activist, and in the 1970s he was a frequent speaker at rallies and meetings on behalf of gay rights. But his greatest impact on the movement for gay and lesbian rights was as a writer, through his novels and memoirs, and only secondarily as a public figure. Several gay men have written about reading *The Berlin Stories* and *Lions and Shadows* and recognizing the gay characters in those books and feeling somehow affirmed in their own sexuality. Similarly, David Garnes, recalling reading *A Single Man* thirty years earlier, wrote: "What I remembered more than anything . . . was that Isherwood had created in this novel an intelligent character whose homosexuality was presented in a natural and life-affirming way."[10] For gay readers, *A Single Man* and *Christopher and His Kind* are probably Isherwood's most influential works.

One of Isherwood's most talked about public appearances later in life was his attendance at the Modern Language Association convention in New York City in 1974. He is listed in the program as giving "A Personal Statement" on a panel called "Homosexuality and Literature." Six months after the USC honors convocation, this speech seems to have had a different topic. No audiotapes or official notes were taken of what turned out to be a historic session for the MLA. Isherwood scholar Claude J. Summers recalls that Isherwood was working on *Christopher and*

His Kind at that time and the memoir provided the background text to the talk.[11] Also in attendance was Alan Wilde, who had already published a monograph on Isherwood. Wilde used the occasion in his essay "Language and the Surface: Isherwood and the Thirties," linking the MLA speech to Isherwood's life in the 1930s.[12] After spending nearly fifteen years lecturing about his life and writing his autobiographies, Isherwood was surely ready to speak the truth to the MLA. One can imagine him delivering this famous declaration on homosexuality and politics from *Christopher and His Kind*:

> [Christopher] became defiant when he made the treatment of the homosexual a test by which every political party and government must be judged. His challenge to each one of them was: "All right, we've heard your liberty speech. Does that include us or doesn't it?"[13]

Isherwood said later that what was remarkable about the MLA event was not that he came out but that the MLA "sat still for it."[14]

Christopher Isherwood's lectures in California in the 1960s provide fascinating documentation of a writer constructing his life story. The lectures are a key to a pivotal period as he shifted away from fiction toward autobiography, and they gave him inspiration and opportunity to examine his life in total as well as the intersections of his life and his work. His lectures in California are crucial to understanding his later work and establishing the American Isherwood.

Reading the American Isherwood

In what is likely to stand for quite some time as the definitive Isherwood biography, Peter Parker writes that "Isherwood's [literary] reputation seems assured."[15] He credits the work of scholars such as Chris Freeman and me as part of his evidence. But a broader survey of contemporary English and American literary scholarship on the twentieth century shows that Isherwood's literary reputation is far from settled.

Literary study as a discipline has been organized since the late nineteenth century on the principle of national literatures: a writer must either be English or American to be taught in the appropriate college courses. These boundaries are less strict when applied to twentieth-century literature, as the lives and careers of Henry James, T. S. Eliot, and Joseph Conrad attest. Yet the boundaries still have a strong influence, perhaps more in Britain than the United States. The easy association of a writer with a place or a period, Virginia Woolf and Bloomsbury, for example, or Charles Dickens with London in the nineteenth century, helps keep the writer's works clear in the minds of teachers, students, publishers, and bookstore clerks. The issues of identity and availability are illustrated by the common problem, in the 1990s, of college instructors who could not find enough copies of *A Single Man* for their students to buy. *The Berlin Stories,* which has been continuously in print since New Directions combined *The Last of Mr. Norris* and *Goodbye to Berlin* into one volume in 1945, has never had this problem.

In his essay "The American Auden," Peter E. Firchow examines the question of nationality and identity regarding W. H. Auden's life and work. Of all the British writers in the United States in midcentury, including Isherwood, Huxley, MacNeice, and Heard, Firchow claims, "only Auden was to identify himself unabashedly as an American."[16] Isherwood presented himself as a foreigner and an outsider in the United States, the better to describe or comment on America. For Auden, however, Firchow writes, "remaining an Englishman in America . . . would have meant remaining content with the role of sympathetic commentator on the sidelines. . . . But if he wished to shape his new world and not merely to observe it, he needed to be part of that world: he needed to become certifiably American" (185).[17]

Firchow also considers the question of Auden's influence on the next generation of American poets, citing the standard, somewhat ironic, view that Auden's early poetry is what mattered. His more difficult early poetry and his homosexuality had a profound impact on many American poets. Firchow cites Richard Howard as a poet for whom homosexuality was a truth

Auden taught others to "speak their minds about," as Howard put it. Firchow concludes, "That is something [gay poets] could not have done if they had not read him first or learned from his example" (195). Firchow maintains that Auden's work at American universities and for the Yale Younger Poets Series was significant: "though poetic influence should not be taken into account as a primary factor in determining Auden's American identity, it needs to be said that the Auden of the American period certainly exercised an influence on the readership and institutions of American poetry" (196). Isherwood likewise recognized that his American work influenced other writers as well as readers; his portrayal of George in *A Single Man* had a similar truth-telling effect on gay male fiction writers in the 1970s. Writers as diverse as Ray Bradbury, Alison Lurie, Armistead Maupin, and John Rechy came to him for help or thanked him for his encouragement.

While examining the American Isherwood, it is important to recognize that Isherwood may never have fully adopted that identity for himself. The combination of being English and being gay kept him feeling like an outsider. He said in an interview in 1960:

> You have to realize that I've never lived, since I've grown up, in any place as long as I've lived in America. I'm so completely habituated to living in America that everything else seems very remote from me. Now I don't mean by this that I don't feel foreign here, because I do. But that I like. And I think it sort of heightens one's awareness of things to feel a little bit out of it.[18]

This is a writer's answer, perhaps, indicating that he feels his powers of observation are stronger when he is somehow apart from the rest of society. How much of this stance is a pose it is not possible to say, but it seems that Isherwood tried to keep at arm's length from a fully American, or English, identity.

The issue of identity is complicated by the fact that Isherwood was strongly influenced by the Hindu notion of the self as an entity not altogether unified in itself and not entirely separate from the rest of the world. That nonunified identity is found in the narrative structure of his final three novels. In *A Single Man,* Isherwood constructs and deconstructs the main character, George, as both less than and more than the sum of his parts. In an early scene, George drives across Los Angeles from his home to his college, and his face becomes tense but his body remains "in a posture of perfect relaxation. More and more it appears to separate itself, to become a separate entity: an impassive anonymous chauffeur-figure with little will or individuality of its own" (35–36). George's body is no more "George" than that which is called his mind or his soul. Later, Isherwood links George to a greater unity by comparing his consciousness to the waters that fill and empty from tide pools on the California coastline:

> Just as George and the others are thought of, for convenience, as individual entities, so you may think of a rock pool as an entity: though, of course, it is not. The waters of its consciousness—so to speak—are swarming with hunted anxieties, grim-jawed greeds, dartingly vivid intuitions, old crusty-shelled rock-gripping obstinacies, deep-down sparkling undiscovered secrets, ominous protean organisms motioning mysteriously, perhaps warningly, toward the surface light. . . . And, just as the waters of the ocean come flooding, darkening over the pools, so over George and the others in sleep come the waters of that other ocean—that consciousness which is no one in particular but which contains everyone and everything, past, present and future, and extends unbroken beyond the uttermost stars. (183–84)

As Isherwood worked out this vision of the self in his fiction, so too he worked it out in his last published works, his autobiographies. In *Kathleen and Frank,* he refers to his child self in the third person, as "Christopher," who is no more his adult self than the "Christopher Isherwood" of *Down There on a Visit.* He continues this practice in *Christopher and His Kind,* retelling the

1930s life he invented for his namesake narrator but again trying to distinguish the self that lived the life from the older self who is telling it.

Certain scholars and critics have been decrying the devaluation of Isherwood's later work since at least 1971, when Alan Wilde identified the issue as "a failure to understand the nature of his vision."[19] The Preface to Wilde's study concludes this way:

> There is probably no living writer less justly valued at the present time than Christopher Isherwood, none, therefore, more in need of revaluation. . . . What has been accepted is Isherwood's importance to the literary history of the 1930s; what has still to be recognized is that, both before and since the war, he has been one of the period's most original ironists and one of its most valuable moral thinkers as well. (5)

Although Wilde's study helped to counter that estimation of Isherwood's American work, as did the few book-length studies (and articles and dissertations) since then, it is still true that what is generally accepted as Isherwood's contribution to literary history is primarily *The Berlin Stories,* and to put an even finer point on it, *Goodbye to Berlin.* For academics (and their students) the neglect of Isherwood's American work can be traced to the dominance of New Criticism in American universities in the postwar period. The New Critics' insistence on looking at "texts" quite apart from their authors hurt the reputation of such autobiographical writers as Isherwood. With the advent of feminist criticism, New Historicism, and queer theory, Isherwood's work has been examined anew in the context of his life, the rise of the gay rights movement, and the great changes occurring in American cultural life in the twentieth century. The Introduction and several essays in *The Isherwood Century* show as much.

Yet the received opinion is still that Isherwood's 1930s fiction is what ultimately matters to British and American critics. This seeming critical consensus is built on a complex set of overlapping assumptions and prejudices that include British and American homophobia, British anti-Americanism, and American East Coast–West Coast rivalries. Peter Parker's biography does not fully escape some of the standard British views of Isherwood's life, but it is more perceptive on the American novels than most British commentators. He writes, for example, "*A Single Man* is certainly Isherwood's most profound and most skillfully written book, one that seems all surface, but is properly engaged with that most important of subjects: what it is to be alive. In particular it is about what it is to be alive now, in the present, in Southern California" (727). For most British critics, Isherwood's American work is inconsequential because it is American; for most American critics, Isherwood does not figure in a discussion of American literature because he was born English and because he wrote from California. Both English and American academics continue to marginalize him because of homophobia. Only for feminist and gay and lesbian critics does the American Isherwood rate serious consideration.

The view of Isherwood as forever and only a writer of the 1930s has been stated and repeated by academics who established the twentieth-century modernist and postmodernist canon. Scholars who attempt a totalizing vision in such texts as *The Modern British Novel* and *The Penguin History of Literature* cite the modernist influences and variations in *All the Conspirators* and *The Memorial* and evaluate at length the documentary style of *Mr Norris Changes Trains* and *Goodbye to Berlin.*[20] When included in such surveys, which are almost invariably arranged by decades, Isherwood's European work is given careful study. In addition to the novels, *Lions and Shadows* (1938) is often seen as the history of the Auden group and is treated accordingly, and *Prater Violet* (1945), written and published from Los Angeles, is sometimes included as a follow-up to the Berlin novels.[21]

Treating Isherwood as a writer of the 1930s allows British critics to ignore the other great productive period of his career, namely, the 1960s. In fact, it seems almost de rigueur to dismiss his later novels in relation to his output of the 1930s. Two works published in the 1990s present this standard approach. In *The Penguin History of Literature,* Richard Jacobs writes that Isherwood's career illustrates "a paradigmatic retreat from the political to the personal" (240). At first Jacobs appears to give the later Isherwood serious attention when compared with the earlier work:

> In other respects, too, Isherwood's work is of a piece. *Mr Norris Changes Trains* . . . and *A Single Man,* for instance, have in common an emphasis on sexual transgression as a focus for meaning . . . and on those who survive against the indifference by treating events and emotions as stimulants to living (single man George's "hate" is a "stimulant—nothing more"). . . . As it happens, history is more urgent in *A Single Man* than in *Mr Norris,* surfacing as it does in unassimilated and casual references to bombs and Cuba, while in *Mr Norris* it functions as a garish stage-set. (241)

The limits of Jacobs's understanding become clear as he continues. Commenting on Isherwood's much-discussed narrator in the Berlin novels, he writes:

> The suppressions of the Berlin texts are more than adequately compensated for in the later works, among which *A Single Man* is notable for its sexual candor. Beginning with a bowel movement and ending with a genital spasm (in one of the period's semi-conscious gestures towards Joyce's *Ulysses*), it may be candid but, if the novel is embarrassing, it is not for this candour but because of its manifest dislike of people, its governing impulse of a disgust that is projected self-disgust. This is manifest in various ways, from open physical hatred of the woman's body, to routine arousal by young men sensed only as animals, to an arch and self-mocking inverted sexism . . . to sentimental references to the supposed mores of classical Greece. (242)

Jacobs is overwhelmed by the matter of the novel, embarrassed not only by its supposed sexual candor but also by its description of bodily functions. (A more dispassionate description of the novel's beginning and end would be that it starts with George waking and ends with his supposed death.) Jacobs's embarrassment stands in stark contrast to George's ironic stance toward heterosexuality being "distasteful" and toward the homosexuality depicted in Greek literature being "wholesome."

Jacobs's reaction to the novel nearly defeats his literary faculties, although he attempts to provide some literary critical perspective:

> Characters are stereotypically drawn, the boy Kenny more or less taken (unconsciously, it must be assumed) from Salinger's Holden Caulfield. Regressive in almost every way (apart from its modishly frank homosexuality), the novel has one scene regressive in a particularly interesting way. In it, George and Kenny swim late at night, drunk . . . The images of purifying, baptism, refugees and borders significantly belong to pre-war and early wartime texts. (242–43)

While Jacobs's complaint about stereotypical characters may have merit, he does not offer any evidence of his claim. Further, he gives Isherwood insufficient credit for knowing what he is doing—identifying his debts to Joyce and Salinger as "semi-conscious" or "unconscious."[22] Even in literary critical terms, it becomes clear that Jacobs does not understand the late Isherwood. I would suggest that the images of purification and baptism are not merely a reaching back to prewar texts (the scene is reminiscent of the "sacred lake" in *A Room with a View*) but also owe a debt to Isherwood's study of Vedanta and Hindu texts as well as his involvement with Southern California beach culture. The images of borders and refugees may relate to Europe and Mortmere, but they owe at least as much to California and Mexico (as we can see from *Down There on a Visit*) and from being the outsider (gay, in this instance) in a world organized against him. Finally,

Jacobs betrays the most common fallacy of literary criticism: *A Single Man* is acknowledged as one of the first and most matter-of-fact treatments of homosexuality in modern fiction, yet Jacobs reduces the entirety of George's sexual identity to an attempt by the author to be trendy.

Richard Jacobs seems at times to be writing in response to Malcolm Bradbury, who includes Isherwood's Berlin fiction in his study *The Modern British Novel.* Where Jacobs sees the place of history in Isherwood's novels, and the novels' treatment of history, Bradbury is not impressed:

> But the later fiction is work essentially of personal narrative rather than historical diagnosis. *The World in the Evening* (1954) deals with what is really sexual boredom in the Cold-War, comfortably alienating USA. *Down There on a Visit* (1962) returns him to his old life in the 1920s and 1930s, but acknowledges his role as essentially that of the tourist in history. (232)

Bradbury's rhetoric is disturbingly dismissive. One could argue that to portray the United States as "comfortably alienating" (if this is what Isherwood is doing in *The World in the Evening*) might in fact be a historical diagnosis. Moreover, Bradbury does not see the overall pattern of *Down There on a Visit* as he ignores its final episode, "Paul," which takes place largely in the southwestern United States in the 1940s. In his discussion of *A Single Man,* Bradbury goes even further: "a work of vivid present-tense neurosis, [it] is a tale of a historyless America and the portrait of a single man who cannot build a full identity and has chosen not to mature" (232). Here Bradbury clearly shares with Jacobs a homophobic reaction to the late Isherwood and adds to it a surprisingly anti-American attitude for its time and author. The literary and cultural image of Los Angeles and all of Southern California is in an almost constant state of vision and re-vision in Isherwood's later work. Even within the confines of *A Single Man,* however, it is ridiculous to call Los Angeles, much less the entire United States, "historyless."

Bradbury's attitude in *The Modern British Novel* develops from an earlier essay in which Isherwood comes up short in comparison to Evelyn Waugh, "Evelyn Goes to Hollywood: Waugh and the Post War World."[23] This essay demonstrates the broader understanding of British attitudes toward the United States characteristic of Bradbury's other work,[24] but it also illustrates that some old grudges remain among the British cultural classes: "When Auden and Isherwood moved or fled to the United States at the outbreak of World War Two, their paths, earlier close, divided" (128). Apparently, Bradbury cannot forgive Isherwood for the twin crimes of cowardice and homosexuality:

> Isherwood chose California and developed "a uniquely self-detached narcissism," a curious and energetic agelessness stimulated by the permissive world under bright blue skies. Even the ambiguities of film-work for Hollywood came to satisfy, transience in artistic endeavor fitting the transience of the landscape and the bodily and erotic celebration it seemed to offer as reward. (128)

The kindest thing that could be said about Bradbury's conception of the American Isherwood is that his preconceived notions inhibit him from reading the work with the same care that he brings to the Berlin novels. Unfortunately, this seems to be the case with most English critics and academics; once Isherwood left Britain for good, he was dismissed as an English novelist. Finally, Bradbury, the kingmaker, tries to shift the blame for this attitude to Isherwood himself or to a general critical consensus he had no part in building: "Isherwood, as he knew himself, stayed eternally a novelist of the Thirties, a novelist whose work was focused and historicized by a decade" (232). What Isherwood knew was that his reputation was as a writer of the 1930s, no matter how substantial his later work would be.[25] Isherwood fares little better with American critics who study English or British fiction of the twentieth century. In *The British Novel since the Thirties: An Introduction*, Randall Stevenson's conception of what the "British novel" is allows him to consider Isherwood's work only through *Prater Violet* and thus he ignores the later writing while still making statements about "Isherwood's career."[26]

For most critics studying the overall arc of American literature in the twentieth century, Isherwood simply does not appear. As easily as the English dismiss him for having gone native in America, the American critics dismiss him as an expatriate or exile in Los Angeles. While Auden was taken up by the Eastern academic and cultural establishment (as far west as Michigan, anyway), Isherwood abandoned the East Coast for the marginality of the west. The obvious exception to this dismissal is his adoption by gay and lesbian (and even feminist) academics.

By ignoring Isherwood's later work, studies of postwar American literature betray a lack of critical attitude to the very terms under study. I have found few analyses of what constitutes "American" or "the novel" analogous to the discussion of the "British novel" that Bradbury engages in the Introduction to *The Modern British Novel.* In such a context, it would be understandable to omit Isherwood's American fiction if it were explained as "immigrant" fiction or another category that would eliminate it as "American." One exception is Frederick Karl's *American Fictions* (1983): in both his Preface and "A Polemical Introduction: Who We Are," Karl attempts to identify what it means to be American and an American writer in the postwar world: "In this period, American fiction is no longer simply American; just as America itself is no longer purely American."[27] The idea that America was ever "purely American" is problematic, but Karl does recognize the impact of global culture and the prevalence of writers who would previously have been excluded from consideration: "The Atlantic, once divisive, has receded in favor of overseas linguistic modes, experiments with structure, a willful difficulty. . . . We cannot read postwar fiction . . . without reference to European models" (xiii). Karl's Eurocentrism notwithstanding, he acknowledges that American writing is less insular than it might have been in the past. He also details the "proliferation of designations" that make it difficult to discuss a "purely American" novel, focusing on ethnic, religious, gender, and sexual designations.

The major element of Karl's definition of "American fiction" is that it is written in "American English," which he claims "is a commitment to American values, no matter what the stresses, attitudes, antagonisms, degrees of separation, and hostilities of the writer" (6). Yet in a study that claims to be "A Comprehensive History and Critical Evaluation" of American fiction, Isherwood does not merit a mention. In other studies that attempt a broad analysis of "American writing," in which the boundaries are self-consciously porous, to ignore Isherwood the authors or editors have to ignore his immigration and his becoming an American citizen.[28] Karl's linguistic criteria excludes Vladimir Nabokov, who was "thinking as a highly sophisticated European with particular reference to Russian culture," and Jerzy Kosinski, who "placed himself in a vastly different literary culture which would affect everything he could envisage or relate." Presumably Christopher Isherwood is English to the core and hence out of bounds, no matter how broad those boundaries might be. This linguistic exclusion begs for a new linguistic analysis of Isherwood's final four novels, which feature American settings and characters and American English.

A recent survey of postwar American fiction, Morris Dickstein's *Leopards in the Temple,* highlights a set of midcentury novelists. He describes them in the Preface: "Instead of old-stock Protestant from New England or the Midwest, many of the newcomers were urban Jews or blacks only a generation or two from the shtetl or the plantation; one was a serious Catholic in the Protestant South; others were gays half-emerging from the closet or Harvard men who came from humble backgrounds."[29] Dickstein concentrates on writers who began publishing in the United States after the Second World War, thus he omits Isherwood from his survey. However much he claims to be looking at outsiders ("This was a moment when outsiders were becoming insiders, when American literature, like the society it reflected, was becoming decentered, or multicentered, feeding on new energies from the periphery, as it had done many times before" [xi]), his study is still essentially a version of the East Coast literary establishment, featuring Saul Bellow, Norman Mailer, Bernard Malamud, and Philip Roth as primary interests. No matter the humble, or even southern, origins of his subjects: they all eventually made their way (many via Harvard) to New York, still the apparent center of a "multicentered" literature. No major West Coast writer is included. Dickstein does provide further evidence, in this multicentered literature, of what he finds to be key to determining whether a writer is "American" rather than, say, Jewish American or African American. Borrowing from Ralph Ellison, Dickstein writes, "Instead of simply exploring his own memories, the Jewish writer first 'had to see himself as American and project his Jewish experience as an experience unfolding within this pluralistic society. When this was done, it was possible to project this variant of the American experience as a metaphor for the whole'" (196). Yet Dickstein doesn't extend this idea to the immigrant writer, who might project his experience of America in fiction. Few immigrant writers are taken up, and none as major topics, although Nabokov is considered an influence on some of the writers studied.

When it comes to the "gays half-emerging from the closet," Dickstein writes with clarity and perception but also with a subtle prejudice about Gore Vidal, Truman Capote, Tennessee Williams, and Paul Bowles. The first three of these, Dickstein shows, can be seen as "consciously posing for a group portrait as a new literary generation, they were friendly rivals then, mainly Southern but not exclusively regional, mostly homosexual but also immensely gifted at portraying indelibly original female characters" (65). Dickstein seems to think that gay male writers would focus exclusively in their fiction on men but then betrays a not-immediately-obvious sexism in equating these four with their female characters, as if Blanche DuBois were really Tennessee Williams in drag. As outsiders, Vidal et al. appear alongside Mailer and the other Jewish writers and Richard Wright and other black writers.[30] Dickstein considers style, character development, and plot content as defining characteristics of the new gay writers, and he traces their influence on subsequent generations of gay men, from Williams's lyricism to Bowles's nihilism. Placing their novels in a broader context, Dickstein writes, "The common coin of the New Fiction was the allegorical fable, which the writers used as a Freudian vehicle for tapping into the unconscious, but like all *literary* fables, they worked best with an abundance of realistic detail. Good fiction is nothing if not circumstantial, full of what Irving Howe calls 'gratuitous detail'" (72). The argument here, in relation to Vidal and Capote especially, would surely be stronger with a nod to Isherwood's documentary style on writing of the 1940s and 1950s. All of Dickstein's roads—the gay coterie, the documentary realism, the notion of the outsider—lead to Los Angeles, where Isherwood received Vidal, Williams, and Capote.[31] Taking only Capote as an example, many readers have found the predecessor to Holly Golightly in Sally Bowles,[32] and the influence of Isherwood's friendship may be seen in the documentary style of *In Cold Blood.* Given such evidence, ignoring Isherwood not only slights his contribution to American fiction but ignores an element that would actually strengthen Dickstein's analysis.

Dickstein writes perceptively about the characters and individual styles in the work of Williams, Bowles, Vidal, and Capote. Yet he sees only the transgressive sexual aspect of the burgeoning of gay American literature:

> If the new gay and bisexual writers were the immoralists of postwar fiction—bold in exploring a dangerous new terrain, lyrical in evoking both lost innocence and a utopia of personal freedom—Jews and blacks were the moralists, weighing the inexorable cost of the historical horrors and psychic traumas their characters experienced. There is no Jewish equivalent to the emotional poetry of Tennessee Williams's plays, to the willed horror or sense of loss in Capote's evocations of childhood, or to Bowles's shocking variations on Poe and Conrad. (82)

In contrast to the somewhat overstated "outlaw" nature of these writers, Isherwood provides an alternative, particularly in *A Single Man* and *Down There on a Visit.* His portraits of gay men struggling to be moral and living a spiritual life offer an alternate stream that will find its tributaries in the works of Edmund White, Paul Monette, and Armistead Maupin, among others, writers who, like Capote and Vidal before them, also wrote literary fables with an abundance of realistic detail. Finally, Dickstein undercuts his argument by seeming to find a higher moral purpose in other writers of the period: "The nightmares of the black and Jewish writers seem more historical, less purely personal, for they were grounded in real traumas, the cultural legacies of their people" (81). The implication is clear: gay men have not experienced "real traumas" as blacks and Jews have. Ignoring Isherwood's influence on his American contemporaries allows the critic to ignore the experience of homosexuals in the Holocaust and the history of persecution of gays and lesbians in the United States. Many minority critics would dismiss the attempt to compare oppressions as passé, but this comparison allows Dickstein to condescend and subtly belittle the work of Williams, Vidal, Capote, and Bowles, while treating James Baldwin—black and gay—as completely "other."

Fighting the established and establishment views on gay and lesbian writers is often the undercurrent (if not the main current) of much gay and lesbian literary criticism. This impulse gives much of the context and urgency to such studies as Claude J. Summers's *Gay Fictions,* David Bergman's *Gaiety Transfigured: Gay Self-Representation in American Literature,* Gregory Woods's *A History of Gay Literature: The Male Tradition,* and Reed Woodhouse's *Unlimited Embrace: A Canon of Gay Fiction, 1945–1995,* to name just a few.[33] Scholars of the British and American gay literary traditions recognize Isherwood's contributions on both sides of the Atlantic and frequently use the term "masterpiece" unproblematically when discussing *A Single Man.*

Gregory Woods, the sole British critic in this list, is more inclusive of non-American authors than any of the others, and he is also more in touch with the literary critical heritage in

Britain. His comprehensive study of gay male literature seems directed to Malcolm Bradbury no less than to Harold Bloom, although he takes on Bloom by name for his attempt to define the Western literary canon. Woods notes that gay writers who make it onto Bloom's list are represented by the work that is the least gay-identified, so for Isherwood it's *The Berlin Stories,* not *A Single Man.* Woods writes of the flowering of openly gay literature in the latter half of the twentieth century:

> This brings me to the exciting changes which gay readers have been able to observe across the careers of certain twentieth-century authors, changes brought about, to a large degree, by gradual liberalisations in state control of both sexuality itself and expressions of it. Certain authors have come out as gay, and their publications have marked the various stages in that process. This is true of Isherwood, but not W. H. Auden; of Thom Gunn, but not John Cheever. I mention the excitement of gay readers as distinct from many straight-identified critics because the latter have often proved petulantly "disappointed" by the later books of gay authors who were at first so unthreateningly closeted. They will never admit that the later books of (say) Isherwood or Gunn could be better than the earlier ones. (337)

Woods takes Isherwood's later career seriously enough to find it both valuable and flawed. He examines several themes that span Isherwood's oeuvre and influence other writers, from the effects of homophobia to the position of gays in the family. Far from equating George's anger in *A Single Man* to the author's neuroses, Woods places George's hostility "to the conventional family of the American bourgeois suburb" in the context of the homophobic society he lives in: "The presence of the neighbouring families combines with the absence of his late lover Jim, who was killed in a motoring accident, to enforce his sense of isolation within American life. The nuclear family next door is the outward sign of the excluded homosexual's disgrace" (345).

Even within this context, Woods finds Isherwood's depiction of George flawed in that George is too singular, too isolated from American gay life in a way that Isherwood himself never was. Not only is George bereft at the loss of Jim, but he has no network of gay or lesbian friends to whom he can turn for community and support.[34] This complaint may be overstated, as it is part of Isherwood's intention to demonstrate the necessity of community by showing a man with little outside support and no spiritual life to fall back on. Woods does display an understanding of the novel, its author, and its context that is missing in most of the writing by the more traditional British academics.

American literary scholars generally ignore Isherwood because they consider him English; they effectively define him out of American Literature. But for American scholars of gay culture, Isherwood's national origin is not an issue. They recognize his contribution to and influence on American literature and culture. This may be because gay culture crosses national boundaries. As scholar and poet David Bergman argues, gay writers in the twentieth century, whether British or American, almost always had to go somewhere else to live as gay men.[35] Bergman's pioneering study of American gay literature, *Gaiety Transfigured,* doesn't mention Isherwood or his work, despite the study's focus on themes, such as gay self-representation, presented throughout Isherwood's writing. Bergman more than makes up for this omission, however, in his study of the Violet Quill group of gay male writers of the 1970s.[36] He argues strongly that Isherwood is central to gay American fiction:

> For . . . the first generation of openly gay writers, Christopher Isherwood was a persistent, pervasive, and profound influence both artistically and personally, not that such a distinction is easy to make. In contrast to such tormented and self-destructive American gay writers as Truman Capote or Tennessee Williams, Isherwood provided a calm, sane, and productive counterexample whose work was imaginatively rich, stylistically challenging,

> and politically and spiritually engaged. More than any other writer, Isherwood gave direction to the gay literary movement.[37]

Bergman examines seven writers, the best known of whom are Felice Picano, Robert Ferro, Andrew Holleran, and Edmund White, who called *A Single Man* "the founding text of modern gay literature."[38] Bergman identifies Isherwood's specific contribution as both stylistic and thematic. In *The Violet Hour,* Bergman quotes Ferro's essay on the gay novel and agrees that "the autobiographical novel is the great contribution that gay writers have made to postwar fiction" (61)—and Isherwood provided the standard with *A Single Man.* Isherwood "uses 'the particularized devices of realism' that Ferro thinks are the tools most important to the gay novelist. . . . For Isherwood, this particularization is not opposed to a universalizing strategy, but the very means of connecting George to a larger consciousness" (63).

The coming-out novel may be the dominant autobiographical treatment by gay male authors, but even after their first novels White and others have continued with autobiographical fiction. Holleran's *The Beauty of Men* (1996), for example, is a fictionalized version of his own life as well as a retelling of *A Single Man.* The same may be said of White's *The Married Man* (2000). We can also see the influence of Isherwood's memoirs in the searing stories of Paul Monette in *Borrowed Time* (1988) and *Becoming a Man* (1992).

Monette was another gay writer who found his way to Los Angeles, and he saw himself engaged in the project begun by Wilde, Forster, and Isherwood: the defining and representation of the truth of gay lives in literature. Monette and Isherwood both adopted Los Angeles, and Los Angeles eventually adopted them. Upon Isherwood's death, the *Los Angeles Times* editorialized:

> His elegant, innovative, and unflinchingly honest prose made him one of this century's most important English-speaking writers. As such, he belonged not only to his

> native Britain and his adopted America, but also to the whole world of letters. He also belonged in a special way to this city, the place which he spent nearly half his life *[sic]* and where he and his art always seemed so much at home.[39]

The editorial was titled "He Belonged." He belonged, in part, because he stayed while so many others came and left. The literature on "expatriate" writers in Los Angeles—or Hollywood, which often stands as a synecdoche for the entire region—is voluminous and includes studies of such native-born Americans as William Faulkner and F. Scott Fitzgerald, as well as (mostly Eastern) European refugees such as Lion Feuchtwanger and Bertolt Brecht. The cliché that serious writers are "ruined" by Hollywood, by everything from the studio system to the weather (see Bradbury), was so entrenched in the early 1950s that Isherwood gave a mock warning to Gore Vidal: "Don't . . . become a hack like me."[40] Isherwood did not disdain Los Angeles or begrudge the living he made through screenwriting; in fact, as Lisa Colletta argues, he was unique in his embrace of Southern California, and "his enthusiasm for the culture foreshadowed post-modern ideas of selfhood, as well as its fascination with surfaces."[41]

Los Angeles boosterism is by now well documented and analyzed by historians, architectural critics, and city planners. A strain of that boosterism attempts to put L.A. on the literary map by profiling all the great writers who called Southern California home. The list of American writers who were either born in California or spent a major part of their careers there usually includes Joan Didion, Kurt Vonnegut, and Ray Bradbury. But boosters, such as the *Los Angeles Times* editorial writers, are also sure to add nonnatives to show that even high-minded intellectuals find Los Angeles a good place to live. The nonnatives invariably include Huxley, who stayed, and Thomas Mann, Bertolt Brecht, and Malcolm Lowry, who did not. Isherwood is infrequently cited among these groups; occasionally he is useful to trot out to lend British legitimacy to the area but not enough of a "name" to stand out. He's no Huxley.[42]

Los Angeles literary boosterism has gone through enough phases that the city's cultural representation has come in for its own critical study. In *Landscapes of Desire: Anglo Mythologies of Los Angeles,* William Alexander McClung analyzes the way Southern California has been seen, created, and written about by the "white, English-speaking visitors and immigrants" who dominated L.A.'s cultural and political life for more than a century.[43] McClung's central trope of L.A. is a common one: the idea of mythmaking. In a rare turnabout, Huxley is merely mentioned in *Landscapes of Desire* while Isherwood, "a famous expatriate," comes in for heavy criticism of his depiction of Los Angeles in *The World in the Evening* and *A Single Man.*

A key issue for McClung is the growth of L.A. and the seeming disavowal by current residents of any responsibility for their own actions. Too often, those who are already in the area blame the newcomers for overcrowding, overbuilding, traffic, and pollution. Isherwood illustrates the problem in *A Single Man* when George decries the growth of the city: "he is oppressed by awareness of the city below. . . . It has eaten up the wide pastures and ranchlands and the last stretches of orange grove" (111). In this instance, McClung is probably correct in equating George's feelings with the author's and for calling out the hypocrisy of George's position. George is no planner: he offers no alternatives to sprawl, no plan for infill development in the already developed parts of Hollywood and Santa Monica. But McClung doesn't consider the novel as a whole to be a depiction of Los Angeles. He doesn't recognize what Colletta argues as the postmodernist appreciation of artifice and pastiche, nor does he acknowledge Isherwood's vision of the city's multicultural future as depicted in George's classroom. Further, McClung misreads *The World in the Evening* as an attack on Hollywood, particularly in the first chapter in which he says Isherwood "writes 'perversion' in a visual code, opening an unbridgeable gap between his readers and the city" (60). McClung equates Stephen Monk's psychological repulsion by L.A. with Isherwood's own views—"God curse this antiseptic, heartless, hateful, neon-mirage of a city" (9)—to provide evidence of the intellectual immigrants' basic misunderstanding of and hatred for the city.[44] No doubt there are plenty of examples of writing in which Los Angeles is shown to be the worst of modern America, but by focusing on "Anglo mythologies of Los Angeles," McClung seems to miss the larger leftist critique of modern materialism, of which Los Angeles, for Isherwood, was a specific example but not the only one.

A more thorough understanding of how Isherwood approached Los Angeles, and how he used the city as a symbol of modern society, can be found in his essays and diaries. He wrote at least two essays about the area: "Los Angeles," published in *Horizon* in 1947, and "The Shore," published in *Harper's Bazaar* in 1952.[45] In "Los Angeles," written and published for an English audience, Isherwood echoes many common attitudes and observations. He plays into the preconceptions of the English literary set and reaffirms their idea of "what Isherwood is doing out there": "in the eternal lazy morning of the Pacific, days slip away into months, months into years; the seasons are reduced to the faintest nuance by the great central fact of the sunshine; one might pass a lifetime, it seems, between two yawns, lying bronzed and naked on the sand" (160–61).[46] Isherwood doesn't see Los Angeles as the worst of America, as the supreme example of materialism and impermanence, but as part of an America and a world that is materialistic and impermanent:

> To live sanely in Los Angeles (or, I suppose, in any other large American city) you . . . must learn to resist (firmly but not tensely) the unceasing hypnotic suggestions of the radio, the billboards, the movies, and the newspapers; those demon voices which are forever whispering in your ear what you should desire, what you should fear, what you should wear and eat and drink and enjoy, what you should think and do and be. (161)

A few years later, Isherwood declares in "The Shore" to an American audience his love for the place he thinks of as home—"the stretch of ocean front running five or six miles south of Santa Monica Canyon to Venice, partly inside, partly outside the city limits of Los Angeles" (162). Again, the Vedantist in him describes the shabbiness of Venice and Santa Monica with appreciative detail.

He closes with what is probably his most famous statement about the area:

> What was there, on this shore, a hundred years ago? Practically nothing. And which, of all these flimsy structures, will be standing a hundred years from now? Probably not a single one. Well, I like that thought. It is bracingly realistic. In such surroundings, it is easier to remember and accept the fact that you won't be here, either. (166)

Despite his embrace of impermanence, it seems Isherwood would prefer that change happen more slowly or even after he's gone. Preparing this 1952 article for reprinting in 1966, Isherwood wrote:

> Los Angeles is changing very fast. The city is being suffocated by its population. The old sleepy valley of farmlands is already a suburban wilderness, the wild hills are domesticated. The glamorous dilapidation which I describe in *The Shore* . . . is being tidied up, year by year. They have torn down the holy places; the mansion of Marion Davies, the St. Mark's where Bernhardt once stayed, the hotel where Tennessee Williams wrote *The Glass Menagerie.* (143)

This is the Isherwood who, about the same time, wrote George's tirades against Los Angeles growth but also expressed his "patriotism" for the freeways. Far from being the complaints of an outsider aesthete, as McClung would suggest, this is written from the position of someone who has witnessed the changes firsthand. There is a note of regret at the loss of his "holy places" despite his earlier appreciation for impermanence. That contradiction reveals an older writer but also one who is human. As McClung points out, Isherwood seems not to recognize his part in the overcrowding of the area. Yet he does not complain just about the numbers of people in L.A.; after all, he has lived in crowded cities before, and numbers alone are never what make cities unlivable. Rather, cities break down if they are unable to absorb an influx of people and plan for change. Isherwood's critique is much more subtle than McClung (or even Isherwood himself) gives him credit for. Isherwood writes here as an insider and, although he is Anglo, he resists (to the extent that an aging and sensitive writer can, and more than many other writers) projecting his "desires" and "mythologies" onto the landscape of Los Angeles.

Isherwood's repeated stance as an outsider or a foreigner notwithstanding, he was as American as any immigrant before or after him. He recognized as much: "California is preeminently a place that you don't have to belong to, in the sense of having been here since birth. If I had settled down in Maine that might be another matter, but here I feel very much at home and quite as much that I have a right to the place as anybody else I meet on the street."[47] One writer even claims that the continued outsider position is common to writers who come to L.A. from other places, even San Francisco.[48] Yet, Isherwood was a participant in the cultural and political life of his city and state: in his diary he writes about protesting the execution of Caryl Chessman in 1960 (*Diaries* 1: 836, 854), and in interviews he discusses voting and his membership in the American Civil Liberties Union.[49]

Although Paul Monette saw himself in the tradition of Forster and Isherwood, he, White, Maupin, and others both embraced and rebelled against the label "gay writer." Indeed, Isherwood warned Maupin against being ghettoized on the gay shelf of bookstores. Nevertheless, to be an American writer in the late twentieth century was to be a hyphenate. Dickstein's postwar writers were mostly from the East or New England, some Jewish; for him, to be an American writer is to overcome the hyphen. Yet postmodern American literature is decentered, as Dickstein argues, and so to be an American writer one must embrace (or acknowledge while rebelling against) the hyphen and its antecedent: gay- southern- African- Jewish- British-

Asian- woman- . As Lisa Colletta so aptly points out and David Bergman confirms, Isherwood precedes our understanding of the postmodern. He early embraces pastiche, multivariable identities, celebrity. As such, one may put as many descriptors before the hyphen as you may, but the final adjective to describe the writer that Christopher Isherwood became is American.

Part I

A Writer and His World, 1960

Editor's Note

A Writer and His World

. . . .

Christopher Isherwood started lecturing at the University of California, Santa Barbara in 1960 with the title of his lecture series given to him by the university: "A Writer and His World." The series is a thematic discussion of his work and his life, beginning with "Influences." The next two lectures ("Why Write at All?" and "What Is the Nerve of Interest in the Novel?") address general questions of the novelist's work. The series continues with topics that Isherwood felt uniquely qualified to comment on, given his own work as a writer: "A Writer and the Theater," "A Writer and the Films," and "A Writer and Religion." "A Writer and Politics" was eliminated from the original plan when one of the other lectures ("What Is the Nerve of Interest in the Novel?") took up two sessions. Isherwood's final lecture honors the academic tradition of retiring professors giving a farewell talk, and he called this final lecture at Santa Barbara "A Last Lecture."

Although "A Writer and His World" is organized topically, it is also chronological, and the chronology suggests the rough outlines of a life. His lectures are made up of stories, anecdotes, and remembrances, as is *Christopher and His Kind.* In the first lecture, when Isherwood speaks of influences, his notes say, "I don't mean Plato, etc. This will involve autobiography." Usually, he says, people talk about books when they talk about influences. "But books don't change you unless you're ready for a change. It wasn't really T. S. Eliot who changed Auden from writing like Frost and Hardy." Similarly, in Isherwood's discussions of becoming a Vedantist, in "A Writer and Religion," he acknowledges the connection he made in 1939 with Aldous

Huxley, Gerald Heard, and Swami Prabhavananda. However, he recognizes that the influence of these men would not have been so strong if he were not ready and looking for a change.

Of his literary influences, Isherwood lists the Brontës and E. M. Forster, as well as the now lesser-known Compton Mackenzie. He continues in his notes for "Influences":

> My life has been mainly occupied in writing about people who don't fit into the social pattern. They may defy society or be terrified of it, or they may lead lives of scandal and alienate everybody, or they may be the gadflies of society, like Socrates, or they may be true Outsiders.

Isherwood is likely thinking here of his characters Sally Bowles and Otto Nowak from *The Berlin Stories,* Stephen Monk in *The World in the Evening,* and George in *A Single Man.*

Isherwood's most general statements about his own writing occur in "Why Write at All?" and "What Is the Nerve of Interest in the Novel?" In "Why Write at All?" he describes the two types of novels he has written, saying that he has alternated between the two of them:

> One is a real constructed, contrived novel—a novel which has a plot in action and also a philosophical plot . . . and it comes to a regular conclusion. The other sort . . . is something which is fundamentally . . . a portrait in depth.

By contrived novels he might be referring to *Mr Norris Changes Trains,* with its criminal plot reminiscent of Graham Greene, or *The World in the Evening,* which Isherwood felt was his least successful novel. The portrait novels would include *Goodbye to Berlin,* a series of sketches interspersed with carefully constructed "diary" chapters, and *Down There on a Visit,* in which "Christopher Isherwood" observes four characters at different times in his life.

The next three lectures return to the autobiographical as Isherwood discusses his work in the theater and movies and his religious affiliations. In "A Writer and the Theater," he describes his long relationship with the theater and his celebrated collaborations with W. H. Auden in the 1930s. This is the beginning of a discussion that is treated in more depth in *Christopher and His Kind.* Isherwood's comments on writing for the theater are closely connected to his talk on writing for the films. In fact, in his notes for "A Writer and the Theater," he often contrasted the two art forms:

> What stays with you in the Theater is character and utterance. What stays with you in the cinema is image and movement.

When discussing his work, Isherwood's observations are those of a practitioner rather than a theorist. At his most abstract, he still relies on the fundamentals of the experience of film or theater:

> The Theater is a box; the cinema is a window. The point of the theater is that the players and the audience are confined together, and among other things the play is about how they escape from this confinement.

One can see here the germ of an idea about theater of the absurd or other more experimental forms. However, his lectures are more involved with his personal experiences in the theater and his interactions with Auden, actors, and directors than they are seminars on theory. Isherwood compared his approach to Auden's lectures on Shakespeare.[1] According to Isherwood, "Auden has a tremendously strong intellectual grasp of everything, and I am much more a kind of intuitive person, a person who can throw off remarks, reactions, metaphors, little *aperçus* of this or that."[2] Isherwood was an avid moviegoer from childhood, and the Christopher Isherwood Archive at the Huntington Library includes an excellent photograph of him with members of the Cambridge Film Society in 1924. His first experience as a screenwriter came in the early 1930s, after he had written his second novel, and his subsequent novels are all influenced by writing for the screen, as can be seen in his descriptive style, plotting, and characterization. As a writer in Hollywood, Isherwood knew and understood that his role in filmmaking was not the most important one. He wrote in his notes to "A Writer and the Films":

> The classic cinema exalted the director. This is right. The Writer is representing sound; therefore minor, the producer is only a back-seat driver . . .

As a writer on the set, Isherwood was also an observer, and he used his observations most famously in *Prater Violet.* It is commonplace now for actors and directors to talk about their work in public forums, but Isherwood's lecture on film gives an insider's view from the perspective of the writer of how films were made in the 1940s and '50s. His knowledge of film history and technique is impressive as this lecture ranges from Sarah Bernhardt to Ingrid Bergman, from D. W. Griffith to the Italian director Michelangelo Antonioni. He took the Hollywood system seriously enough to see it as something more than a paycheck. To him, it was an influential part of culture and worthy of study and discussion.

Isherwood was very aware that when he lectured to a college audience it didn't matter what his actual title was—visiting professor, visiting lecturer, or Regents Professor. He later told Carola Kaplan in an interview that he and his students understood that his role as a visitor was different from that of regular instructors: "I was a privileged person, and I was expected to amuse primarily, rather than instruct."[3] And after he had completed a couple of lengthy lecture series, he might be invited as a speaker to a special event, and he would bring out some of the old material. For example, he used what he had called his "Last Lecture" at Santa Barbara to give general advice about life and writing:

> It is also very important not to tell the young that fame or celebrity is nothing. *Of course,* it is something! As a matter of fact, it is a most valuable and chastening experi-

> ence, and for every one person whom I have known who has been, as they say, spoiled temporarily or permanently by celebrity, I have known at least ten who have been enormously improved by it. It's very sobering to have even a little praise, and it turns the eyes inward, and the true quality of one's work is apt to be seen in a much humbler perspective. As long as one is quite unknown, the ego, in a very healthy attempt at survival, actually forces one to be a little bit arrogant, because, if you aren't, how can you go on? It's very hard. Celebrity (I don't use the word *fame,* but any kind of mild notoriety) brings you back to a sense of proportion, and the serious artist is seldom, if ever, harmed by it.

Isherwood used "A Last Lecture" at least once subsequently, at an honors convocation at the University of Southern California in 1974.

What follows in Part I is an edited version of transcripts produced from audiotapes soon after the lectures were delivered. The version of Isherwood's first lecture, "Influences," at the University of California, Santa Barbara is based on a proof copy that was prepared for Stephen Spender's journal, *Encounter.* The text was corrected by the author on galley sheets but the transcript was never published. In editing the transcripts, I deleted some verbal tics (the various "umms" and "ahs" of a public speaker without a strictly prepared script) but I attempted to retain the voice of the public Isherwood. Without tapes to compare to the transcripts, I had to reconstruct brief passages that the typist could not decipher or that were garbled on the tapes. Rather than invent too much, I omitted passages that could not be supposed logically from the context.

Part of the fun of these lectures is comparing Isherwood's prepared notes to the transcribed talk. As a storyteller, he could spin a tale from the barest of notes. His notes for the Santa Barbara lectures are reprinted in Part III.

Influences

Many years ago now there used to be a poster which I very much liked—it was seen all over Los Angeles—advertising that famous cemetery, Forest Lawn. The poster showed a charming elderly lady, very well preserved, with attractively fixed silver hair and obviously in the best of health, who was saying, "It's better at Forest Lawn. I speak from experience." Just how this experience had been obtained fascinated me. But this is my slogan, for better or worse: I speak from experience.

In the nineteenth century people were very fond of having influences in their lives, and when they became great men in later years they told what those influences were. They used to say that life was never the same after they had read the sixth book of Plato's *Republic,* or whatever it might be. I don't mean anything really like that; I mean something much less pretentious, much less clearly defined, and operating probably at a deeper level of consciousness. I am not going to list great books.

The only member of my family among my ancestors who is worth mentioning was a very curious figure who lived in the seventeenth century: John Bradshaw. At the time when civil war between king and parliament had reached an end with the victory of the parliamentary forces and the arrest and imprisonment of Charles, the Parliament wanted to put on a kind of show trial of the king. So they looked around for somebody to try the king, but most of the important legal figures in England had been on the other side. The only person they could find who was ready to do this was a rather obscure judge, named Bradshaw, who came from the Midlands of England, where my family has always lived. This Bradshaw was hastily made Lord Chief Justice of England and presided at the trial. Considering that after all the trial was a foregone conclusion and more than somewhat of a legal murder in intention, his behavior at the trial was disgusting beyond belief. He insulted Charles, who was powerless, in every way possible and with extreme foolishness, because the worse he behaved the nobler Charles seemed. And while there was indeed a considerable case against Charles, this turned the trial into the ugliest and most murderous travesty of justice—Bradshaw yelling at him, always calling him Charles Stuart to show that he had lost in Bradshaw's eyes any claim to royal dignity, and finally sentencing him to death. Charles died with great courage and enormous style, uttering the best of all such execution remarks, the single word *Remember.*[1]

All this wouldn't be particularly interesting but what follows is fascinating to me—so much so that I've often seriously considered trying to do a historical novel about Bradshaw, but unfortunately there's very little material available. Bradshaw was now a very important person: the chief legal officer of the land. He owes this power entirely to Cromwell. What does he do? He gets into a terrible fight with Cromwell and denounces the use of force, the use of soldiers to create a military dictatorship.

George Fox, the founder of the Quaker Society of Friends, at a time when the Quakers were being persecuted by everybody in England, remarks that Bradshaw and another judge—he is named specifically in the journal—were the only two judges who gave the Quakers a fair trial and behaved decently to them.[2] What happened to this man? What was he really like? This fascinates me.

Well, he died of plague, very luckily for himself, the year before the restoration of the monarchy. And, as he was a prominent public figure, even though somewhat in disgrace and in voluntary retirement, he was buried in Westminster Abbey. Then the monarchy returned, Charles II assumed power in England, and the bones of Bradshaw were dug up and hung in chains from the gallows along with those of Cromwell and Fairfax. This, probably, is incomparably the greatest political honor that any member of my family can ever hope to achieve.

The effect on my family was interesting. Some of them, including myself, say and said—in past generations—"good for him, I'm proud of him, he was an ancestor, a real ancestor." The others were horrified. Interestingly enough, the reaction was that they tended to become Catholic, for the simple reason of course that Charles by this time had attained the status of a venerated figure and his death is regarded as little less than a martyrdom. I had a great-aunt who even put up a shrine to Charles I in the house, and at this shrine she used to pray every day and beg for forgiveness because it was believed that the Bradshaw family was under a curse.

The Bradshaws had lived all of this time in the same house—it's torn down now—but it was an old late-Elizabethan house in a village outside Manchester. It was called Marple, and the house was called Marple Hall. The family, which had been successful farmers, bought this house and, as the generations passed, they took their place in the society of the village as the most important family, and the head of the family was known by that curious English appellation of Squire.

As for the curse on our family, it presumably worked, because the last Miss Bradshaw, in the middle of the eighteenth century, found that there were no successors to the line and married a Mr. Isherwood. Mr. Isherwood was in the timber business, and later the family went into shipping. This is the commercial and rather forthright and democratic and potentially immigrant side of my ancestry. On the other hand, the members of my family endeavored to keep up a sort of "landed gentry" grandeur in this house, which was expressed by calling themselves Bradshaw-Isherwood; my uncle picked up an extra name from another good family in Derbyshire by calling himself Mr. Bradshaw-Isherwood-Bagshawe. We were subtly indoctrinated in a very peculiar kind of snobbery which I think is characteristically English and worth understanding when you read certain sections of British literature. This snobbery has to do with the "landed" families—the families that have no title and are not ennobled, but who have lived in the same place with a certain amount of money, naturally, for two or three hundred years. It was always breathed into me that this upper middle class was the real aristocracy of England; that the people with titles were vulgar, and most of them had bought them anyway, and heaven knows who their ancestors were, and where they had been living two hundred years ago, etc., etc.

I was actually born in another house belonging to the same family, quite near and as old, but smaller—a little Elizabethan farmhouse which was on the very edge of the moorland in the corner where Cheshire touches Derbyshire. This is the moorland of *Wuthering Heights,* except that *Wuthering Heights* and the home of the Brontës is somewhat further north. It's a very strange place, even today. Some of these little stone farms are on the tops of hills and protected from the constant wind by groves of trees which are all bent one way by the prevailing wind. From these little stone farms you can look out in two directions: on one side over the wild, open moors covered with heather and heath and just used for grazing. None of them are great hills, but very beautiful in their undulation, in the utter barrenness of the higher land and the beauty of the little narrow dales in between them. This country was always very much loved and insofar as it is industrialized, the industrialization was bitterly resented. John Ruskin, writing about the introduction of a railroad line which crossed one of the most beautiful dales, Millers Dale, said a dale which Apollo and the Muses might have inhabited has been violated in order that a Buxton fool may find himself in Macclesfield in twenty minutes, and vice versa.[3]

On the other side of the view, on the Cheshire plain and out toward Manchester, is a wilderness of houses, of endless suburbs opening into each other. As J. B. Priestley said about one of the industrial towns further north, the whole place looks as though it had been carefully planned by an enemy of the human race. And yet, this stark, industrial wilderness has its own grandeur, and the great, tall smokestacks, the factory chimneys, pouring out great manes of black smoke across the sky, this rainy sky, which is so suitable for keeping the cotton moist, has its own grandeur and splendor and these two things were very, very much part of my early life, these two views of life—and the reminder that they both existed. For the same reason, I took very naturally to Emily Brontë and through her, at about fourteen, discovered the excitement of her particular sort of romantic love. Preferably the person one is in love with has been dead at least twenty years, and one's favorite way of expressing oneself is to spend the night in the snow, weeping on her tomb. This kind of thing has a great appeal, and the idea of the sternness of the moors, the bitterness of death, and the finality of parting is something peculiarly suited to the taste of a very young man who hasn't yet experienced any of them. This was a great part of my imaginary world.

Another part of it was centered around another author of that region, Beatrix Potter. The point about Beatrix Potter was that in her books she drew the village in Yorkshire which was also part of this moorland country but more smiling and charming—it was down in a dale—and in Beatrix Potter's world the animals lived in some of the houses and human beings lived in others. And they met in a quite uncomplicated way. In one story the little girl Lucy goes to the house where Mrs. Tiggy-Winkle takes in laundry in order to bring dirty laundry to her. At the climax of *The Roly-Poly Pudding,* Beatrix Potter sees the rats leaving their home and hurrying down the street to find a new place to live.[4]

It's impossible to convey the charm or otherwise of such books: everybody has these fixations in childhood upon certain books. In my case, I think they appealed to me because we lived in this very old house where there were indeed rats all the time in the walls, and where one loved to think of little doors leading into another universe, another place. I think out of this inspiration of Potter two things grew up which I'm sure are in me and my imaginative world. One was the idea that, as E. E. Cummings puts it, "there's a hell of a good universe next door"—a feeling that just by opening some little door, by getting through some nook or cranny you will find yourself in another world altogether. Another thing which I have come across surprisingly much in the lives of people I've met is a kind of animal totemism, where two people who live intimately together have a sort of secondary life in which they refer to each other as animals of one kind or another. I don't mean in terms of abuse; I mean preferred animals, animals that are the expression of one's personality. And in this way people who are terribly unhappy with each other, or are just very tempestuous in their temperament, sometimes find it possible to live a secondary life which is extraordinarily satisfactory in this world of being not two other people, but two animals. I won't labor the point, but it was illustrated recently in the play *Look Back in Anger.* Let no one underestimate the power, throughout the rest of life, of the children's book and of the fantasies that arise out of it.

There was another great influence in my own life which again was paradoxical, just like the figure of Judge Bradshaw. That was my father.[5] My father was an officer in the regular British army, and he had been sent there. One didn't have choice in those days; the oldest son inherited all the money, and if there were other sons one would go into the church, one into the army, and so forth. Having decided he didn't want to go into the church or the law, he went into the army, and he was a very good officer: very efficient and much beloved by his junior officers and his men, as I know in meeting them in later life. At the same time, he was an extraordinary athlete in many respects; when he was already in middle age he was the best cross-country runner in the regiment. And the moment that he got home at night he would sit down and either paint watercolors or play Chopin or Wagner on the piano, which he did extremely well. He was also a very spirited ham actor and was much liked in regimental productions of *Charley's Aunt* and that kind of thing. When I was about seven, the regiment was transferred to Ireland. There we were, settled in this beautiful old city of Limerick, very picturesque, very dirty and glamorous in those days. The regiment used to march down to church parade on Sunday morning and people would shoot at them from the tops of the roofs. I would go out on the street and boys would yell at me, "Dirty Protestant!" until even to my juvenile intelligence it became apparent that the Irish did not like our being there. There were, just as in World War II, "collaborationist" Irish families who mixed with the English and whose sons were my friends, and in many cases during the latter part of World War I after the British troops had been pulled out to take part in the war, severe reprisals were visited upon such people: their houses were burned and they had to leave Ireland.

Here I saw—very dimly then but later it became more apparent—the beginnings of a paradox. Here is a wonderful man, whom I sincerely love and admire: father or no father, really a hero. Why does he associate himself with forces that do this kind of thing? Occupy a city, admittedly with every kind of consideration and with no atrocities or brutalities, but nevertheless occupy a city that doesn't want to be occupied. My father's answer was: It's my duty as an officer, I swore an oath, and that's it, and wherever they send me I have to do it. That was as far as he saw. In due course, the war came. My father had always made a good deal of fun of the external side of soldiering. He used to say that one's sword was only used for toasting bread on, and that he hated the bang his revolver made and he never fired it. He was killed in 1915, leading his men in an attack. As an eyewitness saw, he was (this, of course, was quite usual) simply carrying a small cane. He didn't have his revolver in his hand at the time he was killed.

Thinking about this character, I began to feel a great bond with some kind of anti-heroic hero, somebody who laughed at the heroic side and yet who was, fundamentally, a person to whom one could look up as a hero. And I think that a great deal of the feeling that I had in later life for E. M. Forster, both as a personal friend and a writer, stemmed out of this.

My life as a writer has been mainly occupied in writing about people who don't fit into the social pattern, and these people of course are very varied. They may not fit in by sheer defiance, or they may not fit in because they are terrified of society, or they may be just scandalous in their lives and cause offense, or they may be gadflies of society, as Socrates was, or they may be something even, in a way, better. The outsider, the constitutionally born member of a minority, has many voices, all the way from utter defiance, the fury of a Timon of Athens, roaring at the guests and driving them out of the house:

> Live loathed, and long,
> Most smiling, smooth, detested parasites,
> Courteous destroyers, affable wolves, meek bears,
> You fools of fortune, trencher-friends, time's flies,
> Cap-and-knee slaves, vapours, and minute-jacks!
> Of man and beast the infinite malady
> Crust you quite o'er![6]

Which of course he must have loved, to the better-humored but still savage fun of a D. H. Lawrence when he was attacking the magistrate in England who had banned his exhibition of paintings in London. The magistrate's name was Mr. Mead, and D. H. Lawrence, after the trial in which the pictures had been condemned, wrote:

> And Mr. Mead, that old, old lily
> said: "Gross! Coarse! Hideous"—and I, like a silly,
> thought he meant the faces of the police-court officials,
> and how right he was, and I signed my initials.[7]

There is a somewhat different tone, which I think I find more serious—the tone, for instance, of Tolstoy in *A Confession.* Tolstoy is describing how, as a young man, he became successful, he made money, everybody praised him, and so he grew up to his thirties believing and indulging in what he called "the superstitious belief in progress." And then he described how he went to Paris, and for some reason or other which he doesn't state, he was present at an execution, by guillotine. He says: "When I saw the head part from the body and how they thumped separately into the box, I understood, not with my mind, but with my whole being, that no theory of the reasonableness of our present progress could justify this deed; and that if everybody from the creation of the world had held it to be necessary, on whatever theory, I knew it to be unnecessary and bad; and therefore, the arbiter of good and evil is not what people say and do, nor is it progress, but it is my heart and I."[8]

That moved me very much. But still for very obvious reasons, it's not an altogether satisfactory approach, because in a sense the executioners might reply the same thing. To me, at least, one of the great expressions of the ideal character of the outsider is in an essay by E. M. Forster called "What I Believe." I can't quote it from memory, but Forster said, in effect, that in all of the gloom which is gathering, he found that the only reality, the only thing that one can cling to, is absolute loyalty to personal relations. That admittedly people themselves are not real entities—they change—but one must behave as though they were people, and one must be loyal to them no matter what, no matter even if they betray me. And very quietly, in the middle of the paragraph, he works up to a sentence which has shocked an enormous number of people and is quite famous: "If I had to choose between betraying my country and betraying my friend, I hope I should have the guts to betray my country."[9]

Forster then goes on: "Such a choice may scandalize the modern reader . . . It would not have shocked Dante, though. Dante places Brutus and Cassius in the lowest circle of hell because they had chosen to betray their friend Julius Caesar rather than their country Rome." Here is something which is part, at least, of the kind of person that I regard as admirable, worthy to be copied and heroic, as is the best type of the outsider—because the outsider is, should be, really, one of the most socially valuable people in the whole community. Because he often, much more often than not, disagrees, he must not harden into defiance in his disagreement. He must always go along with others as far as he can possibly manage to go, and only when the choice is quite flatly between that and the betrayal of what he thinks right must he very regretfully say I'm sorry, and now there has to be a showdown between us. This kind of character is, to my mind, the highest type of outsider, just as the poor madman lying in the corner of the asylum refusing to speak is, you might say, the lowest. I don't mean that in moral judgment, of course, but it's a whole spectrum of behavior toward them.

I should like to end with something which, like many funny remarks, contains a truth, on the subject of Outsiders. It is re-

Isherwood (left of center) as a university student with the Cambridge Film Society on a visit to a London film studio, 1924.

lated in Tallulah Bankhead's autobiography.[10] The British actress Estelle Winwood was at one of these ladies' luncheons with another actress, Sybil Thorndike; they had been giving a talk, and after the talk they were sitting side by side, and on either side of them was a row of ladies of this particular organization. And one of the ladies, with less than tact, but really because she felt that Winwood and Thorndike were such complete outsiders, and were other than they were, leaned right across them as though they didn't exist, and said to the lady on the other side of the two guests of honor, "They're really quite charming, aren't they?" To which Winwood replied, "My dear lady, *we* are no more *they* than you are."

Why Write at All?

Last time I talked about the influences which worked upon a particular writer, myself, and, in describing these influences, I went into a certain amount of autobiography. I ended up by speaking about a kind of person whom I called the Outsider (as opposed to the Insiders), that's to say, somebody who realizes consciously that he belongs to a minority, and, of course, every one of us does in one way or the other. But, the Cooperative Outsider tries to regard this role as socially constructive. In other words, not merely to go along with his Insiders, his brothers under the skin, as much as he possibly can, but even in his dissent to try to be constructive.

I had said last time that the Outsider goes along with the majority as far as he possibly can, and if the issue is a very grave one, which may involve legal or other types of martyrdom, that he should in every way not try to put the others in the wrong but that when the moment comes where there can be no longer any accommodation, then of course he has to take his position. Someone asked the question, doesn't this immediately make him both aggressive and "holier than thou," in that he is saying I am absolutely in the right and you all are not. Now, I don't think that this is necessarily so at all, because I think that one always has to remember that while we get along very comfortably in the world with a code of ethics, in actual fact, under the eye of eternity, there is no such thing as an absolute code of right and wrong. It is always relative to the individual and his particular problems. There may very well be acts that are absolutely wrong for everybody in the world today, but, if you look over the whole of man's evolution, and the whole past and possible development of history, it's quite impossible to say that all acts can be judged on an absolute standard. This is obvious. Therefore, the fact that

I say that it's absolutely wrong for me to eat cabbage and for you to say that you disagree with me, that wouldn't necessarily put either of us in the right. I am only in the right as far as I'm concerned, and what is really important is what do I believe in enough to make a stand on. Therefore the question of right and wrong doesn't arise, in the sense that you are in the wrong if you martyr me. It's not like that. I also mentioned in this connection the name of E. M. Forster, the writer, and I suggested that in my search for a kind of anti-heroic hero I was drawn towards this great man and writer both by his books and then by getting to know him. This, however, only happened later on in my life, not at first. In fact, I was about twenty-seven or so before I first met him.

Ever since I can first remember, I have been engaged in some kind of writing or another, and there's almost no kind that I haven't tried. Of course, one of the forms of writing, with which many of us start and which I think is of enormous value, is the journal or the diary, a kind of autobiographical self-expression. Stephen Spender, in his autobiography, *World within World,* says that autobiography is the characteristic art form of our time,[1] and that probably the best expression of the mental life and spiritual life of our time is to be found in autobiographical work of one kind or another. Much of this type of writing is still under wraps, because it has inevitably a relation to real people and in some cases therefore cannot be published until much later. Harvard, I believe, is bursting with manuscripts by all sorts of people to be published in the year 2000 or even later, according to the scandalousness of the material involved.

All my life I have had an instinct to record experience as it is going by and somehow to save something out of it and keep it. The only thing which is a little bit heartening about diaries and things is that the moral to be drawn from it, though reassuring, is extremely simple. The moral is: cheer up, you're not dead yet, maybe it won't happen. If you read your diary of ten years ago, the thing that really strikes you is that, after all, it all came out all right in the end. From this point of view, of course, diary-keeping is a great moral support. Again, I think that for anybody who is going to write or who, indeed, is in any way interested in what is happening to them—the actual meaning of their experience—to keep any sort of notes is absolutely fascinating, and it's the one act that I never, never regret. I always wish I had written more. For me, art really begins with the question of my own experience, and what am I going to turn it into? What does it mean and what is it all about? I suppose that I write in order to find out what my life means and who I am, to find out if there's meaning in the external world, and then, I suppose, if I decide that there isn't, to impose a meaning of my own. There are many other motives for writing, but as I promised to speak always out of my own experience, this has been my motive, by and large, as I became aware of it. For many years I didn't think of it quite in those terms.

You have this material, this thing is passing by, what does it all mean? Who are these people? Why am I here? What is it all about? And so you grasp at this thing and try to understand it. But in order to understand it you have to simplify and modify and arrange it in various ways, and this is how one gradually approaches the idea that the journal is not enough. The journal is hopelessly messy, for one thing. People show up and are immensely important in one's life for a while, and then disappear for several years, show up again for no reason whatsoever and perhaps are not important, or are much more important, or are important in a different way. Artistically speaking, this is deplorable, it's so untidy. Then, of course, people have far too many relatives and they have to be reduced. Like somebody trying to produce Shakespeare, you discover that a number of the parts can be doubled, and there again you find that it's good to do this.

The kind of writing that I've been concerned with has belonged to two categories all through my life, and I've alternated between them. One is a real constructed, contrived novel—a novel which has a plot in action and also a philosophical plot (I shall explain what I mean by that in a moment)—and which works out. It has motifs as in a symphonic work, and it comes to a regular conclusion. The other sort of literary work in which

I've been engaged is something which is fundamentally a portrait, a portrait in depth. In this sort of work you take a character and you show him or her to the audience as a magician shows a card, rather quickly, which allows the audience to get a superficial view of that character. It's a view that you would get if you came into the room at a party and saw somebody at the other end and heard them talking and saw them in a rather public and therefore slightly deceptive manner, not quite as they really are. And then the object of such a piece of fiction—I hesitate to call it a story because often there is really no story to it, as such, or very little—is to penetrate more and more deeply into this character, removing layer after layer, and resorting to a certain amount of artifice, so that the reader is perhaps always a little bit wrong. Every time they think, "Oh, I was wrong. He's like *this,*" I say, No. "Oh, all right, then. He's like that." No, no, not quite. And in this way you lead deeper and deeper into this person. It's not so much that at the end you express the truth about the person—you don't dig out a little shining nut of wisdom at the end—but by placing all these different people in a kind of order, a relation in perspective as well, you create a composite portrait. This is the real object of such writing.

When I started to write I became enormously influenced, as I said, by the novels of E. M. Forster. There were many other people whom we admired very greatly at that time, but Forster seemed somehow to express exactly the kind of artwork which we longed to produce. "We" were a college friend of mine, named Edward Upward, who has since written very few, but extremely distinguished, works, and myself.[2] We spent almost all of our time at college together in a state of raging cerebral excitement, which is only possible at that particular age and in those particular situations. It was absolutely wonderful. Nobody was taken on trust. I remember the time when I came tearing down the stairs to Edward's room to tell him that *Hamlet* was really quite good after all. And Edward would be reading some book, let us say Gide's *Les Faux-Monnayeurs,*[3] and would suddenly dash in and say, "He's ruined everything!" Books would be burned or thrown into the can symbolically if they seemed to be particularly vile.

Our response to art was absolutely maximum on all occasions. People of whom we disapproved were not merely bad writers but deadly enemies to society, fiends, and part of an enormous conspiracy to destroy all artistic life upon the earth. Many of these were perfectly respectable, second-rate writers whose names I wouldn't even like to repeat now. Forster got some very severe criticism, too, because nobody got off altogether, but Forster was thought to be the nearest thing to the kind of writer we wanted to be. Edward, who was the leading spirit of the two of us in making these kinds of decisions and was always stating new slogans for us, said that we were essentially comic writers: "Tragedy has become impossible nowadays." I was very interested in reading Mr. Trilling's book on Forster; right away at the very beginning he says that Forster is essentially a comic writer.[4]

Another thing that we loved about Forster was a kind of toning down of the tremendous tragic and melodramatic scenes which frequently occur in his work. As you know, one of the characteristics of Forster's novels is great and very abrupt violence. About one of the characters he says quite casually, "So and so died that afternoon. He was broken up on the football field." Of course it's perfectly true that he elaborates on this later, but what is so shocking is the quietness of the announcement and the refusal to lead up to it in any way.[5] Also, many quite important figures die offstage, as it were, between the end of one chapter and the beginning of the next—for example, Mrs. Wilcox in *Howards End.* Now this toning down of melodrama and relating it to everyday life seemed to us extraordinarily fascinating. We found a phrase for it which was in consequence extremely obscure, like most of the phrases coined in the course of a private relationship which exists almost entirely by telepathy, because when you know somebody very well you hardly need to explain anything. We called it "tea-tabling": what we meant was that we hoped to reduce all kinds of violent actions, which had hitherto been presented in the biggest way by the great masters of the nineteenth century, to the polite mildness of the tea table.[6] That's to say, the sort of "Won't-you-have-some-more-bread-and-butter, Do-you-like-it-with-or-without-sugar" kind of tone. In other words, we felt that you could be truly shocking with a minimal range of notes. Why this appealed so tremendously to us is very hard to say, but I think it was in reaction against other forms, and it is true that fiction is constantly alternating between these two voices. For instance, in the early writings of Camus there's a very definite kind of tea-tabling in another sense. One of the epoch-making literary pronouncements after the war was when the Doctor in Camus's novel *The Plague* says that really he doesn't like being a doctor in a plague at all. He'd much rather there wasn't a plague. This was very daring after the cult of danger and death which characterized the Hemingway period, for instance, where you feel that the characters would be extremely uncomfortable if all this would stop. So what you come to is: it's just a matter of taste. Nevertheless, this is the way we wanted to write. I suppose I have held to that attitude ever since, much as I enjoy of the opposite school.

The first two or three novels I wrote were in this highly contrived and constructed manner—that's to say, *All the Conspirators, The Memorial,* and a sort of seriocomic melodrama called *The Last of Mr. Norris.* Then, however, I switched right over to the other thing, these portraits, which come in *Goodbye to Berlin* and in a short book I did about the British movie industry called *Prater Violet,* which is really simply the portrait of one man. Then I did a novel called *The World in the Evening,* which was extremely contrived, and what I'm writing now is right back to the autobiographical portrait thing.[7] It's simply four portraits which are linked psychologically in no other way than by the fact that they're all observed by me at different ages in my life. The continuity is really in my consciousness of the people, rather than in any circumstances tying the people together.

The question always arises—how do you start to write a story or a novel? What is the first thing which sets you going? We all know the conventional idea of an artist getting an inspiration: the composer is walking along a road, he hears a lark singing, and immediately this is the theme of his Forty-second Symphony. And down it goes, with variations, and everything's built up from that. Then again, writers are supposed to hear yarns from old sea captains, or people they meet in bars, and they write them down. Now it's perfectly true that this kind of thing really happens. Somerset Maugham, for example, has written many of his stories that way and even some of the most extraordinary ones. There's a story in one of the late volumes, called "The Kite," which was also made into a short film.[8] The plot of it was that there was a young man who wanted to fly kites, and his wife didn't like it. She disliked it more and more and became downright jealous of the kite. She finally destroyed it. He was furious and hit her and went to prison. Now, every word of this story is absolutely true, and it was told to Maugham by a friend of his who used to be a prison visitor. This is one way of getting stories. The only trouble is that stories seldom spring full-armed like this out of experience, and it's only when they're absolutely right, in this sense, that they can be transposed into art without any trouble.

Something that I do, however, and I believe this applies to many writers, is that I get interested in a situation or in a person. For example, one time I was in South America, and we met a man at a party in Quito, in Ecuador. He said, I'm a representative of the Shell Oil Company, and down in the jungle we have a camp in which we're drilling for oil. Would you like to come down and see it? I went down to his camp, and I think it was the most marvelous natural situation for a novel of anything I've ever seen in my life. It was almost too beautiful to be true.[9]

Down at the foot of the mountains there was a large level space with airstrips and all kinds of prefabricated buildings in which to get Coca-Cola and hot dogs and everything, just like home. And there were living on this base not only the oil drillers, who were all Texan and Oklahoman, but also the pilots who flew them out to the wells, who were very disgruntled ex-RAF pilots of World War II, who hadn't got anything else to do and were restless and inclined to be drunken and violent. There were also a large population of wives and children of all these people, and the oil executives. Beyond this was a trackless jungle. So think that it would take you twelve days to get to a place to which you could fly in about twenty minutes. And during the twelve days you would be exposed not only to the hardships of hacking through the jungle with machetes and being stung by sand flies and annoyed by very large snakes, but on top of that there were the Indians, who were absolutely not kidding and killed everybody they met. Which was very natural, because some unpleasant rubber prospector had gone through there about twenty years ago, and they have very long memories.

These people had to fly to different spots where the ground crews thought there might be oil. Of course there were geologists to find the oil. And then planes would fly over and drop parts of machines which were put together, became bulldozers, and broke down the trees. Airstrips were made, and then the parts of the derricks were put in and then the drilling began. And all the time, all around this little world which was completely British–American in atmosphere, there was the jungle full of Indians. Spears used to fly out of the thick of the forest and kill people on the airstrip, and nobody ever saw who threw the spears, nobody could ever catch them. And yet, other Indians belonging to river tribes, or for some inscrutable reason not afflicted by this kind of feeling, would arrive in the calmest manner and request to be transported from one airfield to another. I watched their faces very carefully as they were taking off in this plane, which was loaded with pigs and drums of gasoline and all kinds of machinery—not the slightest trace of fear. You would have thought they'd been riding in those things all their lives, and they presumably rejoined this primitive culture when they got there.

Now, this is all to convey to you what I call a situation, a place, which is tremendously attractive to a writer, not necessarily to me personally, but to many writers it certainly would be. When you have a place like this, it's really fundamentally the same as when you have a character. You meet somebody, and you can't tell what it is, but it's just as irrational as love. You say, Ah, she's one of them; he's one, he'd do. This interest seems to grow, and you feel that this person is too good to live among mortals. He must live also *sub specie aeternitatis*[10] in the world of art, where there's no right or wrong. So you start to try to put him there. And then the question arises, how can this person, or this situation, be best presented? The other day I was talking about this, and I used the simile of a horse: you want to show the horse off, so therefore you put the horse through its paces. You show it in different gaits, and you show it jumping, and so forth, and lead it around the ring. Well, in a way, the whole of the piece of fiction which grows out of meeting this person or encountering this situation is really a way of putting the person or the situation through its paces. If it's a person, he or she must of course have a supporting cast and they must go through adventures, but the object of all these adventures, the object of the plot and the action, is simply to show how this person reacts and to get them to react in the maximum way so that you see every facet of this person. This is more or less how the circumstance of the story and how the setting and everything else grow up, out of the first initial excitement. If you've been given a situation like the camp at Shell Mera, then of course you have to populate it. You have to populate it with people who will represent the essence of the place in different ways and express what it's all about. Because you're not merely exhibiting the life, the liveliness, of a character or of a situation, you also are trying to say, what does it mean? If you asked Conrad to describe *Heart of Darkness,* he'd tell you how Marlow went up the river, how he heard tell about this Mr. Kurtz, how some people seemed to regard him as a swindler and a criminal and others regard him as a great saint, a great hero, and so forth. And the whole story is unrolled: Kurtz dies, and Marlow comes back down the river. If you asked Conrad, Yes, but what is the story about? What does it mean? Then he would say, Oh yeah, it means . . . I was writing about the darkness in the human heart.

There are in fact two aspects of a work of fiction. One is the attempt by every means possible to bring the aliveness of the person and the circumstances to the reader, to make the whole area that you've chosen glow with life. But there is this other thing, which is to engage to say, however indirectly, what does it signify? And it seems to me that however much people may disclaim the intention to either of these things, in fact, every writer of fiction is trying, in his own way, to do both. To say what is the aliveness of the situation and to convey that aliveness, and also to say what does it all mean, what does it signify?

In the Forsterian kind of novel, and also in the Conrad novel and in many other types of novel construction, there are these things which become a weariness and a burden in academic circles because we have to discuss them so much: symbols. But all that a symbol is, in fact, is a sort of a rivet which runs through from the one aspect of the novel and connects it with the other one. Because what is a symbol? For instance, in Forster's *Howards End,* among many other things, there's a tree. Now this tree is a tree, and it is part of the scenery, and it's just as much alive as the flowers around it or the people who live in the gardens where the tree grows. The tree is there. But the tree isn't just a circumstance of the story, it also stands for something. As the novel goes on you begin to realize that the tree means the enduringness of life in the face of death, or it means England, or it means goodness knows what, it has some sort of symbolic value which the author hasn't even intended. Of course, there are symbols which are not intended by the author but are detected by people whose business it is to discover symbols later. So the symbol, the tree, lives in a double world. It is both the enduringness of England, and also it's a tree. This is what I mean by saying that a symbol is a bolt which connects the two halves of the novel and holds them together. Of course, novel writing, or indeed any kind of artistic creation whatsoever, is such a strange mixture of conscious intention and subconscious evolution that many, many symbols are projected into the novel that aren't conscious intentions. This happens again and again—it's only other people who then find them and show them to you, and you're amazed at your own subtlety at having put them there.

In concluding these remarks for today, I want to say just a little bit about that mysterious thing, the enemy of the writer, the force inside himself which is trying to prevent him from writing. It is sometimes referred to as writer's block. One dismisses it, of course, by describing it as sloth, which indeed it is. Or one dismisses it by pretending that one is too busy to do it, because one has all kinds of other things to do. That's neither here nor there. One has to accept the reality of its presence, to realize that it will never, never yield, that it will return to the attack again and again all through your life, completely unconquered, and that therefore instead of wondering exactly what it is or making moan over it, one has to develop techniques for fighting it, or rather, getting around it. It appears, in my own experience, that it is something, a kind of terror, to do with the formal act of writing. Talking to other people I've found that many of them share this. That's to say, a lot of people have a terrible resistance to sitting down at a table and writing. It's therefore true that a number of very distinguished writers, including Sir Walter Scott and Bertolt Brecht, to name two who are sufficiently dissimilar in every other respect, always wrote standing up. This is not nearly as silly as it sounds, because you can avoid this terrible thing by pretending that you aren't really going to write at all. You walk about the room, look at books, fiddle with this or that, and then suddenly go over and there are the papers all on top of some high piece of furniture or a specially constructed desk if you've gone that far (and both Sir Walter Scott and Brecht did), and then you write something. Once you start the momentum a little bit it gets that much easier, and so you can edge your way into writing enough to get you interested, and as soon as you're interested you begin to overcome this resistance. There is, however, another method which I discovered was practiced by Henry James, and which I've found very helpful. That is, to turn the whole thing into a lecture. One may not be able to write, but one can always talk. I've found that it's amazing what you can do with a really sympathetic secretary. [The audience laughs, and Isherwood admonishes them playfully.] Now really. Do you realize they're going to hear that on the air tonight? What'll they think of you?

What I mean by that is you begin, not to dictate—that, of course, is difficult—but you begin to talk about the problems that you see in the work. Theodora Bosanquet, who was James's secretary in later life, wrote a very interesting small book, I guess it's out of print now, in which she actually describes how James approached a novel in the very first mood, in which he talked about the basic nature of the interest.[11] I mean, in other words, if he'd been going to write a novel along the lines that I've been indicating, he would have described this person or this situation, and then he would have said: At present that's all I can tell you, except that so and so. He was thinking aloud, as they say. And then he'd say, No, I see more than that.

This whole technique and its humors and successes and the whole fun of the thing is something that I would like to talk about at considerably more length another time. As for now, I feel that we have reached a point in the discussion where I would like to stop, because next time I want to begin rather more with chapter and verse, and read you a considerable number of extracts from various books, to give you an idea of what it is that I personally find valuable and exciting in fiction. I believe it's very, very important to come down to examples and cases and not remain in the world of generalizations any longer than we can help.

What Is the Nerve of Interest in the Novel?

My talk today is probably going to be the most unsatisfactory in the series, because what I'm going to try to do is to a certain extent attempt to define that which cannot be defined, that is, what actually makes a novel vital, alive, good—great, if you want to use the word, which I rather dislike. Anyway, the question arises always: how can one get down to the nerve of the novel? What is the nerve of the interest? A friend of mine, a British painter named Francis Bacon, told me once that when he painted he was always trying to "get down to the nerve." Well, what is the nerve of life in a novel? Can we somehow come close to this?

Now of course it's very little use attempting to generalize in these cases. All one can really do is to take a number of writers and speak about them, and this is what I shall endeavor to do. But I will make a few general remarks first. Henry James wrote in a review of some modern novels to this effect: "Yes, yes—but is that *all*? There are the circumstances of the interest . . . but where is the interest itself?"[1] One knows very well what kind of book he was referring to, a book in which everything that is conventionally considered exciting or interesting is thrown in, but—just because it is *thrown* in, because it's thrown in quite irresponsibly—nothing is really described but only used as a kind of move in a chess game which is supposed to interest the reader, so all these escapes, murders, love affairs, flights and pursuits, wanderings over mountains all end up to nothing. Just the circumstances of the interest. Just the thing which ought to be interesting, and would be interesting except that in this particular book it isn't. Because there is no vitality within the narration of the experience.

There's a strange quotation from Robert Louis Stevenson, which haunts me a good deal, and I'm not even sure if he meant by it what I choose to mean by it, but we'll go into that in a moment. In an essay called "The Lantern Bearers" he says: "True realism, always and everywhere, is that of the poet: to find out where joy resides, and give it a voice . . . For to miss the joy is to miss all."[2] Knowing Stevenson, I still have an awful suspicion that perhaps all he means is that one should look on the bright side of things. But what I mean by the joy, and why this remark seems to me extraordinarily stimulating, is a kind of higher fun, a kind of mad vitality which exists in the universe. And I think in this sense that none of the writers that we call great have in fact missed the joy. In other words, that however apparently sordid or distressing or tragic or grim the circumstances of a novel may be, underneath all of this there is a great lift of exhilaration in reading about it. Let us try to think why this is so. The saints have almost all been unanimous insofar as they've expressed themselves on the subject in saying that in some way which the rest of us can't understand everything is finally all right. It is marvelous.

In one of the Hindu scriptures is the saying "In joy the universe was created, in joy it is sustained, in joy it dissolves."[3] Now of course on the level of our everyday experience this is a hard saying and seems to be an unfeeling saying, a saying which expresses a kind of indifference toward human suffering. And what I want to point out is that this is not at all the case. But the fact remains that some of these great men of compassion and mercy did in fact, in the midst of terrible suffering which they were working all through their lives to alleviate, nevertheless rejoice. There is a charming anecdote in the life of Ramakrishna of one of the wandering monks who used to visit the temple at Dakshineswar on the Ganges, where he lived. He used to come out of his cell twice a day and sit on the edge of the Ganges as though he were a spectator in the theater, and clap his hands and say, "Bravo! Excellent!" as though the whole universe were an enormous theatrical performance.[4]

This brings us to the question, What is a great novelist? And in what sense does he experience joy, and how can he experience joy in the face of evident human suffering? And it seems to me that the novelist works simultaneously in a novel on two levels and that he must, as it were, succeed and come through to us on both of these levels if he produces work of a first magnitude. On the level of human suffering and struggle the novelist obviously has to be involved, engaged. He has to mind that people suffer, he has to condemn the bad and rejoice in the good. He has to depict the circumstances of everyday life and he has to make them vivid and not in any way conceal their reality—what we call reality, the everyday reality. On this level he can be passionately involved, as I say, get very angry, and he can have a set of ethics. He has to have a moral code. Every writer who really has any kind of vitality has some sort of moral code. Whether this code of morals is a good one is to my mind absolutely immaterial. One can read with the very greatest enjoyment art which is founded on quite different ethical principles from one's own. That doesn't matter. What matters is the intensity with which this struggle on the human level is realized. But, surely, in a great novel, there's something else again. While all this struggle is going on the novelist is not only down there, covered with mud and blood, fighting and suffering with his characters, but he is also up above. He is also the eternal, who looks down upon everything and enjoys it. Because, of course, in the world of art if something is well done it is enjoyable. One has to face the fact that the most dreadful descriptions of agonizing death are, artistically speaking, just as enjoyable as great love scenes or charming scenes of domestic happiness with children. It is quite, quite immaterial. This sense of joy, of contact with life, of the vitality of life, can be related to any set of circumstances or characters you choose to name.

What is it that the novelist has to have on the upper level, on the level of looking down with the eye of eternity upon the characters? He has to have, I suppose one can say, compassion. He has to see the just and the unjust as being all his children. Just as we say that in the human world God looks down and says, "They are all My children and, in the last resort, I care nothing for their righteousness or unrighteousness. I only love them."[5] And so, in this joy in experience we find a kind of transcendental vitality to a book. Now it is entirely possible for the novelist to fail in either the one or the other, because the compassion can be false or absent or coarse; on the other hand, there can be a failure on the lower level to depict the struggle with vividness, a failure of involvement, and all kinds of other failures which make the book just the circumstance of the interest and not the interest itself.

When I say compassion (and this is why I dislike the word), I don't just mean a kind of sentiment, or even a sense of pity in the emotional meaning of the word. No, the compassion of great writers seems to be quite dry—as, for example, in Flaubert. Nevertheless, you feel the compassion. You certainly feel the compassion for Madame Bovary, and a great joy, from the upper level, even in the villainous apothecary. The other side of compassion, of course, can be quite noisy and melodramatic and yet at the same time strike us as genuine. The first of the examples of this kind of thing that I am going to read you is from Dickens. Here is Dickens describing the situation—being thoroughly embroiled in it—and yet at the same time obviously reveling in it. This is *A Tale of Two Cities,* and I'm going to read you just a little bit of the opening of the book, because I think it's so marvelous. And you will see how, in these passages, Dickens is both above and below, both in the midst of the battle and looking down over it.

> France, less favoured on the whole as to matters spiritual than her sister of the shield and trident, rolled with exceeding smoothness down hill, making paper money and spending it. Under the guidance of her Christian pastors, she entertained herself, besides, with such humane achievements as sentencing a youth to have his hands cut off, his tongue torn out with pincers, and his body burned alive, because he had not kneeled down in the rain to do honour to a dirty procession of monks which passed within his view, at a distance of some fifty or sixty yards.

> It is likely enough that, rooted in the woods of France and Norway, there were growing trees, when that sufferer was put to death, already marked by the Woodman, Fate, to come down and be sawn into boards, to make a certain movable framework with a sack and a knife in it, terrible in history. It is likely enough that in the rough outhouses of some tillers of the heavy lands adjacent to Paris, there were sheltered from the weather that very day, rude carts, bespattered with rustic mire, snuffed about by pigs, and roosted in by poultry, which the Farmer, Death, had already set apart to be his tumbrils of the Revolution. But that Woodman and that Farmer, though they work unceasingly, work silently, and no one heard them as they went about with muffled tread: the rather, forasmuch as to entertain any suspicion that they were awake, was to be atheistical and traitorous.[6]

It's the vice of this method of illustration that it's very difficult to convey one's own preferences. But I read this because it seems to me to have this combination of furious indignation, compassion, and fun, which coming all together gives Dickens—in spite of his melodrama, in spite of his hamming—his effects: this greatness. Now, a lesser writer, perhaps, would have conveyed the killing of the child but would somehow have brought the camera down too close to the events and not given us the overall sense which you get in this passage of a whole state moving towards a tremendous catastrophe. Another kind of writer, by dwelling on the broad outlines of the catastrophe, would have lacked the vitality of the day-to-day scenes, the specific instances. Always we find in great writing that there's a constant reference back and forth. I don't mean explicit reference, a spoken reference, but a reference which you feel, back and forth, between the individual incident which is being described and the general predicament of man. And this is why you don't need necessarily very startling effects—why you don't need the drastic means employed by Dickens, because if this reference between the particular and the general exists right down to the nerve of feeling and vitality, art is, as it were, caused like an atomic fission—a tremendous discharge of artistic vitality and power takes place.

The other day I was talking about the novels of E. M. Forster and saying how much Forster's technique had influenced me. Now Forster in a way is an opposite pole of Dickens. Forster, usually with very small, domestic effects and situations which do not have as a rule any kind of life-and-death gravity, creates nevertheless the sense of tremendous issues at stake. The circumstances of *Howards End,* for example, are just as moving as anything which dives into the depths and ascends to the heights of human violence and feeling, because there is a tremendous sense in Forster of the underlying significance. I was asked by one of you who was kind enough to write to me why, if I liked Forster, had I, on other occasions, expressed a preference for melodrama of another kind and, in fact, rather like Dickens, rather like Balzac. Of course, the answer is that one is not bound to any one way of doing things. And though one's admiration goes out in many directions, when it comes to trying in a small way to be an imitator or disciple, one chooses one master rather than another. One owes a great deal to many masters. It's such masters, such writers and their different approaches to this question, that I shall try to speak about, not only for the short time that's remaining now but also I think in my next talk, because there's a great deal I want to say about a great many people.

I said already that the question of compassion is not a question of sentiment, and sometimes the extremely dry, clinical approach also covers very, very deep feeling, and I instanced Flaubert. Another writer who means a very great deal to me, and who is fundamentally a very clinical writer, a writer without sentiment, a writer who is enormously truthful and exact in his observations, is Proust. I think of all writers that I've ever read, Proust is the one who most often reduces me to despair by saying something which I would like to have said, ever so much better. It's of course ridiculous in a short space of time to give you any impression of the quality of Proust's perception. But I am going to read you just one short passage, because it makes such a pleasing contrast to the feeling that you get out of Dickens.

The things in Proust that I most like are in the early part of the novel. I like best, I think, the first three novels. And one of the things that I like particularly is Proust's study of jealousy. Now, jealousy is one of the most boring human defects. And the fact that Proust can make it so fascinating is just one more example of what I'm talking about—that one can use absolutely any material. Why Proust makes it so fascinating is that he is simply fascinated by jealousy. As a phenomenon, as a way of life, as an indoor sport. And in this very close and loving observation of the jealousy between Swann and Odette, there is, in fact, the most wonderful kind of compassion. But it's a very dry compassion—not an outspoken, sentimental compassion.

> There can be no peace of mind in love, since the advantage one has secured is never anything but a fresh starting-point for further desires. . . . Actually, there is in love a permanent strain of suffering which happiness neutralises, makes conditional only, procrastinates, but which may at any moment become what it would long since have been had we not obtained what we were seeking, sheer agony.[7]

Here's another passage from Proust that I want to read you anyway, except it hasn't anything to do with jealousy. This is a very strange passage, a kind of dream experience of seeing his grandmother again after death. Proust was very devoted to his grandmother—I mean, the "I" of the novel was very devoted to his grandmother—and this is the passage where he describes this experience. The passage has this apparent sentimentality and a tremendous clinical observation underneath and a very sad, austere understanding of death. I'm not quite sure which of the novels in the series it comes from, but it always appealed to me.

> World of sleep in which our inner consciousness, placed in bondage to the disturbances of our organs, quickens

the rhythm of heart or breath because a similar dose of terror, sorrow, remorse acts with a strength magnified an hundredfold if it is thus injected into our veins; as soon as, to traverse the arteries of the subterranean city, we have embarked upon the dark current of our own blood as upon an inward Lethe meandering sixfold, huge solemn forms appear to us, approach and glide away, leaving us in tears. I sought in vain for my grandmother's form when I had stepped ashore beneath the sombre portals; I knew, indeed, that she did still exist, but with a diminished vitality, as pale as that of memory; the darkness was increasing, and the wind; my father, who was to take me where she was, did not appear. Suddenly my breath failed me, I felt my heart turn to stone; I had just remembered that for week after week I had forgotten to write to my grandmother. What must she be thinking of me? "Great God!" I said to myself, "how wretched she must be in that little room which they have taken for her, no bigger than what one would take for an old servant, where she is all alone with the nurse they have put there to look after her, from which she cannot stir, for she is still slightly paralysed and has always refused to rise from her bed. She must be thinking that I have forgotten her now that she is dead; how lonely she must be feeling, how deserted! Oh, I must run to see her, I mustn't lose a minute, I mustn't wait for my father to come, even—but where is it, how can I have forgotten the address, will she know me again, I wonder? How can I have forgotten her all these months?" It is so dark, I shall not find her; the wind is keeping me back; but look! there is my father walking ahead of me. . . . "But tell me, you who know, it is not true that the dead have ceased to exist. It can't possibly be true, in spite of what they say, because grandmother does exist still." My father smiled a mournful smile: "Oh hardly at all, you know, hardly at all. I think that it would be better if you did not go. She has everything that she wants. They come and keep the place

> tidy for her." "But she is often left alone?" "Yes, but that is better for her. It is better for her not to think, which could only be bad for her. It often hurts her, when she tries to think. Besides, you know, she is quite lifeless now. I shall leave a note of the exact address, so that you can go to her; but I don't see what good you can do there, and I don't suppose the nurse will allow you to see her." "You know quite well I shall always stay beside her, dear, deer, deer, Francis Jammes, fork." But already I had retraced the dark meanderings of the stream, had ascended to the surface where the world of living people opens, so that if I still repeated: "Francis Jammes, deer, deer," the sequence of these words no longer offered me the limpid meaning and logic which they had expressed to me so naturally an instant earlier and which I could not now recall. I could not even understand why the word "Aias" which my father had just said to me, had immediately signified: "Take care you don't catch cold," without any possible doubt. I had forgotten to close the shutters, and so probably the daylight had awakened me.

I've decided that in order to speak much more fully about these other writers, I shall take the next talk and speak at some length, particularly about D. H. Lawrence and about Tolstoy and about various others.

What Is the Nerve of Interest in the Novel? *(continued)*

This week's talk and last week's talk are the only two that are kind of closely connected together, and for that reason I must recapitulate very briefly what I said last time. I said that I was going to attempt the very difficult task of trying to define what it is that makes for greatness, or supreme vitality, in the novel. And I quoted a saying of Robert Louis Stevenson: "True realism, always and everywhere, is that of the poet: to find out where joy resides, and give it a voice . . . For to miss the joy is to miss all."

I said that I thought this meant that Stevenson was referring to a kind of super joy, a joy in experience, which contains both the ordinary concept of pleasure and happiness and also the ordinary concept of sorrow. In other words, it is a joy that accepts the whole of the human experience, artistically speaking, and says about it that it is ultimately wonderful. It follows from this that no great book, if we accept this definition, can ever be depressing no matter what it's about. I suppose one of the severest tests of this theory is the long short story of Tolstoy, "The Death of Ivan Ilych," a story which begins with the words "Ivan Ilych's life had been most simple and most ordinary, and therefore most terrible."[1] And it goes on to describe, in considerable detail, his death from cancer. Well now, all I can say is that in my opinion this book meets the requirements of Stevenson's kind of joy and is in fact not depressing in spite of its appalling subject matter and leaves one with a strange kind of exultation, whereas an extremely brilliant book on a lower level might be so depressing on this particular subject that one simply couldn't bear to read it.

Then I put forward briefly the theory that in order to produce greatness in art, you had to have the coming together of two things which the artist does, the writer does. The writer, in telling a story, must be passionately engaged in the action. He must delineate the characters vividly, describe the scene, make it all come to life, and he can—if he likes—enter with great violence into the battle, take sides with the hero, and denounce the heavy in no measured terms. I don't say this is absolutely necessary, but it is absolutely possible in a work of great genius. But, at the same time, another part of the writer must look down on the action with what—for want of a better word—one could call compassion. That is to say, he must look down on it, saying "These are all my children, and although you heard me going on just now against Mr. So-and-So, of course I love him too in my own strange way."

I suggested that these two attitudes have to be in some way, like two points of view, brought into focus before art can be created which has real vitality. We all know the kind of book which has compassion without any kind of engagement on the lower level. This also can be a brilliant novel, the author looks down on them all and says aren't they amusing . . .

But how in the world do you manage to do it? Everything else that one can say on the subject is really what is called in theological terms the *via negativa.* You arrive at truth by saying Not this, not that, not this, not that, until you possibly, ideally speaking, illuminate the one thing which is. For instance, one thinks at first that perhaps realism is necessary to great art. But, then again (of course, you may not agree with my particular opinions, but I think you'd agree with the implications), you take the writing of Virginia Woolf, that great master of the reverie, who gives us, I think, like no other writer, that strange kind of subterranean movement in consciousness which takes very little account of the dates and intervals but somehow makes the whole of life one great graph or curve in a winding river. The book which is her most vivid attempt to create this effect is *The Waves.* I personally also like very much, indeed prefer, *To the Lighthouse.* Neither of these books, by any stretch of the language, could be called realistic. Then again we take Melville. I have more to say about Melville later, but Melville undoubtedly was not in any ordinary sense of the word a realistic writer.

Very well then. Is it perhaps style, fine writing, which makes for this vitality, this greatness? No. It would seem not necessarily. I personally find something of this greatness in the novels of Theodore Dreiser, and I suppose nobody could write in a more clumsy manner than he does. Again, at the other end of the scale, it often seems to me that a writer like Henry James succeeds almost in spite of his style. At first one sees, to use his own metaphor, this great carpet, which is almost formidable in the complexity and variety of its colors; this is to be likened to the style particularly of the middle and later James. But then when you come closer you see what he himself called the figure in the carpet, and this is in fact the whole meaning of the work. But here James surmounts style or comes through style to something beyond style.

Then again, it's hardly necessary to say that a great scope is not the point. There are people who think that a great novel should have a vast extent. Well, of course, that particularly squalid little tale of small-town murder, *The Brothers Karamazov,* is by all standards one of the greatest novels ever written. E. M. Forster, too, confines himself to a very small scope; and, in a different way, although there are parties and receptions and in a certain sense French society, even Proust has in many respects a very small scope in his writing. He doesn't need vast areas and enormous casts of characters. In Proust's case there are many characters, it's true, but you need in fact neither great extent nor do you need a great number of characters. Then again, it's not a question of being restrained. Some people feel that the great thing is to keep a firm restrain on one's loquaciousness. If you talk too much, then you say too much, and it all dissipates, as some of us think it does to an extent in the novels of Thomas Wolfe. But then on the other hand you have Dickens, and Dickens is the most copious, the most unrestrained person imaginable. And yet he, too, achieves this vitality in his own way.

Is it perhaps necessary to have great warmth, to have great emotional heat? Should one have very much heart, as they say?

This is also a thing which has been promoted in some quarters. But then when we see Flaubert or George Moore,[2] his pupil, of whom I shall speak in a moment, you see that in fact there can be great restraint and even apparent coolness. In fact, there is, I maintain, a compassion which looks down from the eyes of Flaubert and George Moore just as real as the compassion of Dickens. But nevertheless, obviously the one is all over the place and the other is playing its card with the greatest care, as though it were poker, and dealing out one after another these little clues leading up to an effect which leads to another effect. Everything, you feel, is planned.

I'd like to speak a little more of Moore because I admire him so greatly, and he's rather in eclipse at the present. His most famous novel, I suppose, is *Esther Waters* (1894), and there are many others: *The Brook Kerith* (1916), *The Lake* (1905), *A Mummer's Wife* (1885). But the novels of which I want to speak for the moment are the two related novels, *Evelyn Innes* (1898) and *Sister Teresa* (1901). It is, in fact, the story of how an opera singer named Evelyn became a nun. And this story shows the most marvelous insight into a change of this kind in the life of a human being. There's a scene, which I always think very wonderful, in which Evelyn Innes is in a convent and is listening to the excruciatingly trivial chatter of the nuns, talking about their daily affairs with a little rather pretty piety thrown in. And she thinks, If I stay here any longer, I shall go mad. And then suddenly she remembers the days of the theater, and of the theatrical life, and she remembers the excruciatingly trivial chatter of the dinner parties after the theater, among actors and actresses, and she thinks, If I went back there, I should go mad, too. And so she finds herself passing through the agony of belonging no place, and this, of course, is the beginning of her understanding of why she is really in a convent and what the religious vocation has meant to her. However, that is not what I want to read.

The last chapter of *Sister Teresa* (that's to say, the end of the second volume) seems to me to express in the most beautiful way the extreme of restrained compassion in which there is no overt sentimentalism and almost a kind of coldness on the part of Moore towards the characters—and yet, I feel, such great love for them.

> In the middle of the following year Mademoiselle Heilbron called to see her, and Teresa came into the parlour, and with ready smiles and simple glee she entered into conversation with her old friend. . . . A little embarrassed to know what to say to her, Louise talked to her about a new part in a new opera by a new composer.
>
> "I've brought the score with me. Would you like to see it? Shall I leave it?"
>
> Teresa said that once she would have liked to see it, but now such things were far behind her, and with a merry laugh she spoke of herself as a broken spirit. And then, as if speaking out of some vague associations of ideas, she spoke of her pupils—of one who really had an aptitude for the piano, and another who could really sing a little. She would like Louise to hear her, and Louise was not certain if she were speaking in bitterness or in jest, or if her present mind was her natural mind. . . .
>
> They walked around the garden twice, carrying on the conversation as best they could. Louise remarked a nun reading her Office, and Teresa told her who she was. Louise affected an interest in the flowers, and Teresa told Louise she must hear her favourite pupil.
>
> "I really don't think you will be disappointed, she has got a very pretty voice, and I have just taught her a song out of one of Handel's operas."
>
> "I remember a song of Handel's that you used to sing beautifully. Do you ever sing it now?"
>
> "No, I lost my voice last winter; a heavy cold took it all away," and Teresa laughed just as she had laughed when she spoke of herself as a broken spirit, and Louise left the convent uncertain, thinking that perhaps it was this loss of her voice that had decided her to remain in the convent.
>
> "So this is the last stage," she said as she drove back to London. And then Louise thought of her own life. She

> was now forty-five, she might go on singing for a few years—then she, too, would have to begin her packing up, and she wondered what her end would be.[3]

There is one kind of writing which most people do think of when they think of a masterpiece. And that's a great big book, with an enormous number of characters and an epic line under it of the rise and fall of something, or growth of something, or what have you. But if one casts one's mind back over the best-seller list of the past few years, you'll find that there are many such books of the most desolating boredom and enormous length that do just exactly what they promise. They have enormous scope, they're full of characters, and they describe the rise and the fall of something. And they couldn't be more dreadful. On the other hand, we have *War and Peace.* I think that one is quite apt to spend one's life alternating between two moods: one in which one loves *War and Peace* more than *The Brothers Karamazov,* and then vice versa. But anyway, *War and Peace,* even if you're not attracted to Tolstoy, is a great example of one thing I've been talking about, and that is the sense that all Tolstoy's creatures, that all these people, live and exist vividly in Tolstoy—in the element of Tolstoy. There isn't a waiter in a restaurant or a soldier bandaging up his foot, or anybody anywhere, who isn't uniquely interesting. And Tolstoy pauses very often and talks to them for us just for a moment and indeed we see always something unique, something wonderful about these people, which nevertheless is all part of his expression of the genuine situation, the great movement of youth into age, and the alternation of war and peace which makes up what we presently call civilization.

We here in this country have—this is a rather broad generalization—two writers of the first eminence, one who is a Dostoyevskian (I refer to William Faulkner) and one who is undoubtedly a Tolstoyan (and that is Hemingway). And if I had more time, I should in fact read you (but in fact you'd much better read yourself) a story which to me expresses the very best in Hemingway, "The Capital of the World."[4] It's a very simple story about a hotel in Madrid in which there are bullfighters.

And there is a young waiter in the kitchen who adores bullfighters and thinks that he would like to become one. Another of the boys in the kitchen, a dishwasher, says, No, you wouldn't, you'd be scared just like I would be scared. Everybody is scared, and that's why there aren't more bullfighters in Spain. And so this boy, he's called Paco, says, Let's try it. And they tie two great kitchen knives onto a chair, and by an accident he gets fatally stabbed and dies. Hemingway really invests this story with what I can only speak of as greatness. That's to say, a perfectly vivid interaction between these particular characters in this place and the entire human predicament. And the story also satisfies the second qualification: it is not in the least depressing. It is in fact full of this strange joy in the experience of all these people. However, as I've said, I can only recommend you to read that. It is among the best of all the things that Hemingway has written.

Curiously enough, it's paralleled by a scene in *War and Peace.* This comes very late in the novel, and it's an account of how the youngest of the Rostov boys, Petyr Rostov, finally arrives at the front. He's a boy who all his life has been longing to get into this war with Napoleon which has been going on all through his adolescent life; now he's only sixteen or seventeen, and the war is practically over. The French, in hopeless rout, are retreating towards the frontier pursued by the Russians. But to this boy, Petyr, the war is glorious and exciting and romantic. And Tolstoy devotes two or three chapters to describing Petyr's night at the front. He gets himself sent up to the front on some errand and then meets two different officers who are friends of his family and persuades them to let him take part in an attack on the French the next morning. These attacks are really only in the nature of harassment, because the French are in retreat. They very seldom turn and defend themselves, only just to beat off the Russians as one beats off some kind of stinging fly. And so the retreat goes on toward the frontier. But to Petyr this is the most dramatic and most heroic action in the world; he gallops ahead, disregards other people's warnings, and is shot dead. And here again this incident is profoundly moving in the most universal sense, and is filled with a very strange kind of exhilaration. So I beg you to read that, too. If I were to do so it would take at least thirty-five minutes.

The rest of the time that I have I want to spend on a writer who is in some respects nearer to me than the other writers I've mentioned, and that is D. H. Lawrence. Lawrence seems to me to have achieved something which in fact happens very, very seldom in any art, and that is a real revolution. Something new. Now, of course, nothing that is really vital in art is absolutely new; only tricks are new, or sensations or stunts are new. But Lawrence did something which I don't feel anybody had really quite done before. And it's very hard to describe what it is. It is as if he came much nearer in a physical sense to the characters, animals, landscape, and objects than anybody had ever come, so that he established a relation with his material that is almost more like sculpture—or again, from another point of view, like impressionist painting—than like writing. He had first and foremost in his work a great sense of the physical, of the physical presence of people. The other thing which is very striking about Lawrence is a kind of fearlessly subjective approach. That is to say, he seems to be absolutely himself looking at people, and he doesn't fear to make judgments of all kinds about them, and he's so full of his attitude and himself that he can look at a landscape, or anything, and charge it with this personal, subjective significance. Now, you may think that this is in contradiction to what I've been saying about the other self that looks down in compassion, but of course there is that, too; if not, Lawrence would not be Lawrence. And to my mind, he is incomparably the most exciting writer who's lived in my own time.

Lawrence had all kind of theories, about which people write books and spend a great deal of time talking. The idea that we have somehow become divorced from what he described as the dark—he was very fond of the word *dark*—instinctive part of our nature, and have become too cerebral, too mental. That we didn't feel things, we only thought them, and thought we knew them. Now this may or may not be true, but this approach of Lawrence's to life has really only indirectly something to do with this. And I think that what one learns from Lawrence, if one's a writer, is not a philosophy of life but an attitude toward material. I don't think that any writer who has read Lawrence can ever be quite the same again, because in his case it really changes you to look at anything in the world if you once feel the thrill of Lawrence's sensibility. If I were recommending Lawrence from the point of view of a reader coming to him for the first time, I should not recommend any of the big novels, all of which seem to me to go on far too long. Lawrence wrote and wrote and wrote. He did very little correction, I understand, although very occasionally he rewrote a book entirely, as in the case of *Lady Chatterley's Lover,* of course. The versions are quite different, and *The First Lady Chatterley* is a complete uncensorable book.[5] Therefore the story that I would recommend as being, in a sense, as good as a novel—it gives you all the essence of what Lawrence projects into his novels—is a short story called "The Blind Man." This, too, is too long to read to you. And what I do want to read is a passage from a novelette called *St. Mawr* (1925), to which I'm very attached. This novelette, or long short story, novella, is probably the most disgraceful mess ever produced by a major writer from the standard of a creative writing class. Because the plot is utterly crazy. What happens briefly is that there's a young painter in London, whose name is Rico, who marries an American girl. The American girl admired him very much because he's handsome, enormously attractive, and she thinks it would be wonderful if he rode in the park on a horse that is really beautiful, to suit his appearance. So she shops around, and she finds a great stallion, named St. Mawr (it's a Welsh name), and this stallion, she thinks, is just the right thing for Rico to ride in the park. But the stallion, of course, is Lawrence. Lawrence is always somewhere in the story. And the stallion takes one look at Rico and sees that he's no good at all—he hasn't got a dark center! He only lives in the head, and altogether he's a great mistake. So the stallion chooses a strategic moment and throws him and jumps on him. Rico is very angry. He's hurt, of course, injured. But aside from that—he recovers from that—he thinks the stallion ought to be shot. Whereupon his wife is so indignant, especially as Rico is convalescing with another girl, that she goes off with the following people: her mother, the stallion, the Welsh groom who looks after the stallion, and then they go over back to America and pick up another groom who is to make it a foursome, you might say, who is Mexican.

> It was the New England wife of the trader who put most energy into the ranch. . . . Her cabin faced the slow downslope of the clearing, the alfalfa field: her long low cabin, crouching under the great pine-tree that threw up its trunk sheer in front of the house, in the yard. The pine-tree was the guardian of the place. But a bristling, almost demonish guardian, from the far-off crude ages of the world. . . . And the wind hissing in the needles, like a vast nest of serpents. And the pine cones falling plumb as the hail hit them. Then lying all over the yard, open in the sun like wooden roses, but hard, sexless, rigid with a blind will. . . .[6]

That to me is the most wonderful kind of descriptive writing, because it's doing two things simultaneously: it's conveying the extraordinary magic of this place and also describing the character of the woman who sees it. And I remember reading this in the twenties in England and thinking how I would love to go to Taos, and it was a great moment for me when I could go there and make the pilgrimage up to the ranch and spend the night out sleeping under the great trees, and it's all exactly as it's described here, provided of course that you're a New England woman and have to live there.

Now, for the sake of making a rousing conclusion to all this, I'm going to return to a writer of whom I spoke briefly, Herman Melville. And I want to do this because I think that *Moby-Dick,* and specifically the very last portion of the last chapter, illustrates almost more vividly than anything that I know in literature this point about this joy, this underlying, enormous exhilaration, the wildness behind the actual events of the story. The events of the story are, of course, tragic. Captain Ahab has pursued the white whale—they're out in a boat trying to harpoon it—and the whale suddenly turns and sinks the ship. But my goodness, what a ball they are all having, and how in a strange way you feel that Ahab and the white whale and everybody else all adore each other and are part of an extraordinary kind of cosmic fun going on. So I'll see whether you feel the same way about it. I'm sure you've all read it, but, of course, one's apt to read these things a little under the spell of the rest of the book, of what other people have told you you should feel about them, and so forth.

Melville is a writer who fundamentally derives from Shakespeare.[7] That's to say, the way in which he attempts to be and often succeeds in being great is on the scale of the largest kind of Shakespeare speeches—the great roarings and bellowing of Shakespeare when he becomes quite beside himself. This is the kind of thing that Melville does. Another thing he does is the Shakespeare soliloquy, of which there are a number in *Moby-Dick,* such as this one by Ahab:

> "I turn my body from the sun. What ho, Tashtego! Let me hear thy hammer. Oh! ye three unsurrendered spires of mine; thou uncracked keel; and only god-bullied hull; thou firm deck, and haughty helm, and Pole-pointed prow,—death-glorious ship! must ye then perish, and without me? Am I cut off from the last fond pride of meanest shipwrecked captains? Oh, lonely death on lonely life! Oh, now I feel my topmost greatness lies in my topmost grief. Ho, ho! from all your furthest bounds, pour ye now in, ye bold billows of my whole foregone life, and top this one piled comber of my death! Toward thee I roll, thou all-destroying but unconquering whale; to the last I grapple with thee; from hell's heart I stab at thee; for hate's sake I spit my last breath at thee. Sink all coffins and all hearses to one common pool! and since neither can be mine, let me then tow to pieces, while still chasing thee, though tied to thee, thou damned whale! *Thus,* I give up the spear!"[8]

After that there is nothing to be said.

A Writer and the Theater

Today I am going to talk about the theater, and my dabblings in it. I say dabblings in relation to the theater, because, as a matter of fact, I have never really been totally involved in any theatrical production. Although some people refer to me as a playwright, there isn't any play that I ever wrote the whole of, except for one play, my very first, at the age of about six or seven.[1] This play anticipated Somerset Maugham by being called *The Letter.* Only it was called *La Lettre,* and it was entirely written in French. The plot of the play was simple. A middle-aged woman, played by myself, receives a letter to say that her son is killed. She opens the letter and speaks the only line of the play: "O! Il est mort!" She then falls with tremendous force, senseless—or maybe lifeless—to the earth. Perhaps some of you think that this reminiscence has a Freudian flavor. But not at all. It was the most natural thing in the world. You see, my first intimations of the theater were given me by my grandmother—a wonderful lady who was passionately devoted to the cult of Sarah Bernhardt. It therefore seemed entirely natural to me that acting should be done by a middle-aged lady, that the acting should be in French, and that it should end with a fall—for which Madame Bernhardt was famous. And the fall, of course, was the part of the play which I most enjoyed doing.[2]

After that, I had really no contact at all with anything theatrical as far as I can remember until the time when I began to work with W. H. Auden, who had been a friend of mine since the days in our first school when he was seven and I was ten. Around 1933 when he published his first book of poems, he also published a short play in verse called *Paid on Both Sides.*[3] This play was based on one of our favorite kinds of literature, the Icelandic saga, and contained those speeches of heroic understatement for which the sagas are notable. In one of the Icelandic sagas, a lady whose husband has gone away for several weeks to attend the Althing[4] looks out of the door and sees the neighbors, who are notoriously unfriendly, advancing with axes and torches across the hill. She has nobody in the house except the old grandfather, some young boys, and some women servants. Looking at them as they advance, she remarks, "I think this day will end unluckily for some."

This type of dialogue was what fascinated Auden, and there's an echo of it in this first play of his, *Paid on Both Sides* (1930). Soon after this Rupert Doone, a friend of ours who had been a dancer for a while in Diaghilev's ballet, shortly before Diaghilev's death, founded The Group Theatre with a number of friends.[5] Doone asked Auden if he would write a play which had a silent part for a dancer and spoken parts for a number of other characters. Auden and I talked this over, and I provided a few ideas (but it wasn't in any other sense a collaboration) for a short play that he then published called *The Dance of Death* (1933). This play was in due course performed, and Rupert Doone took the part of Death, which was a mimed part, as a dancer. This started Auden off on writing plays, and our first collaboration was a play called *The Enemies of a Bishop* (1929). This was actually the basis of *The Dog Beneath the Skin* (1935–36), our first published, performed play. After we'd written *The Enemies of a Bishop* (which couldn't possibly have been performed at that time—although nowadays you could probably get away with it in the Village, at least for a while, before it was raided), Auden then wrote a play called *The Chase.* He sent me the manuscript, we got into correspondence, and after much back and forth met and worked together on this play, so that it became a collaboration. We intended to call it *The Chase,* but it was Rupert Doone who invented the much more exciting title, *The Dog Beneath the Skin.*

The Dog Beneath the Skin is a sort of modern fairy tale in which a man is chosen to go out and search for the missing heir, an ordinary fairy tale structure. Every year such a man is chosen, and they have all failed to come back. But this year, the hero is chosen, and he sets off on his errand and is accompanied by a dog. This dog is not a realistic dog, but rather like the dog in *Peter Pan,* that's to say an actor obviously inside a dog suit. After going through all kinds of adventures which are supposed to show the state of Europe and society at that time, in various symbolic and farcical styles, it is revealed that as a matter of fact the missing heir has never left the village at all, but has simply turned himself into a dog in order to observe people. He has gone along with the hero on the quest, and in due course he reveals himself. The virtue of the play, such as it is, is simply that we were completely reckless, completely irresponsible, had no idea that the play would possibly be performed, and indeed if it had been performed in its entirety at any time it would be far longer than *Hamlet,* and so we wrote in that kind of uninhibited way that you can only do once. This play contains some very beautiful poetry by Auden. As a matter of fact, it is being revived off Broadway next spring.[6]

To our astonishment, and due to the enterprise of Rupert Doone, the play was cut and put into shape and performed, and it was quite a fair success. We then felt that we must absolutely write another play, simply because we'd written one and because people said why don't you write another. So we thought we would like to write about mountain climbing. The reason we wanted to do this was that Auden's brother was a distinguished mountaineer and in fact had been quite a long way up Everest in one of the expeditions. Also, under the guise of mountain climbing, we wished to describe the career of a man in whom we were passionately interested at that time, Colonel T. E. Lawrence, Lawrence of Arabia. So we devised a kind of melodrama describing the ascent of a mountain, called *The Ascent of F6* (1936–37). This play really had quite a success in England, and to this day is constantly being restaged in various versions. The most dramatic performance that I ever heard of, which I did not see personally, however, took place in America. There's said to have been a performance by students at Harvard, in which a mountain about as high as this hall was constructed and an extremely serious accident occurred on the first night in which almost the entire climbing party fell and landed in the orchestra pit.

William Devlin in debut production of The Ascent of F6.

The other staging of the play that I did see in America took place in a studio in New York. It was extremely interesting because it was performed without any scenery whatsoever on a flight of steps at the end of the studio leading up to a door. All the climbing was done by the actors rising and stumbling and scrambling about on these steps. In order not to remind the audience that there was no scenery, they had the lights out and used flashlights during many of the climbing scenes. They were not dressed like people are at twenty thousand feet; on the contrary, I think they wore T-shirts and jeans and sneakers. But the effect was curiously powerful—it was very well directed—and among other things I always remember one theatrical effect which, in its own way, was one of the most interesting psychological effects I've ever observed in the theater.

On the mountain, one of the characters is killed by an avalanche offstage. The others lean over looking offstage and tell the audience that an avalanche is coming. They see this friend of theirs in a hopelessly exposed position—he cannot get back. The avalanche is coming down, they yell, he can't even hear them, and then it's over. When this play was performed in the studio in New York there was no attempt to convey the sound of the avalanche at all. The actors just shouted at the tops of their voices. Then, at the climax of the excitement, somebody offstage slammed a door, as hard as he possibly could, after which there was complete silence. This conveyed, in the most curious and shocking way, the sense of finality of a tragedy.[7]

The first production of *The Ascent of F6* took place in a very small theater called The Mercury, which was extremely intimate and in which every sound made in the audience could be heard. When the play was staged, Auden was still away in Spain where he had gone with the intention of joining an ambulance unit, from which he had been sidetracked into making speeches in favor of the Spanish government's cause. He only found out later that they were inaudible to anyone outside Spain because the radio was being jammed by the opposing forces. So Auden didn't arrive until the fourth or fifth night after the production opened. Naturally, as in all plays, we had made very considerable last-moment changes, cuts, and so forth. The play started and ran for three or four minutes, when suddenly Auden's voice, in an intense and indignant stage whisper, was heard saying, "What have you done to it?" Which absolutely broke up the audience in roars of laughter.

Two years later, in 1938, we produced our last play, *On the Frontier.* It was a play more or less about the contemporary situation with its acute threat of war. This play was very well acted, very well staged, politely received, and an utter flop—I think because it was too near the reality of the contemporary situation. It was notable for a scene at the beginning which was unrehearsed and had nothing to do with the play, in which Auden had been asked to appeal for some fund or other for needy refugees, and he stepped forward, wishing to say, in effect, that the state of the world at that time was worse than anything that we had portrayed in the play, more tragic and more terrible. What he actually said was, "Ladies and gentlemen, as many of you know, much worse things have been happening in the audience than happened on the stage tonight."

More about the method of these plays in a moment. I want to pass on briefly to refer to my other contacts with the theater, which took place very much later, when my old friend John van Druten decided to my great delight that he could make a play out of one of my books, *Goodbye to Berlin.* He constructed a play out of two of the stories, "Sally Bowles" and "The Landauers," and a section called "Berlin Diary." This play was called *I Am a Camera* and was put on the stage in the fall of 1951.[8] It's a most curious experience to be associated with a production which actually arrives on Broadway, and what you always feel is how incredible that so few people can possibly manage to confront the mass, formidable clump of the audience. You go backstage, and there are so few of them—just somebody looking after the curtain, the actors in their dressing rooms, looking terribly lonely, and you go on the stage and it doesn't look like anything very much. I remember going on the stage, just before the curtain went up, and sitting down at the desk where the character who's named for me is going to sit, and trying in some way to hex the desk so that some wonderful kind of power would come out of the play from the very first moment. And then going back and coming out front and standing right behind the audience, right at the back of the theater, with van Druten and, as the play started, we began to walk back and forth in opposite directions. From time to time as we passed each other we exchanged glances, like animals who scarcely know each other and are vaguely suspicious. I hardly remember looking at the stage. Julie Harris, who was our supreme good fortune and treasure in the play as Sally, was, as it were, opposed to the audience. And it came to me strongly that the play was really very much like a boxing match in which you were praying for Julie Harris to knock them out. Sometimes she hit them very hard and you felt they were on the ropes, then they came back again, then you couldn't bear to look—they seemed to be winning (because the silence meant they were winning) and again, and again, and again, and then you thought, Now they're down! but No . . . ahh . . . again! Those of you who have had plays produced will know exactly what I'm talking about and how one feels under those circumstances.

The thing that I learned from working in what one might call the professional theater—the theater of the good playwright, of the craftsman, as opposed to the theater of the expressionist, of the poet—was that the thing that matters supremely is not plot or situation, but it is character. The great vice of the professional (one might almost say the representational) theater is neatness: the danger that you tie up the whole thing too neatly, that it adds up like a sum and is balanced, and there's something about it, a kind of coldness and artificiality in consequence. What rescues this is character. If you can put a character on stage, if the character having been put on stage is marvelously acted also, then you have something which takes a great deal of destroying. Once an audience is really interested in the character, the audience will forget about the weaknesses of the structure of the play. I noticed this very much in the case of this play of ours that what really mattered was Julie Harris. In London the part was played with equal brilliance in another manner by Miss Dorothy Tutin, and it also ran a long while. I noticed very much that as long as Julie Harris was on the stage, the audience was happy, and that this was, in itself, satisfactory.

Now I've deliberately sketched over the merely historical account of my relations with the theater before going back to the question of theory, and the question of approach, which is what

I really want to discuss here. The theater is a box, a place of imprisonment in which the audience is shut up with the actors. The effects are created by means of claustrophobia: you can't get out. Of course, you can get out, and if you do you break the spell, not only for yourself but, if enough of you go out, for everybody in the place. But this simple fact of imprisonment in a box applies to all kinds of theatrical representation, including such a thing as this lecture. I'm really here, and you are really there, and we are all inside this building, and this lecture is a means by which we all get out of it. That's to say, if I can navigate it to the end, then the doors will open and we can all be released. Similarly, a play is a way in which one is allowed to leave the theater at the end. This is, as I shall endeavor to point out next time, the fundamental difference between the play and the cinema: the cinema being not a box, and not claustrophobic, but a window through which you look outside. The frontal human drama of really having live actors on the stage is something in which the cinema does not and cannot attempt to deal.

When Auden and I became interested in writing for the theater, we had very much criticized the conventional play of that time because we said that there the actors were unnecessarily divided from the audience. In our 1930-ish way, we equated this with the undesirable separation of the private life from the life of the common good, and we equated the audience as it were with the great mass of society, and the actors with the people of the ivory tower. However much nonsense this may have been, the fact remains you could make such remarks in 1930 without the audience throwing anything at you. It was taken as being probably true, or at least worth discussion. So we said what we want to do is to liberate the actors from the confinement of the stage, and hence we were very much in favor of all those devices which, goodness knows, even in those days were not at all new: the device of having people get up in the audience and yell out, the device of having people rush down runways to and from the stage, the device of having no scenery but maybe showing the bare back of the theater or a cyclorama on which lights are thrown. In other words, to exchange the atmosphere of conventional theater for that which much more resembled a kind of animated political meeting.

Now of course in saying all this we were really not changing the fundamental fact at all. If you break down the barriers between the stage and the audience, you are heightening the sense of claustrophobia, increasing the involvement of everybody inside the box with each other, and so in that sense not being at all revolutionary. When we first came to New York, we were taken by our publishers to see a performance of a review which we immediately realized was the great masterpiece in our sort of playwriting—a reaction which shocked the publishers very much, because the review was dreadfully uncultural and was called *Hellzapoppin'* with Olsen and Johnson. Olsen and Johnson produced the sense of claustrophobia, the confinement in a box, to the greatest conceivable extent by means of sound effects and tarantulas that were supposed to be passing under our seats. At one notable moment in the performance a very large gorilla seized a girl out of the audience and began climbing up the side of the boxes—either Olsen or Johnson or both drew automatic pistols and fired repeatedly at the gorilla, but missed. Finally, Olsen remarked, "Well, I daresay they'll be very happy," as the gorilla with the girl over his shoulder disappeared through the entrance to one of the boxes.[9] So this was in fact the sort of theater that we were interested in at the time we were working together.

There is another thing that one learns from being in the theater, and particularly from being in the theater of poetry, the theater of expressionism, and that is the enormous importance of speech, of sound, of what is said. This again is a fundamental difference between the theater and the films, in my opinion. In the theater, you can dominate by sound, by speech, just as on the film you dominate by image and movement. In the theater you can remain perfectly still and deliver speeches which cover four or five pages, and, if you know your business as an actor, and if the speech is of real quality, people will listen to you. I always imagined that if you said more than two or three lines and didn't switch to another character, people would leave the building. Not a bit of it. Now just as the characteristic danger in the professional theater is neatness, a too cut-and-dried, too mechanical plot, so the great danger in the theater of poetry and expressionism is double-talk. We have seen a great deal of that nowadays among dramatists, many of them French, who have played such a large role in the life of our theater during the last ten years. You all know those tremendous utterances by one of the characters which sound pretty good, but you spend the rest of the night wondering what it meant. I was trying to parody such an utterance the other day and thought of this: a character says, "No, Prince, 'tis not the birds that fear the sea, it's the sea that fears the birds."

This kind of line is absolutely usual and is accepted in good part by the audience and is thought to be necessary to the sense of mysteriousness which such a play endeavors to create. Auden and I were of course also guilty of double-talk in this respect from time to time. We were often accused, and I have thought about this very often since, of not taking the theater seriously. I think this was both good and bad insofar as it was true. I think that a certain irresponsibility in the theater is very exciting and desirable. The only trouble is that one is so apt to get carried away by it. But there is no doubt that we did exhibit an enormous amount of irresponsibility, and even a certain faint sadism toward the audience as much as to say I wonder if they'll stand for that. Without the least reason to say this, without the advantage of knowing Samuel Beckett, I have often felt that he is working toward such effects in another way. Beckett's provocation in a play like *Waiting for Godot* (1953) is extraordinary. Remembering that the whole point of the play is that the people are in the theater and cannot leave until they have been dismissed by the working out of the play itself, remembering this, think of Beckett's extraordinary use of pauses. Think how he brings the whole action on the stage to an absolute standstill, and with incredible daring confronts the two characters. There are places in *Godot* where such remarks are made as "Well, say something."

And the other looks and says, "I've got nothing to say."

And the first one says, "Neither have I."

And then there follows a pause which is technically of enormous interest. When I first saw *Godot,* I hadn't read it, and I really wondered if somebody wasn't going to scream or rush out of the theater.[10] And yet one saw that this use of pauses was deliberate, exceedingly effective, and that it created a certain psychological situation which corresponds absolutely with situations in our daily lives, and that the play seems full of meaning and relevance, and was in fact very moving. You find this to some extent in all of the plays of Beckett. And, indeed, perhaps the technique of pauses, of slowing down, is something that has been in the air ever since the early singing of Frank Sinatra. You probably recall those early records—there's one in particular where there was a line about a star falling, and he sang it like this: "Why does its flight make us stop . . . in the night, and wish, as we all do." I used to tremble when he sang this. I thought, this can't go on. Something has got to happen. Somebody must intervene. This silence is scarcely bearable.

In conclusion, I want to read you a little from *The Dog Beneath the Skin,* the first of our plays together. The passages that I'm going to read are all exclusively by Auden. Among the many misunderstandings about me, one is that I am a playwright and another is that I am a poet. As a matter of fact, all that I ever did with our plays was, first of all, make structural suggestions, and secondly, write scenes that are entirely in prose and indeed, not all of those. But now I would like to read you two examples of Auden, one in verse and another a kind of heightened poetic prose which he dearly loved, which I think he has stolen from the sermon in *Moby-Dick.* The first one is right at the beginning of the play and is a speech spoken either in unison or alternating verses by the leaders of the chorus. When this was performed, an actor and an actress, both in modern evening dress and wearing small, black eighteenth-century masks, spoke the lines. What these two people represent is just as much your guess as mine. They call themselves The Two. And it seems that they are some kind of force in life, perhaps laws of nature, which we willfully and in our arrogance ignore but which will catch up with us sooner or later.

LEADER OF SEMI-CHORUS I: The young men in
Pressan to-night
  Toss on their beds
  Their pillows do not comfort
  Their uneasy heads.
  The lot that decides their fate
  Is cast to-morrow,
  One must depart and face
  Danger and sorrow.
VOICES: Is it me? Is it me? Is it . . . me?
LEADER OF SEMI-CHORUS II: Look in your heart
and see:
  There lies the answer.
  Though the heart like a clever
  Conjurer or dancer
  Deceive you often into many
  A curious sleight
  And motives like stowaways
  Are found too late.
VOICES: What shall he do, whose heart
  Chooses to depart?
LEADER OF SEMI-CHORUS I: He shall against his peace
  Feel his heart harden,
  Envy the heavy birds
  At home in a garden.
  For walk he must the empty
  Selfish journey
  Between the needless risk
  And the endless safety.
VOICES: Will he safe and sound
  Return to his own ground?
LEADER OF SEMI-CHORUS I: Clouds and lions stand

Before him dangerous
And the hostility of dreams.
Oh let him honour us
Lest he should be ashamed
In the hour of crisis,
In the valleys of corrosion
Tarnish his brightness.
VOICES: Who are you, whose speech
Sounds far out of reach?[11]

At the beginning of the action we had a scene which was based on musical comedy, and there I discovered something for us to steal in a very strange place, Edmond Rostand's play *L'Aiglon* (1900), the play about the son of Napoleon which Sarah Bernhardt used to play in when she was already in her late fifties, this being a boy of seventeen. It was one of her great successes.[12] Rostand, who also wrote in verse, had the device of scattering a whole number of actors all over the stage, each of whom said two or three words of a speech, and then somebody else said something else quite unrelated, and they always built up to rhyming couplets. If this is done very slickly on the stage it's quite amusing.

A strange sermon occurs late in the play and, as I say, owes more than something to the sermon in *Moby-Dick.* It's amusing as an early example of something which Auden did repeatedly later.

Incidentally, this reminds me that Auden was always fascinated by sermons, and by the ecclesiastical manner of English clergymen. I told you that we went to the same school, St. Edmund's, named for a kind of Anglo-Saxon version of St. Sebastian—he was a martyr who got shot full of arrows. On St. Edmund's Day, we always had an outside clergyman who came down and used to preach, and he used to repeat this sermon so much verbatim that most of us knew parts of it by heart, and it had a great effect on Auden's style.

I see how long the sermon is, and I don't think that it's any use reading it unless one reads all of it. So, I'll read you something else, which is the very first passage, even before the chorus that I read to you, with which the play is supposed to open. This was cut out in production because if you read the whole of the chorus like everything else in the play it would be enormously long, it would probably take about twenty minutes before the curtain went up. But this is very characteristic of the doom-laden manner of Auden's early work.

The Summer holds: upon its glittering lake
Lie Europe and the islands; many rivers
Wrinkling its surface like a ploughman's palm.
Under the bellies of the grazing horses
On the far side of posts and bridges
The vigorous shadows dwindle; nothing wavers.
. . .
Hiker with sunburn blisters on your office pallor,
Cross-country champion with corks in your hands,
When you have eaten your sandwich, your salt and your
    apple,
When you have begged your glass of milk from the ill-kept
    farm,
What is it you see?
I see barns falling, fences broken,
Pasture not ploughland, weeds not wheat.
The great houses remain but only half are inhabited,
Dusty the gunrooms and the stable clocks stationary.
Some have been turned into prep-schools where the diet is
    in the hands of an experienced matron,
Others into club-houses for the golf-bore and the top-hole.
. . .
Man is changed by his living; but not fast enough.
His concern to-day is for that which yesterday did not occur.
In the hour of the Blue Bird and the Bristol Bomber, his
    thoughts are appropriate to the years of the Penny
    Farthing:
He tosses at night who at noonday found no truth.

Stand aside now: The play is beginning
In the village of which we have spoken; called Pressan
    Ambo:
Here too corruption spreads its peculiar and emphatic
    odours
And Life lurks, evil, out of its epoch.

A Writer and the Films

Today I'm going to talk about "A Writer and the Films." This is a companion piece to my talk "A Writer and the Theater," and I must recall a few of the things that I said then. I suggested that the art of the theater is based, to some extent, on the fact that the actors and the audience are together in a box—a place of confinement—and that the story of a play, among all the other things it is, is the story of how at the end of it everybody is going to be released from that box. The excitement of the theater is to quite a large degree the excitement of being with living actors in the same room. They really are alive, and that's what's so shocking. The same thing, of course, is true of minor theatrical representations, such as this lecture. I am really here and you can't be absolutely sure of what I will do, in consequence. The events on the stage are not absolutely predetermined. This is important to remember; it sounds very obvious, but I think it does have a bearing on the attitude with which we watch a movie and a play, respectively. And it applies far more in the case of a lecture. Indeed, perhaps it is the only kind of dramatic excitement the lecturer is able to exploit. You simply don't know if I won't fall down dead in front of you. If I do, that will be a new event, something not planned—and well worth having been here to see.

The same is true of live television, and this is why, as I shall endeavor to show, from this angle television has more affinity with the theater than with the screen, because these people are simultaneously alive and doing what they are doing at that very moment. Now you may say that this is just a mere technical detail and that very often the audience is being fooled—very often the show has indeed been taped and the whole thing happened in New York hours before. Nevertheless, as long as the audience believes this, the audience is getting a certain kind of thrill which it otherwise only gets in the theater or in the lecture hall or in those forms of athletic competition which are also dramatic—notably boxing and wrestling matches where the opposition between two individuals becomes extremely dramatic and highly exciting.

The theater is all these things. What is the cinema? The cinema to me is a window—a magic window which you look out of. You may look into the far world and see events enormously distant in time and place, and you may look over vast areas of landscape, as in extreme long shots, or again you may enjoy a closeness of observation which is quite impossible on the stage. Not only can you come right up to a person's face until it looks like the moon at about thirty miles over the surface (you see all the pores and the holes and the hairs growing out of the nostrils) but also you can dwell on certain actions of the actor; these actions can be isolated, so that one looks at nothing else. One can see the hand alone holding a revolver or flower. One can go in very close and observe the habits of the smallest insects, if one wants to. And so the film has an immense range of view—a kind of range which, until the invention of the cinema, simply didn't exist for human beings on the earth. They hadn't ever had these kinds of experiences which were made possible by the cinema. But, however great the illusion, however much you may lose yourself in the images on the screen, you are not in a box, and you are not confined with the actors in the same sense. Perhaps people who have never been to any plays (and there are many such people) might disagree with this, and might say that they are able to identify with the photograph on the screen so closely that they forget that these photographs are not three-dimensional, that they're not living and breathing people. But if such people do go to the theater then they see the difference, and the difference is there, and one is certainly aware of it psychologically all through one's viewing of a play.

I suggest further that the theater is primarily for speech: for the excitement of the human voice in great poetry or rhetoric, or in wit, in epigram, in the quick give and take of brilliantly conceived dialogue. The theater is for speech, and the theater is also for character. I mean that when a character is performed and portrayed on the stage it has a kind of added dimension, because as I say the actor who is portraying it is alive. He is really there with you. And in the sense of intimate theater and in the case of the various devices by which the actors are brought even nearer to the audience than usual, this contact can become quite shockingly direct. When a play called *The Connection* (1959) was performed in New York, the audience was told that the actors were real dope addicts, which was not true, and that they would solicit the audience during the intermission for money in order to buy more heroin.[1] This daring theatrical effect, probably one of the closest contacts between the audience and the actors, was unfortunately not witnessed by myself and my companion, because we were so bored by the first act that we left. But I can see where something of this kind is the ultimate extension of this question of being confined in a box with actors. And this is the sort of effect which cannot be produced in the cinema under any circumstances. The thing can't get down, can't come off the screen; it can't come through the window, it can't come right down into the audience. It's true that Mr. Huxley, in *Brave New World,* conceived the idea of something called "Feelies" in which, by means of electrodes, the audience experienced all sorts of sensations connected with what they saw on the screen. But this, of course, would be a purely mechanical device and wouldn't really disprove my argument.

Very good. I contend that the stage drama is primarily for speech, for utterance, and for the presentation of character. What is the film for? The film is primarily for image and for movement. This thing about image, about the actual, visual effect of something on the screen, can sometimes be very disconcerting. The other day I went to a movie theater with a friend of mine who is an artist, and a scene in a film adapted from a well-known stage play began to take place on the screen. Two ladies, two actresses, both very talented, were conducting the scene with great spirit, saying their lines, acting like mad, and what were we doing? We were absolutely fascinated by a grape-purple stained glass window which happened to be in the set and was in between them, and was so inconceivably beautiful that it distracted one's attention altogether from the acting and from the opposition of the characters and from everything else. I have known this to happen really quite often in the films, that some prop, some moment of movement, something perhaps related to the story but only indirectly, was so arresting, so memorable, that five years later you couldn't remember anything else about the film. You say, Don't you remember how wonderful it was: there was first a great black explosion and then a white explosion. You remember the way the smoke trailed away from the train as it took off? Do you remember that great field of yellow flowers contrasted with the darkness of the barn? Do you remember one time when, in an almost black-and-white film, where you saw a barn in winter surrounded by the snow, a boy in a red mackinaw came out of the barn—it was like firing a shot right in your face. These are memories, actual memories of actual films that I've seen, which haunt me when I can't remember any longer what the film was about, how the people acted, or anything else. Now, admittedly all of what I'm saying to you is extremely subjective and open to many protests, but for me this is primarily what the film does. It gives you the wonder of movement and the shock of image.

In the very early silent films, for instance, of the great Russian masters, Eisenstein, Pudovkin, and others, this alternation of movement and image was a deliberate part of their technique. In one film, the milling crowds in the streets during a revolutionary street fight were constantly being contrasted in their violence and powerful eddying movements with intercut shots of absolutely immobile eighteenth-century statues looking down on the square in which the fighting was taking place, or with shots of great cumulus clouds moving quietly in the sky, as though entirely above the battle. Such was the art of the silent film. The silent film was essentially poetic. The silent film didn't pretend so much to particularize and say, There was a boy named Joe Black; there was a girl named Mary White. It tended to say, There was a boy; there was a girl. One felt in such films a poetic generalization, so that the film could have had the overall title of *The Lot of Man* or

The Human Condition, some title which suggested that this was an eternal process of human life upon the earth. The characters were always seen in very close relation to their environment; for instance, if there was a man who hunted in the woods, one was made to feel the relationship between him and the woods very, very closely. This was part of the poetry of the silent film. The first film ever made by Josef von Sternberg, who later became famous as the director of Marlene Dietrich, was called *The Salvation Hunters* (1925). This film began very characteristically with a subtitle which said, "A city. Like all others. Houses, a river, mud. And sometimes, the sun." In other words, a generalized poetic note was struck right from the beginning of the film.

Before going on to speak about the intrusion of the sound film into this situation (and it was a real and most dramatic intrusion), I have to say that right from the very beginning an entirely different development was taking place in the cinema. This development was connected with the fact that the cinema is also a most marvelous appliance for popularizing and universalizing anything that you want to show. People didn't only want to see poetic visions of man's life upon the earth—although as a matter of fact what one would call quite average audiences were surprisingly sophisticated in this respect, in comparison with nowadays. I remember once, in a part of Berlin which was quite poor and inhabited entirely by the working class, going into a film theater and seeing some film in which some horses, young foals in a field, cantered up a hill and there was a line of trees. The absolute justice of the photography of this movement, and the beauty of the trees in their exact position within the frame set against the sky, was so startling that the whole audience applauded quite spontaneously. They were applauding an aesthetic experience, an immediate experience which held only for a few moments, and then passed on. But nevertheless there was a very different function that the cinema was fulfilling: the function of bringing to the masses all kinds of material which hitherto had been inaccessible to them, of turning stage plays into a canned film version, and of presenting the fascinating creatures known as the stars.

One might say that the first star, or the first movie star, scarcely ever acted in a movie, except at the very end of her life, and this was Sarah Bernhardt. Sarah Bernhardt had all the glamour of the stars of the great tradition. She had fascinating hobbies, she slept every night in her coffin to show that she was exotically aware of the brevity of her fame, she had very dramatic adventures in her private life, and on one occasion she paid a train to dash over a whole line of track on the way to New Orleans when it had been condemned because of floods, in order that she could make an appearance there. She was enormously dramatic in her private life, and she let her private life spill over onto the stage, and vice versa, to the great indignation of her colleagues, both in France and elsewhere. She was the first film star and appeared in a number of films, but quite briefly and indeed, it must be said, rather ludicrously, since her idea of gesture for the camera was to raise both arms and then let them fall again a number of times. She obviously had very few resources as a screen actress and seemed to be unaware of the power of the human face to convey, at that range, emotions by mere nuance. However, she was followed by a whole procession of great stars—people whose lives were in themselves a kind of story and whose appearances on the screen were intimately connected with the public idea of those lives, so that it was in fact very important for them to appear only in the kind of picture which the public wanted to see them in. Hemingway makes an amusing point about Garbo's appearance in *Anna Christie*—that it shocked the people of Madrid inexpressibly to see Garbo in poor clothes as an unfortunate girl, an outcast and a prostitute. They felt that she should always wear jewels, magnificent gowns and furs, and be exotic and mysterious.

The great star was of course a kind of aristocrat in his own right. I remember, for instance, the German star Conrad Veidt, certainly one of the great stars of the German theater, who later had a considerable career in Hollywood and died there. I remember one time in England they were shooting a film version of Lion Feuchtwanger's novel *Jew Suss* (1934).[2] Conrad Veidt was playing the leading role. Everything was set up for the execution scene—the most elaborate scene in which a whole set had been built as the town square, vast numbers of extras were waiting, and a very unpleasant kind of cage was hanging down from the gibbet in which Veidt was to be strangled. Veidt himself, all made up and in costume and ready for his great entrance, was sitting in a cart with his hands chained together, surrounded by guards, and he was about to be driven onto the set and into the range of the cameras after which he would be taken out of the cart and dragged to the place of execution. At this moment, as constantly happens in the studios, something was wrong with the cameras, and there was a wait for about ten minutes. This is where I saw that Veidt was a great star. He sat in the cart. A stenographer, one of the studio girls, came up to him and offered him some candy. Now, a lesser actor would have done one of two things—I should say, a lesser *star.* Veidt was also as a matter of fact a very good actor, but I'm speaking of the quality of being a star. A lesser star would have either been annoyed because this stupid girl was interfering with his mood and he was trying to hold the mood of a condemned man and not to be offered candy; or else, anxious to show that he was "regular" and just one of the gang, he would have laughed and joked with her, taken the candy and, in fact, behaved just like anybody waiting for his job to start—would have thrown off the whole mask of being Jew Suss, this great aristocrat who'd been unmasked as a Jew and who was being cruelly punished by the prejudices of his time. So, what does Veidt actually do? He looked down. He saw the girl. He didn't see her as a little twentieth-century stenographer; he saw her as the only girl in this town who took pity on him as he went to the scaffold. His eyes filled with tears. He could hardly thank her, he said nothing, he nodded a little, he stretched out his manacled hands, took the candy, put a little to his mouth yet could hardly bear to eat it, was deeply moved, bowed his head, and went on waiting for the execution. This was simply magnificent, and one saw what it is to have real style in this manner.

When the silent film gave way to the invention, or forcible intrusion, of sound, a major crisis took place. There was an economic crisis caused by the fact that the studios had to get an enormous lot of new equipment, and that much of this equipment, as always happens in the early days, was almost instantly obsolete and had to be junked and more equipment bought. Aside from this, many of the stars, who were most valuable properties, turned out to have heartrending, dreadful accents of various kinds. They couldn't under any circumstances be allowed to speak, or they squeaked in little high voices, or this was wrong or that was wrong, and so a number of people's careers came abruptly to an end. But, in fact, something far more serious than all of this happened, which was that people now tried to behave as though one of the fundamental laws of the cinema had been abolished and had never existed. They tried to believe that the cinema is for sound. And they introduced immense scenes of talk which slowed down the precious life of the film, the life of movement, in favor of voices speaking to each other. This mistake was recognized and to some extent rectified in that people cut down the dialogue as much as they could. Only the very greatest directors have understood that it's not that simple. It's not just that, on the screen, you have to have less dialogue than you can afford to have in the theater. It's that the words spoken on the screen should have an entirely different relation to the image. They should have a relation to the image which is not akin to the relation between what we see in the theater and what we hear. The sound in the film should always be, as it were, balanced against the image and not go with it. For one thing, the fact that you can see everything on the screen makes it only about one-quarter as necessary to let the audience know what is happening. The audience is very quick at guessing and, by long training, has developed a sixth sense. It's a very common thing to hear said in the movie studios "the audience is way ahead of you," and so it often is. It takes very little, a gesture, a certain relation between two scenes, two shots, the introduction in a rather prominent way of some prop which has already acquired a dramatic significance in the story, and immediately the audience says, Why yes, of course, now I know what's going to happen.

Therefore, we do not have the necessity that exists on the stage very often of speaking in order to explain just what is going on. On the stage, it's really quite difficult—and for people in the back almost impossible—to see the finer niceties of gesture and business between two people, and these often have to be backed up by dialogue. On the screen this kind of thing becomes absolutely ludicrous, and never more so than when, as if becoming very fashionable nowadays, a stretch of silent film is backed by a spoken narration. "I felt blue that morning. I didn't know what was the matter with me. I took a tram, I went out to the park, I looked at the ducks. Stupid creatures, I thought. Their life is as dull as mine." Every bit of this narration is absolutely unnecessary. And yet we see film after film in which, by God, the hero gets out of bed, looks blue, looks like he doesn't know what's the matter with him, goes downstairs, takes the trolley car and rides out to the park, sits down, sees the ducks. The whole thing is photographed, and yet this voice goes yakking on as though contributing to the situation, and of course it isn't in the least. This is one of the things that you have to learn when you write for the film—you have to try your best to somehow oppose the words and the image.

There's another thing about the films nowadays that is, to say the least, questionable, and that is the endeavor to pack enormous quantities of material into them. Years ago, I heard Robert Flaherty say, "The film is the longest possible distance between two points." Robert Flaherty was the great documentary director who made *Nanook of the North* (1922), *Man of Aran* (1934), and discovered the young Hindu actor, Sabu, and made a film with him called *Elephant Boy* (1937). He meant by this that his conception of films was to take some quite small piece of material, a short story, or a simple dramatic proposition, and explore it and exploit it and play the variations on it. See it from every angle, and, in other words, make the longest possible distance between two points which is consistent with keeping the interest of the audience and keeping this precious thing, this tightrope walking movement which is the nerve of the film.

Nowadays entirely the opposite is so often attempted, and we get entire novels decanted into films in this way, with the unfortunate result that the most interesting parts of them are—and I would suggest always must be under these circumstances—left out. You see, you take the most complicated, subtle work of fiction, and if you reduce it and get something onto the screen, it all ends up with the fact that the boy is running after the girl, he gets her or he doesn't, very simple, very crude movements, and all the marvelous irrelevancies which make up half of the charm and atmosphere of a great novel utterly destroyed. The mainline characters are the characters that we follow. The minor characters—although they're always introduced at first—are progressively cut out and even if scenes with them are shot, these scenes are necessarily the first to be destroyed. This isn't just bad taste; this is really the logical consequence of having bitten off more than you can possibly chew. I can imagine some entirely different kind of film, a kind of film which I believe has never really been attempted, in which one gave impressions of a great novel—a sort of symphony—something analogous to those records that contain a sort of potpourri of airs out of the best-loved operas of Verdi or someone. I know that in this particular case this sort of thing may be regarded as undesirable, but it is conceivable that you could do such a thing with a film dealing with an enormous novel on the epic scale and by creating hundreds of little moments and not dwelling so much on the fortunes of the principal characters perhaps really bring the book not only to life but into a new meaning and significance in another medium. This is something, however, which has, to the best of my knowledge and belief, never or almost never been attempted.

I should speak about my own work in the movie industry. I do so with great hesitation because, as I've already conveyed to you by my theoretical remarks, I really don't feel that there are very many films that are at the moment in the truly live line of cinema. Most of them tend to be, to a greater or lesser extent, conveniences for conveying stage plays and novels to a mass of people who are unable or unwilling to see or read them. And I have never been engaged in the other sort of film at all. I have been engaged in a number of films of a commercial variety in the big studios. This isn't to say that such enterprises aren't very worthy in their own way, and that they aren't a great deal of fun to do. Packing calls for great ingenuity, and packing enormous novels into a two-and-a-half or at most three-hour film also requires ingenuity and is very challenging, and is perhaps in a way more fun to write than to see on the screen. Anyway, I started off by becoming involved in London with a movie director, an Austrian, whose name was Berthold Viertel. I have described this experience in a novelette of mine called *Prater Violet* (1945). We made a picture together, and then later in my life, after I came to California, I worked on several pictures for the big studios, Warner Bros., MGM, or Twentieth Century–Fox. As a matter of fact, the two jobs in which I had a more or less free hand and of which I am proudest (insofar as I am proud of any of it) were scripts which have never been shot because they both involved considerable expense and also great casting problems. The first was quite an amusing project. Some Indian filmmakers came over and, in a strange hour, persuaded the front office of MGM to make a film about the early life of the Buddha. Why they ever consented to this I don't know. But as a matter of fact, as no doubt many of you are aware, the early life of the Buddha is extremely dramatic material if you regard it in a very simple way as the conflict between the father who doesn't want his son to go out into the world and fulfill the prophecy of becoming a monk, and the son who is impelled by this mysterious restlessness without knowing what it's all about. The father adores his son, provides him with every luxury, with companions, beautiful girls, and finds him finally a beautiful wife. But he lives always in a kind of dream world inside the great park of the palace, and the question always is: Will he leave it and what will happen if he does? Along these lines we wrote a screenplay, and I still think that if you could possibly find anyone to play the young prince, Siddhartha, who later becomes the Buddha, and if it could be done in the proper setting, it might be extremely effective.

What actually happened was something which very often happens when you're working for the studio, primarily for the

A staged studio photo of screenwriter Isherwood "relaxing" with stars Lana Turner and Marisa Pavan on the set of the MGM film Diane. *Also shown is producer Edwin H. Knopf.*

producer. This means that one's writing a literary rather than a cinematic work—you have in some way to make him see the visual side of the whole production. And so one writes in all kinds of details, rather recklessly, just to create atmosphere. I remember that what really sank this film was that I had put in one scene, without very much knowing what I was talking about, that the king was sitting on a throne in the form of a giant cobra, fashioned out of gold and obsidian. I liked the obsidian because it sounded kind of reptilian and sinister, and it's such a beautiful word. Well, they rushed out and priced obsidian, and found that it's very expensive and hard to come by, and there was a big financial lobby against the film at once as being hopelessly expensive.[3]

The latest project that I've been engaged in (it's some while since I've worked in the studios), and one which I think will certainly be put into action one day, is a film version of Romain Rolland's novel *Jean-Christophe.*[4] This is eminently actable material. The only trouble is in the book it goes on forever—he had about sixteen girlfriends, and a great many of the scenes are repetitious. It's the story of a very brash young German of peasant extraction who comes to Paris with great gifts as a composer, absolutely no tact, and very little knowledge of the world, full of violent idealism and very little sense of humor. I will conclude this talk by telling you a short sequence out of this film because I think it would play amusingly on the stage. You are to imagine this very husky young man, looking kind of like a younger Brando, let us say. Here he is looking out for somebody to perform an oratorio that he had written based on the biblical story of the boy David and his fight with Goliath. He goes out into Parisian artistic society and makes a lot of rather rash and loud remarks—he's very shocked by the triviality and sophistication as he sees it of the people in this group. He feels alien to them. But suddenly a handsome and very cultured man comes up to him and asks to be introduced, and this is a man named Goujart, who is the great musical critic of Paris of the time. And Goujart, to Jean-Christophe's delight and amazement, shows the greatest interest in him and his oratorio, and says in fact, I have a marvelous singer for you . . . a soprano who should sing David. And he produces a rather passé lady named Mlle de Sainte-Ygraine, and says, She's a wonderful singer and just the person for you. Well, Jean-Christophe has slight doubts, even from the beginning, but still he thinks it's so kind of him to suggest it, and he is ready to appear, and they go into rehearsal and she's simply awful. He struggles with it, but it really is too much. Here is this vast, enormously fat woman saying, With these tender arms of mine I, a young boy, will vanquish the giant Goliath. Then, Jean-Christophe discovers that Sainte-Ygraine is the mistress of this critic, Goujart, that she had a lot of money, and that she's determined at all costs to appear on the concert stage, and that they've been looking out all season for a sucker who would let her perform something. They have victimized this young man.

Jean-Christophe is furious; he breaks up the rehearsal, goes right down to the café where Goujart is sitting, and makes a terrific scene. Goujart calls a waiter and says, Here is my card. Give it to this gentleman. "He will wish to arrange our next meeting" (78).

So here is Jean-Christophe involved in a duel. Jean-Christophe takes the duel terribly seriously. He's certain that he'll be killed, but he doesn't care. Anything is better—his honor has been insulted, his work has been insulted. He's going through with it. Everybody else in Paris is enormously amused. In the first place, this is the very end of the century, and under these conditions the opponents used pistols which could scarcely carry the range anyway, and great precautions were taken so that nobody would be seriously hurt at all. Jean-Christophe is the only person who doesn't know this, and all his friends come to him and say Goujart is the best shot in Paris, you'd better watch out. The next morning Christophe, like a man going to a heroic death, drives out to the Bois, and they have a meeting outside a little restaurant. Goujart, as the injured party, has the first shot. With the utmost negligence, he points the pistol somewhere vaguely and fires—the bullet drops practically at Christophe's feet. Christophe, with enormous care, aims right at Goujart and misses. Goujart comes over with his hand out, says, My dear fellow, all that little silliness is over and now let's be the best of friends. Christophe, who is utterly frustrated by this whole thing and doesn't understand dueling at all, simply flies at Goujart and seizes him by the throat, which is of course a most appalling thing to do after a duel. Nobody had ever seen anyone do anything like this before, and he's dragged off by the seconds, whereupon he's so embarrassed that he rushes off into the woods and hides. He won't come out for hours, after all the others have left.

Well, he gets another soprano, they perform the oratorio, and on the night of the concert they arrive there and Goujart is in the audience. And Christophe's backers have hired, as is usual, a claque to applaud at the right moment. But, unfortunately, as he realizes when it's too late, Goujart has paid the claque some extra money, and they change their allegiance. In the middle of the concert, after the first pieces have been performed, Goujart gets up very noticeably, so that the whole audience sees him, and with a sort of charming bow as much as to say, Sorry to eat and run, walks off with Sainte-Ygraine out of the concert hall. Now the claque starts, and at the end of the next duet they start to shout, and they take the usual chauvinistic attitude and shout, Take it back to Germany. We don't want your German music here . . . this kind of thing. The whole audience is in an uproar, the concert comes to an end, Christophe is absolutely furious. He comes downstage, looks at the audience, and says, Oh, so you want something French. And with one finger, very carefully, he picks out on the piano "Frère Jacques," then he turns and walks off.

A Writer and Religion

Religion is a vague word that immediately needs to be defined because what I'm going to deal with is the figure of the saint in literature—the difficulties of dealing with him, and the rewards of success in dealing with him if you do succeed. I am not proposing to talk about literature dealing, for instance, with the various religious organizations or churches, and I will talk only indirectly about the literature dealing with monasteries and convents. I'm thinking more of the saint as a fictional character. Now, of course I must start by defining what I mean by a saint. And I take, arbitrarily, this definition: a saint is a man, primarily, of experience—an experience which has led to enlightenment.

It is necessary, before using the words *experience* and *enlightenment,* to make clear that there is here a hypothesis which, if it's absolutely rejected, makes it impossible to write about saints except from an entirely objective point of view as eccentrics or madmen. Or possibly as benevolent figures with utterly mysterious motivations. But if you accept this hypothesis, which Aldous Huxley referred to as the minimum working hypothesis, then you can go a little further in understanding what is meant by a saint. The minimum working hypothesis is simply this: that there is within ourselves and all around us and within every other creature and object something other than individual being, something which we call God, or the Godhead, or the Reality or various Sanskrit or other names. That's the first hypothesis. The second part of the hypothesis is that this Reality can be contacted within ourselves and known, not in the sense that you know the alphabet but in the sense of self-knowledge, of an absolute unity of experience of knowing the self as one's true self and being united with it. This kind of knowing leads, of course,

Isherwood with two Hindu monks in India, where he came up with the idea for his final novel, A Meeting by the River.

by extension, to the recognition of this Godhead within other people. In order to know this self, there is, according to the third term of the hypothesis, a way of life. In other words, the practitioners of this kind of knowledge which leads to union with the Godhead and self-enlightenment have agreed that there's a right way to do this and a wrong way to do this. Speaking very broadly, the way of life that must be followed is one that recognizes the existence, at least hypothetically, of the Godhead in other people, and therefore for that reason a charitable attitude toward them (in the very widest sense of that word): we mustn't try to kill them, or to swindle them in any way, or to tell lies to them, or show them any kind of cruelty. On the contrary, we must try to help them as though they were indeed ourselves.

This being the case, the saint as he's conceived of in terms of this hypothesis is a person who develops. He develops through stages to an increasing self-awareness and always, primarily, by the light of his own existence. This struggle toward self-knowledge is attended, as I say, by acts of what you might call a positive rather than a negative nature, and the crown of the whole thing, the sainthood, is in the illumination, in the enlightenment, and is attended by a sense that all the creatures and the objects of this universe are at one within the Godhead, and that therefore all are infinitely lovable and are to be served because of their essentially divine nature.

Most of us tend to take a rather opposite view of the saint; that's to say, instead of stressing the importance of his experience, of his struggle for self-knowledge, we dwell upon conduct, and we all have a general idea of the kind of conduct which we require of a saint, which includes immense quantities of meekness and sweetness and a rather low-wattage light shining forth in a kind of soft dreamy beam around his figure. We are therefore extremely disconcerted, when we start to read the historical lives of the real saints, to find certain other characteristics—in the first place, the wildest kind of eccentricity, farce, and fun, also actions which appear on the surface quite drastic and impulsive and domineering, and indeed not meek at all. So these two views of the saint are at odds, and the truth is that we find it extremely difficult to imagine what the real saints were, or are, or should be like. Now, if you approach the saint quite objectively as a novelist, and say, I would like to write about him, I would like to create this figure, you have at once a great incentive to do so, and also enormous difficulties. The saint in many ways is the most exciting character that you can possibly pick for a character in a work of fiction. Why is this so? Because all the rest of us are to a lesser or a greater degree necessarily bound within the confines of our lust, our desire, our greed, our ambition, and our fear. And therefore we repeat the same kind of responses over and over again. But the saint is subject, in his perfected form, to none of these bondages and is absolutely unpredictable in his behavior. And this makes for the most exciting and extraordinary scenes of all kinds, because you just don't know what he'll do next. You know the limerick:

> There was a young man who said, Damn,
> I really can see that I am
> A creature that moves
> In predestinate grooves
> In fact, not a bus, but a tram.

Well, a saint is a bus. A tram is what most of us are, confined along certain lines. The bus can decide to change its course because, at the same time as it is a public convenience, it's also an automobile, and it can go anywhere.

And so, we have as a matter of fact rather a paradoxical image of the saint, because the saint is a kind of public convenience who is at the disposal of everybody, but only to go in certain directions. Sometimes he will say, No, I'm sorry. If you insist on going along Hate Street to Murder Square, I am turning off here, and though I urge you to stay with me and will gladly take you to some other place, I must now ask you to get off the bus. The driver of the trolley car, or tram, on the other hand, of course can only go along one route the whole time, and so he does. And whatever you may think about it, he takes people to the bad streets as well as the good. I perceive certain holes in this analogy, so let's not push it any further.

Very good. Now I've suggested why one may want to write about saints but also why it's extremely difficult to do so, because the saint as an end product is a very, very strange and eccentric being, profoundly other than we are. But I stress the point when I say as an *end product.* Oscar Wilde says in one of his plays, "Every saint has a past, and every sinner has a future."[1] In writing a work of fiction about a saint, we have to deal with the saint's past, either by implication or by going back in the narrative itself, to show how he got to be that way and how he started.

The way that we can take the reader with us and convince the reader that the saint's evolution is something believable is to show the saint back at the point of starting, when he was just like anybody else, when he was a sinner with a future.

Now this problem has been faced by a great number of novelists, and I'm only going to mention comparatively few of their creations. They are Larry in Somerset Maugham's *The Razor's Edge* (1944) and a much greater creation to which I will refer in detail later, Father Zossima in *The Brothers Karamazov* by Dostoyevsky (1880). In both cases we find that these authors have started with extremely reassuring, normal hundred-percent figures. Larry is the all-American boy: athletic, handsome, popular, fond of girls, a good mixer—absolutely charming. And Father Zossima is the all-Russian boy of the '40s of the last century, a young military officer, perhaps not so charming because very loud and quarrelsome but absolutely usual in every way. Very fond of girls, and of drink, and of creating a lot of noise and excitement, full of vitality and animal high spirits. Of such material are saints made. It may be said, however, that in real life they frequently are made in a very different way—out of acute neurosis and acute troubles of one kind or another which have driven somebody to a point at which he either has to make the negative decision of suicide or madness, or the positive decision of some kind of mutation of his whole character. Be that as it may, it is entirely possible for a saint to start off like Father Zossima did or like Larry did in *The Razor's Edge.* Now, in other words, what we're telling the reader is that Mr. Smith, Mr. Jones, and Mr. Brown are all potentially saints, and that therefore we needn't think that this character of ours is so strange. And Maugham does a very good job, I think, of reassuring us on this point. He makes Larry absolutely ordinary before he starts to make him extraordinary, and he introduces, with a great deal of art, little hints of the strangeness which gradually comes over the character. However, it is an extremely difficult thing to indicate, to describe, the moment of vocation—the moment at which the young man or young woman suddenly is struck by some sort of insight which causes the first beginnings of gradual movement of life away from the pattern, away from the trolley-car line tracks. I think that Maugham is a little unsatisfactory; the moment is passed over rather vaguely. Dostoyevsky, on the other hand, produced a scene of unexampled farce, warmth, charm, and beauty with the account of Father Zossima's duel. But there is something that I must add at this point, and that is, historically speaking, it is known that a great number of major saints made this mutation—experienced this moment of vocation—in the form of what is called a vision. Now, there are no two ways about this. Whether you believe any of the things I have been mentioning, undoubtedly the people in question thought that they had had visions. And, after all, what is a spiritual experience? It is something which leaves a tremendous change on the character. The only thing that you can argue about was whether it was the vision—whatever it was—that did it, or whether it wasn't. We know objectively speaking that something happened to St. Francis, and afterwards he was different. We know objectively speaking that something happened to Bernadette, and afterwards she was different. But from the point of view of literature, visions are obviously out, because they are a form of cheating. Visions are something which can only be created in literature by the author, and therefore are just like killings performed by the author: they prove nothing either way. And therefore I would exclude visions from my ideal religious novel because they are entirely too simple. They prove nothing and provide the reader with no psychological truths that I can see, since it's impossible to communicate to the reader the intense kind of revelation which a vision is.

The situation in *The Brothers Karamazov,* you understand, doesn't really answer the question, but it happened to the young man at a particular time. It only describes in a way, although the man himself is speaking and retelling the story as a much older man, the outside of the experience, and perhaps in some ways that's all we can do. It goes down several layers, with Dostoyevsky's marvelous insight, but it doesn't quite tell you what it was that triggered the whole mutation. He describes how, as a young man, he fell in love with a girl, that this girl treated him with absolute correctness, never encouraged him in any way, she liked him, she did not love him, and presently she got engaged to someone else. And Zossima, being an arrogant and aggressive young man, deliberately picked a fight with this older man and forced him into the position of fighting a duel. He knew that by doing this he couldn't win the girl's love—it was a simple act of vindictiveness and brutality. And yet such were the morals obtaining at that time in the army that all his brother officers thought it was a normal and natural thing to do. Then suddenly he begins to feel very badly about the whole thing, and the duel is to take place very early that morning, and he remembered how his brother, when he was dying, said:

> "My dear ones, why do you wait on me, why do you love me, am I worth your waiting on me?" Yes, am I worth it? flashed through my mind. After all, what am I worth that another man, a fellow creature, made in the likeness and image of God, should serve me? And for the first time in my life this question forced itself upon me. . . . Suddenly my second, the ensign, came in with a pistol to fetch me [to the duel].
>
> "Ah," he said, "it's a good thing you're up already, it's time we were off, come along."

Now the night before Zossima had flown into a rage at his servant, Afanasy, and struck him violently, so that his face was "covered in blood." So he runs back to Afanasy's room.

> "Afanasy," I said, "I gave you two blows on the face yesterday, forgive me," I said.
>
> He started as though he were frightened, and looked at me; and I saw that it was not enough, and on the spot, in my full officer's uniform, I dropped at his feet and bowed my head to the ground. "Forgive me," I said.
>
> Then he was completely aghast.
>
> "Your honour . . . sir, what are you doing? Am I worth it?"[2]

In another part of the book we see him as a very sick, dying man and a great saint—a man of extraordinary insight. That's why, when he realizes the terrible fate that lies in store for Dmitri Karamazov he bows down before him to the ground, just as, in another context, he bowed down before his servant in his full uniform.

Now, I've said that one important thing with regard to making the saint credible is that he shall be presented as an ordinary or believable person, a person with whom we can identify at the start of the story. There is another aspect, however, which is of deeper importance, or greater importance. When our would-be saint sets out on his career, when he goes into a monastery, or when he devotes himself to some kind of social service for others, or whether he lives in strict retirement in a cave and meditates—in each case we, the readers, will find something at once chilling and forbidding about his behavior, and we will say to ourselves, I can't understand that. How is the novelist to meet this objective? The saint has apparently taken a step right off the main highway of human life and conduct. How are we to explain it? Well, I would suggest to you that one way of doing this is to indicate that the others, his friends, his neighbors, the other characters in the book, are in fact themselves searching for the same thing that the saint is searching for. Only they're searching for it in the wrong direction and with the wrong means. This is, in a way, the reason why books about saints also require sinners in them, in large quantities—not just for the effect of light and dark, but really to show the enormous universal human struggle. Because all of us, of course, are searching for some deeper insight than the outer appearance of life.

Even the riddle of boredom is a riddle which, if it is solved, leads into deeper insight into the nature of life and understanding about its interestingness and significance. And many of the people who are suffering from the dullness of their everyday apprehensions try to escape from them into drink, which, of course, although it is an extremely inefficient drug and soon brings on all kinds of other symptoms, does contain within itself undoubtedly a moment of insight before the intoxication becomes too advanced. Other people, seeking safety and relief from fear, another of the great torturers, think that they will get it by secure jobs, so-called, and by the amassing of wealth. Others, going considerably further, engage in various kinds of violent actions for the removal of those who seem to be menacing their lives. But all these people are in fact struggling towards the same kind of thing that the saint is struggling toward: all of them are dissatisfied with the subject, appearance, texture, and nature of life, their daily lives, and are trying to break through in one way or the other into something else, and of course this includes also the whole of artistic endeavor and the whole of any sort of endeavor to know, to penetrate, into the nature of phenomena, in any field whatsoever. And so, I think that one of the things that you certainly have to show in such a novel is the general human predicament of the rest of the characters. Maugham has certainly done this in *The Razor's Edge,* and in *The Brothers Karamazov* it is carried to absolutely alpine proportions—the ups and downs have a range of about twenty thousand moral feet. Again, in another remarkable book, Aldous Huxley's *Time Must Have a Stop* (1944), these problems are faced; the only thing is that in that book there is no account of the development of a person. The chief character, Sebastian, is an extremely unregenerate and rather uncertain little boy at the beginning of the book, and then there's an enormous time lapse and we suddenly find him as a mature and considerably enlightened man.

There's another important aspect about the saint and his life, be it in the monastery, be it engaged in social service, be it in whatever way that he is trying to evolve toward his self-knowledge. The struggles of such a person are usually regarded as very gloomy and very depressing. And I suggest that this is an enormous mistake, both artistically and also in case you happen to know any saints yourself. We none of us shed a single tear over the thought that someone training for an athletic event might have to go through appalling austerities, as many do. All this seems the most natural thing in the world. Nobody is the least bit sorry for a boxer during his training in the training camp, which is perhaps the meaning of Gertrude Stein's poem which begins

"Gaily the boxer, the boxer, very gaily, depresses no one." And in the same way I think that the saint's struggles, misadventures, temptations, yieldings, and so forth should be told with considerable gusto and fun, like "Mishaps in Learning to Cook." Why should the temptation of St. Anthony be a dreary scene? Why is it not amusing? Why is there not a certain joy, a certain glee, in this whole process? This is, however, something in which I feel art has been rather backward, and it's very difficult to convey this adequately, because if you go too far in the other direction you do what I think Maugham does in *Razor's Edge*—you make it sound as though becoming a saint is just no trouble at all. Larry's adventures are too agreeable. What you have to convey somehow is a sense of the struggle of a peaceful evolution, but at the same time not raising the thing into a kind of gloomy grandeur, but seeing it with a certain amused eye. I think that the two novels by George Moore, *Evelyn Innes* and *Sister Teresa,* also suffered from this defect. The passages in the convent, wonderful as their insight is, are sad. There's a kind of sadness about them which is very depressing, and I think lowers the quality of the impact of the book.

What I do think is a successful religious novel in this context is by a very great name, and yet probably very few of you have heard of it. At the end of his life, Tolstoy produced a novelette called *Father Sergius* or *Father Sergei,* depending on the translation.[3] It's really an outline for a novel, but it's fundamentally a novel in form. It was only published after his death: he died in 1910 and it was published in 1912, so it's the very last work of his. In *Father Sergius,* Tolstoy engages to tell the entire story of the evolution of an extremely unregenerate character to the point of sainthood. He does it as follows.

There's a young officer (not unlike the man who became Father Zossima in Dostoyevsky's novel) called Stephen Kasatsky, who is very brilliant in every way and a tremendous eager-beaver. There's no kind of study which he doesn't excel in. He also excels in his tactical skills, horsemanship, fencing, and all the military arts. And he is a burningly ambitious man. When he was a cadet, like many of the other cadets, he conceived a passionate reverence for the Tzar, Alexander. He thought of Alexander as a father—he himself was an orphan—and he felt that the only thing worthwhile in life was to live to be the best possible officer in Alexander's army and, if necessary, to die for him.

In the army Stephen Kasatsky mingles with Petersburg society, and he meets a young girl. At first he has merely ambitious motives because she is a good match, belongs to a good family and has money, but very soon he falls ardently in love with her, and she seems suddenly very much interested in him. At first she was repulsed by him, but now suddenly she seems extremely interested in him and agrees to marry him. He is delighted.

And yet, all around him there is whispering, and the whisperings are because everybody in St. Petersburg knows one thing about this girl that he doesn't know. For a short while she was the mistress of the Tzar. The girl knows that everybody knows this—it's not the kind of thing that you could keep quiet, and she knows that sooner or later Stephen will find it out. And being a girl of some character she makes up her mind that the only thing possible to do is to tell him before they are actually married. One day, profiting by a moment when he has been expressing himself in the most burning language about his love for her, she tells him. He simply cannot take it. His vanity is tortured. If it had been any other man, of course, he could have gone out and challenged him to a duel and at least killed him or been killed. That's the way officers reacted at that time to problems of this sort. But here was the great father figure, the adored Tzar, the guilty person. He couldn't bear to think of living in society with this girl and having everybody know this. He hit instinctively upon the most spectacular revenge he could think of: he resigned from the army and went into a monastery.

This created a tremendous amount of talk in St. Petersburg, and everybody was wondering why he did it. Then the truth came out, and everyone was intrigued. Meanwhile Stephen set himself to be the perfect monk, just as he had set himself to be the perfect officer, consumed with pride in himself and consumed with ambition. But now all his pride and ambition was turned in a completely different direction. If the other people prayed for four hours, he prayed for six. If there were penances to be done, he did twice as much. If people had to be humble, he was humbler than anybody. He exceeded in every way, and all this excess over the others was of course a mark of his passionate pride. Some of his fellow officers came out to the monastery to see him, and the Abbot, who was rather socially minded, was flattered by the monk's connections and brought them together. Stephen snubbed them brutally by the most extreme humility, bowed down to the earth, turned his back on them, and asked for permission to withdraw. Nevertheless, he found the life in the monastery disturbing for this reason and sought permission to go to a monastery out in the country that also contained a hermitage. According to Tolstoy's description, there were caves at considerable distance from each other, and one of these caves had been occupied until very recently by a holy man of great renown who had died. Father Sergius, as he was now called, was told that he could take over this cave. So now he spent the second phase of his life in the most tremendous self-discipline and in strict silence, in long hours of prayer and meditation, receiving food only that was left for him by one of the novices who went away again without speaking to Father Sergius.

In a nearby town there was a woman who was very bohemian and daring, who was always thinking of something exciting to do, and who thought it would be very amusing to make a bet with her friends that she could spend a whole night in the cell of this famous Father Sergius. She had herself driven near the place by a friend in a troika and got out, went over to his cell, knocked on his door, and said, Oh, she was out in the cold, she'd lost her way, she was miserable, and so forth. She came into the cave, and Father Sergius was very disturbed by her. He could hardly bear to look at her—he found her insanely attractive and he was so troubled that he was very rude and distant, and said, All right, you can sleep in there. I'll stay out in back. But she insisted on making a fire, and then she took her stockings off because they were wet. And she kept calling to him through the door and saying, Father Sergius, I'm taking my stockings off. Oh, my dress is wet. I'm going to take my dress off, too. Now I'm taking my dress off. And she went on like this, torturing the unfortunate man. At last, realizing, she thought, that she was getting nowhere at all, she covered herself up decently and said, Do please come in. I promise you I'm in bed. I'm all covered up. I just want you to help me get something. She was quite unaware of the fact that Sergius was going through a hell of temptation, and that he'd remembered the line in the Scriptures: If thine eye offend thee, put it out. And he went to the wood block, on which he cut wood for a fire, and cut off one of his fingers. He then wrapped his stump of a finger in his robe, came to the door, and said, Yes, was there something you wanted? The woman saw the stain of the blood on the robe, rushed outside, saw what he had done, was absolutely horrified, overcome with horror by the pettiness of her life and the triviality of this attempt, the sheer malice behind this attempt to change Sergius's life for no reason in the world except that it infuriated her to think of somebody being different from herself, and she went away, and in due course entered a convent herself.

Now Sergius passed the third stage. By this time he'd really overcome, it seemed, his more violent passions. He went back into a big monastery where there were a lot of other monks, and one day they brought him a child who was sick, and said, Father, won't you bless this child. He was unwilling to do so, but then he thought, After all, why not? Why not bless the child? There's nothing in that. And the child was cured. He had developed some kind of psychic power (which is by no means unusual), and a large number of those who came to him were in fact cured when he laid his hands on them or blessed them.

And now another phase started, in which he became enormously famous, in which he didn't have to do any austerities, in which he was waited on hand and foot and introduced like a great star at a certain hour and all the cripples and the poor people and the sick people bowed down before him and he blessed them. And now his vanity began to assert itself in another way, and he began to think to himself, After all, I am a saint, this is the way saints behave. And he was very gracious, but at the same time he allowed other people to push the sick around and say, Hurry up there, hurry up, come on. Be quick. You can't keep the father waiting all night.

Then one day somebody brought a girl who was almost an idiot, a very strange girl. She was a grown-up and exceedingly sensuous. And she looked at Sergius with a terrible kind of recognition, as much as to say, You and I, we understand each other. And Sergius became very disconcerted, and yet he had to let the experience develop. The father said, I will leave you two alone together, and Sergius said, Where's your pain, and where do you feel sick? She said, Oh, I feel sick all over. Put your hands on me. And Sergius did.

An hour or two later, horrified, humiliated to the earth, absolutely disgusted with himself, wearing peasants' clothes, he hurried out of the monastery by a back door and went to a cliff near a river, thinking that he would kill himself. It was then that a voice said to him, Don't you see that what is really happening to you is that your pride has been wounded once more, fatally wounded? And that's all that has happened. And suddenly he remembered a girl whom he used to play with, an ugly and weak girl named Pashinka. A voice said to him, Go and see Pashinka and ask her what you should do. And so he went. She was of course an elderly woman. She had married, and so forth, and he went to see her, and he found that she was a housewife, that she had many, many causes of unhappiness in her lifetime, and she didn't think of herself as anything special at all. She was overwhelmed with the honor of the visit from Father Sergius, and after spending a short time with her, he left. And he said to himself:

> "That was the meaning of my vision. Pashinka is what I should have been and was not. I lived for man on the pretext of living for God. She lives for God, imagining she lives for man! Yes; one good deed—a cup of cold

water given without expectation of reward—is worth far more than all the benefits that I thought I was bestowing on the world." But was there not, after all, one grain of sincere desire to serve God, he asked himself. And the answer came: "Yes, there was; but it was so soiled, so overgrown with desire for the world's praise. No, there is no God for the man who lives for the praise of the world. I must now seek *Him.*"

He walked on, just as he had made his way to Pashinka's, from village to village, meeting and parting with other pilgrims, and asking for bread and a night's rest in the name of Christ. Sometimes an angry housekeeper would abuse him, sometime a drunken peasant would revile him; but for the most part he was given food and drink, and often something to take with him. Many were favorably disposed toward him on account of his noble bearing. Some, on the other hand, seemed to enjoy the sight of a gentleman so reduced to poverty, but his gentleness vanquished all hearts.

He often found a Bible in a house where he was staying, and he would read it aloud, and the people always listened, touched by what he read them, and wondering, as if it were something new, although so familiar.

If he succeeded in helping people by his advice, or by knowing how to read and write, or by settling a dispute, he did not afterwards wait to see their gratitude, but he went away directly, and little by little God began to reveal himself within him. . . .

For eight months Kasatsky tramped in this fashion, until at last he was arrested in a provincial town in a night-shelter where he passed the night with other pilgrims. Having no passport to show, he was taken to the police station. When he was asked for documents, for his identity, he said he had none; that he was a servant of God. He was numbered among the tramps and sent to Siberia. . . . He works in the vegetable garden, teaches the children to read and write, and nurses the sick. (88–91)

With this deliberately quiet, matter-of-fact ending, Tolstoy tries to convey what he means by being a saint. And although I think that even in this remarkable work the kind of fun which I would like to see is absent, I can't help feeling in many respects this is the best account that I know of a life progressing in this manner toward sainthood.

A Last Lecture

This is in two senses a last lecture, the last of a series of talks I have been giving at the University of California, Santa Barbara, entitled "A Writer and His World." In another sense, I am going to try to give you what is called a "Last Lecture." This is something which is done from time to time. My great friend Professor Douwe Stuurman gave such a talk quite some time ago,[1] and the idea is that, without becoming melodramatic, you attempt to say the kind of thing you would say if this *were* your last lecture—where you really try to sum up your beliefs or the results of your experience, and you try to express these results briefly, and this is what I am going to try to do tonight.

First of all, I should start with the suggestion that a writer always should write as an individual, first and foremost as an individual. Because, after all, what does he really have? He has only his individual experience. What he knows is his own experience, not somebody else's—that is only filtered through his experience.[2] Furthermore, I would suggest that one not only writes as an individual but one writes for other individuals. There may be just a few thousand of these, there may be millions, but ideally speaking one writes for each one of these individuals and not for the mass taken together. This is rather an important point. Anyway, it's important to me psychologically to think of writing in this way, and I would even suggest that the opposite—writing for other people as a mass, rather than as a collection of separate individuals—perhaps is one of the differences between art and propaganda. I'll return to this idea again a little bit later.

Being an individual doesn't necessarily in itself mean that you are cut off from other people or that you feel yourself at variance with them. A writer may belong to a political party which is in the majority and is in power. He may hold opinions which

Isherwood speaks at a tribute to W. H. Auden at the University of Southern California, May 12, 1974.

are generally shared by the majority of people in the country he lives in. But nevertheless, I suggest he must hold these opinions in a slightly different way and with a slightly different emphasis. He must always hold them with the possibility of dissent. Without the freedom to dissent, he is just that much less valuable to the community. This is not the same thing as belonging to a so-called loyal opposition, because an opposition party, with the best will in the world, cannot help being contrary by its very nature, in face of the things done by the party in power; whereas the individual reserves the right to judge *both* the party in power and the opposition and at every moment to make adjustments to them. That is why the writer who is really an individual is absolutely sure to be in trouble in a country which is totalitarian, no matter whether it is of the right or the left, and indeed it is very hard for me personally to see how a writer can be, in any sense of the word, free in such a country, even though he may be lavished with privileges and petted and approved of by the State. Because, even if he agrees with the general policy of the State, he must have this little nagging insistence on his right to dissent or assent at any given moment. As a writer, he is not what is thought of as a good party member of any party. He always has this certain distance, this certain independence which he maintains.

In my first talk, I spoke a good deal about what I called the "outsider," and I want to remind you of certain points I raised then and perhaps amplify them a little. It follows, from what I have just said, that every writer must, in fact, be an outsider, and I think I've already indicated what is meant by an outsider. It doesn't mean somebody who is *necessarily* in opposition but somebody who may at any moment get out of step, who reserves the right to be out of step, and boldly says, "You may be glad if I *am* out of step." In other words, the kind of outsider of whom I approve is one who is very, very anxious to share his reactions with the others, the insiders, or whatever you want to call them. He is not doing this out of aggression or hostility. He is trying seriously to report his own reaction. His dissent is not important *as* dissent. He may be absolutely wrong, and, let's face it, the majority *are* sometimes right! He may be wrong and even idiotic in his dissent, but an outsider properly used by the community is nevertheless a very valuable instrument, because he shows another point of view, and therefore widens our appreciation of any given problem, shows another facet of it, and shows us how to think about it in a larger way. Therefore, I maintain that the truly cooperative and social outsider is one of the most valuable members of the community, and a writer should strive to be such an outsider, sometimes assenting, sometimes dissenting, but always, one hopes, in some way illuminating the problem under discussion.

Now sometimes the outsider's dissent must be something a little more than merely polite. Sometimes he must dissent absolutely. Sometimes he must say, "I am very sorry, but here we've really got something." And under certain circumstances, this can lead to his being fined or imprisoned or even put to death. And this is where the test of the outsider really occurs. I don't mean just the test of his fortitude, that he is ready to stick to his opinions. I mean something much more than that. I mean *the way* in which he sticks to them and the degree to which he can go on cooperating right up to the last—even in dissent. That is to say, his dissent should illuminate the situation right up to the moment when they drag him out and cut his head off, or what have you. And this is the moment at which he will be beset by terrible temptations, to be holier than thou, to be noble, to be aggressively humble in a manner which condemns other people utterly. It is at this moment that the outsider's function, as I say, is not to shut off the lights before it is absolutely necessary, not to relapse into aggression. Some of the very greatest figures in history have managed to do this. What sustains them in such a situation is the realization that their fellow men are about to commit a crime by suppressing them, and, if they are truly great, they will endeavor not to save their own skins, but, for the sake of their fellow men, to prevent them from committing this crime as long as it is humanly possible. When finally the crime is about to be committed, then, of course, the moment occurs at which the outsider can do no more. All he can do then is to accept the tragic circumstance. This kind of person I called "the anti-heroic hero," and what I mean by an anti-heroic hero is the hero who goes beyond the mere tragic fact of absolute opposition. Socrates was such a hero, and he went on until the last moment shedding light upon the situation and not freezing into the rigid gesture of tragedy. The anti-heroic hero is not tragic in the sense that the ordinary tragic hero is tragic. The anti-heroic hero instinctively avoids tragedy in this sense of the word because this kind of great tragic death is an act of defiance, an act of aggression against the others, and this is exactly what the anti-heroic hero is determined to avoid.

From the sublime to the ridiculous, or to the minor, I can say that I myself am more than usually an outsider in certain respects, temperamentally speaking, because I really enjoy being a foreigner. I am a foreigner by temperament, and I've always liked to live in countries other than the one I was born in, because I find that a slight edge of foreignness prevents me somehow from taking life too much for granted. I don't know if I can convey to you quite what I mean but there is just this slight remove which makes everything that the people around one do interesting, because it has always that faint quality of strangeness. After more than twenty years in this country and fourteen years as a United States citizen I can say with satisfaction that I still feel just a tiny little bit foreign, and now when I go to England I feel foreign too, and so I appreciate England very much more than I did formerly. I also, in an earlier period of my life, lived in Germany for quite a long time and there enjoyed, of course, a very considerable measure of foreignness.

Now, not to be mealymouthed, I shall be expected to tell you at this point just in what ways I do, in fact, dissent from what can be called the majority opinion, although in some cases the majority is a great deal smaller than in others. To me the individual is the paramount fact. To me the State exists for the individual and not vice versa, and I believe that loyalty to the State is something which the State must win from the individual by good treatment, just as a university, for instance, can win loyalty from its members of the faculty.

I am, therefore, constitutionally opposed to loyalty by test just as I should have been opposed to religious orthodoxy by test in the days of the Inquisition.[3] I am opposed, and I expressed my opposition in the last World War, to the use of armed forces between nations or in civil strife under any circumstances whatsoever. I am opposed to and see no utility in capital punishment. I am opposed to the interference of the law in the life of the private adult individual. I do not believe that the law should interfere in his life while he is harming no one other than himself, which is always a matter of argument, and I, therefore, am opposed to those laws which interfere with his sexual life, with the life and occupations that he chooses to lead in private, and with the kind of books he chooses to read. You may say that I have no right to express such controversial opinions without backing them up by a lot of arguments, but I must remind you that this series of talks has never been argumentative in tone, and if this is indeed a last lecture it is too late for opinions to have any real validity, because what we leave behind us is, in fact, not our opinions but our examples. We all know of people we admire who have held certain opinions of which we greatly disapprove and yet when these people hold them we just smile and say, "Isn't he marvelous! The silly old thing believes that so-and-so is so-and-so!" On the other hand, we have also constantly had the unpleasant experience of hearing the very noblest opinions and sentiments, unanswerable in themselves, expressed by people whom, in our hearts, we regarded as fiends. And so opinions are indeed relative to the individual, and I have only confided mine to you because I feel this is part of a description of a writer and an indication of what I personally happen to mean by dissent in my own case.

Now, getting on to writing itself. The first thing I would like to say, addressed chiefly to the young writer but indeed to all writers, is that the first necessary act for a writer is to write. There used to be a song, around the turn of the century in England, a patriotic song so-called. This kind of patriotism is sometimes called by another name, jingoism, and I often wonder if this name doesn't derive from the song. "We don't want to fight, but by jingo if we do, we've got the men, we've got the ships, we've got the money, too." Well, an awful lot of young people spend their time saying to themselves, "I don't want to write, but by jingo if I do . . ." In other words, they keep thinking about how wonderful it would be if they were to write, or to embark on any other art. I know by my own experience, and I would implore anybody else in the same situation to believe me, that the great thing is to get something down on paper. If I were allowed to give only one piece of advice, I would choose to say this because it is obvious and yet is so necessary, and thinking about writing and getting excited about the wonderful writing that *you are going to do* is the most dangerous occupational vice of a writer. The thing to do is to *get something down on the paper,* and then you have something to work on.

The second thing I would say applies to one's colleagues. I might express it as "Don't shoot the pianist. He's doing his best." If you live long enough, you have to endure the unpleasant experience of seeing work which you consider third, fourth, fifth, sixth, seventh, eighth, or ninth grade, or utter trash, praised to the skies, compared to Tolstoy, awarded the Pulitzer, the Hawthornden, the Nobel Prize, heaven knows what, and also earning fabulous amounts of money while your own book sells a few hundred copies. One is very apt to give way to envy and malice and somehow feel that these writers have done something wrong. No! No act of creation is wrong, and no person who creates is the enemy of another creator. The enemies, if any, are the dishonest boosters, the jumpers on the bandwagon, the promoters, the bought critics, and all such people who push an inferior product knowing it to be inferior. But the creator himself always has the dignity of having done his best, like the pianist. And maybe in his heart of hearts he doesn't think any more of his work than you do!

It is also very important not to tell the young that fame or celebrity is nothing. *Of course,* it is something! As a matter of fact, it is a most valuable and chastening experience, and for every one person whom I have known who has been, as they say, spoiled by celebrity, I have known at least ten who have been enormously improved by it. It's very sobering to have even a little praise, and it turns the eyes inward, and the true quality of one's work is apt to be seen in a much humbler perspective. As long as one is quite unknown, the ego, in a very healthy attempt at survival, actually forces one to be a little bit arrogant, because, if you aren't, how can you go on? It's very hard. Celebrity (I don't use the word *fame,* but any kind of mild notoriety) brings you back to a sense of proportion, and the serious artist is seldom, if ever, harmed by it. At least that's my belief. However, on the other side, it's very important not to be too grandiose in one's view of one's objectives. They always say, of course, you should aim at the stars, etc. It's all very well to talk like that, but actually one should be glad if one can accomplish even a little. The writer Norman Douglas, in a fit of bile on one occasion, said of the much greater writer D. H. Lawrence: "Lawrence opened a little window for the bourgeoisie. That was his life work."[4] My goodness, if I could open a little peephole for the inhabitants of Goleta I should be proud to tears. One must realize what it means to make even a small contribution, if that contribution is valid, and not go into absurd megalomaniac daydreams of some kind of universal art.

I get on now to a philosophical point that is connected with my own beliefs. I have been now for many years deeply involved with, and under the influence of, Hindu philosophy, and particularly as it is expressed in the so-called gospel of Hinduism, the Bhagavad Gita. In the Bhagavad Gita there is a verse which says, "You have the right to work, but for the work's sake only. You have no right to the fruits of work" (40). In other words, writing (or any other kind of worthy occupation) must be, whether we like it or not, its own reward. One must do one's very best, and that's it. What happens to the work, the effect it has on other people, is anyway outside our power, and we only make ourselves wretched if we pin all our hopes on what the Gita calls "the fruits of work." The reward, the effect, even the good effects, even the benefits to other people, all these I seriously believe we have to renounce. We have to concentrate entirely on the act itself, on the act of work and on the attempt to perfect that work just as much as we know how, and then send it forth and try to be content with that, and to know that our real happiness is in doing the work, not in what happens to it afterward.

Why should you do your best at all? There again, Hinduism has an answer and these answers, of course, are found in many other kinds of philosophies and religious systems. I simply express them in this language because I am accustomed to it. The Hindus have a concept which they call dharma, and dharma in the Sanskrit language means the duty related to your own nature. Everybody has their own dharma, that is to say the duty which is important to themselves and which is a part of their profession or vocation. And a writer has his dharma: there are certain things which he should do and certain things that he should not do. It is very, very important to follow one's own dharma and not somebody else's. We are all tempted from time to time to try to follow the dharma of somebody else, and it always leads us into trouble; we must always try to find our own. This is a matter of a great deal of discrimination and a great deal of thought—to ask ourselves what is really the duty of our own nature. What is it that our own nature demands and what does it tell us to do? We must not be turned aside by the fact that perhaps the dharma of another may cause him to do totally different things. We mustn't feel offended by the behavior of another person if he is obeying his own different kind of dharma.

And now, if you will bear with me, I must moralize a little, and please remember that what I am saying is with reference to my own work and my own experience as a writer. I personally have found it difficult, psychologically, to accept the Christian concept of sin. The Christian concept of sin, as I was taught to understand it when I was a child, was that certain actions offend a supreme Being and that we should feel guilty because that Being has been offended by our actions. In Hindu philosophy I found a concept which to me was much more helpful, and might be more helpful to some of you, and that was to regard the sins not as sins in this sense but as obstacles. By doing certain things we do not offend some other Being but we create obstacles to our own advancement, our own worth, spiritually, artistically, any way you want. There are artistic sins, and I, personally, have always found it much easier to work on the basis of thinking that I have created an obstacle for myself, rather than that I have offended another Being or some code of laws laid down by some other Being. This, of course, is an entirely personal reaction. I do think one thing stands firm (this is particularly evident to a writer who spends his time trying to practice it): the most important thing in all of conduct is truth. Insofar as we tell the truth, we're doing pretty well. We may not be perfect, but we're not far off course. Insofar as we lie, and particularly insofar as we lie in various indirect ways, obliquely, we are losing direction, and we are in danger, and artistically speaking our work suffers. It is extraordinary how lies in various forms—lies about experience, lies about perception—creep into one's work and vitiate it. I believe that as in art so also in life: telling the truth is the most important of all virtues and the one real compass needle pointing out the way for us.

In the great Taoist scripture that is called variously *The Way and the Power* or *The Way of Life* or *Tao Te Ching*, there is a sentence which haunts me a great deal: "Heaven arms with pity those whom it would not see destroyed."[5] What this means, at least the part of the meaning that is valuable to me, is this: we are very often apt to think that cruelty is something which is bad because it is practiced toward another person. Very true. But what we don't always see is what I have to keep reminding myself—that the person you are really harming by cruelty is yourself, and that is the tremendous power of this sentence. Just think of it. "Heaven arms with pity those whom it would not see destroyed." You are given pity, compassion if you like, for other people in order to protect yourself from destruction. This is something which comes into my mind very often.

On the other hand, it seems to me that in this period we perhaps overemphasize the value of that extremely attractive virtue, courage. I think that courage is enormously admirable and that cowardice is to be deplored. But I also think all that really matters about cowardice is not to conceal it. If you can have the courage to say I am afraid to do this or that, no great harm is done. If, however, you conceal your cowardice, people are apt to rely on you and get let down later. Concealed cowardice is a great breeding ground of cruelty. Cruelty is fear disguised. Insofar as I think the virtue of courage is a necessity, all you really need is the courage to say, when necessary, "I am afraid," "I am scared," "I'm sorry, but I'm not going to do it," "I'm not with you in this, I don't care to be."

As for the so-called weaknesses of the flesh, I think these must really be judged in relation to one's dharma. If too much indulgence in this or that vice is interfering with your life and work, of course it has to be given up, but we must see that people have a varying tolerance in this respect and we mustn't be too hasty to judge others. Just because, let us say, they can drink us under the table that doesn't mean that they are wickeder than we are, or vice versa.

The great besetting difficulty of the writer is sloth: a mysterious kind of dead calm with fog down to the water that comes over one so that one absolutely cannot move, cannot navigate, doesn't know where one is. I have found that it is better not to regard sloth in the light of a vice or a failing but more to treat it as though it were the weather. To say, "Well, the airfield is shut down today, but at least don't let's lie on the runway staring at the fog. Let's go off and do something else." I think that many people in the creative arts know what I mean and know that on those occasions sometimes you can even make the fog lift by simply turning your back on it and saying, "Very well, I'm going to read a book, or I'm going to the movies, or I'm going out." Suddenly the perverse thing says, "Oh, no, you're not," and it blows away again. Even if it doesn't, it has to be borne with and endured as it is endured and has been by sailors ever since the world began. One must bear with it, and one must wait for it to lift, and then one must go on. The great thing is to go on, when it does lift.

Now we come to those appallingly august and massive questions. I myself am what I choose to call an existentialist. Not in any terribly complicated meaning of the word, but simply somebody who believes primarily in his own experience. I believe the most that anybody can do is to follow his experience, to try to understand what it means, to try not to lie to himself about its meaning, and that is all. Some of the noblest and best people I have known were unable to go beyond this. I have met other people who were able to see farther into the meaning of life and to share some of their experience. Constantly ask yourself what it means, trust it, don't lie about it. That is true of the writer and of the human being.

There are, of course, at the end of all experiences two famous mysteries. The first I shall allude to very briefly: it's death. Death is something which nowadays we play down, try to make agreeable, to pass over, to minimize in every way possible. This probably is a terrible mistake. There should be a serious art of dying just as there is an art of living. It should be something prepared for and approached with reverence, more reverence and less fear, but, be that as it may, we don't do it, we just hope we'll get by, somehow or other.

The other mystery I have already referred to in these talks, and that is the mystery of ultimate joy. The greatest saints report to us that, in some way in which they are not even able to explain to us, the universe appears to them ultimately joyful. All is well, beyond ordinary happiness, beyond ordinary sorrow, somehow or other everything is all right and functioning and, therefore, a state of joy exists beyond what we normally call happiness and beyond tragedy. This is a very great mystery and a very difficult subject. I tried to speak about it a little bit in relation to Art in earlier talks, saying that, in my opinion, there is no such thing as a really depressing major work of art; it is only second-rate work which is depressing. In great art, no matter what the subject matter, there is a curious sense of joy, of exhilaration in the experience. I believe this to be also true of life, but it is a very bold man who dares say that he has known this in his own experience. It has nothing to do with the facile optimism which penned such lines as used to be written on a calendar in my grandmother's house: "It ain't no use to grumble or complain. It's just as cheap and easy to rejoice. When God sorts out the weather and sends rain, why, rain's my choice." One wonders what the author would have said if God sorted out the weather and sent a typhoon. This kind of shallow meliorism just will not stand up. When Dante says, "In his will is our peace," then we feel that at least he went through something tremendous before he could say it. And it is in this final kind of joy in the nature of life, joy which is only reached after great suffering has been experienced, that the ultimate truth about life seems to reside.

I think I've been put off this by the rather unfortunate cult of tragedy which stems back to the attitude toward the great Greeks that was inculcated throughout the nineteenth century. It was always held that in some mysterious way tragedy was the thing, but the great thing was to suffer, and the highest truth was destruction and the heroic hero standing up grim and aggressive against the disaster. In some rather confused way, I instinctively rebel against this idea and feel that there is a state beyond that can only be inhabited by the anti-heroic hero. As Forster wrote in 1939, under the imminent shadow of the Second World War, in "What I Believe":

> The above are the reflections of an individualist and a liberal who has found liberalism crumbling beneath him, and at first felt ashamed. Then, looking around, he decided there was no special reason for shame, since other people, whatever they felt, were equally insecure. And as for individualism—there seems no way of getting off this, even if one wanted to. The dictator-hero can grind down his citizens till they are all alike, but he cannot melt them into a single man. That is beyond his power. He can order them to merge, he can incite them to mass antics but they are obliged to be born separately and to die separately, and, owing to these unavoidable termini, will always be running off the totalitarian rails. The memory of birth and the expectation of death always lurk within the human being, making him separate from his fellows, and consequently capable of intercourse with them. Naked I came into the world, naked I shall go out of it! And a very good thing too, for it reminds me that I am naked under my shirt, whatever its colour.

Part II

The Autobiography of My Books, 1963–65

Editor's Note

The Autobiography of My Books

The compilation of this second series of Christopher Isherwood's lectures, which he called "The Autobiography of My Books," proved problematic. There are two extant documents to which this title might apply: the first is an audiotape recording of two lectures given at the University of California, Berkeley, on April 23 and 30, 1963. Isherwood and the university intended to present a two-part lecture, but Isherwood covered less material than he had planned on the first night, and so the series was extended to a third session. The first two sessions were recorded, but the third, on May 8, 1963, was not. The audiotape is labeled "The Autobiography of My Books."

A second version exists as transcripts to a series of lectures delivered two years later, in April and May 1965, at the University of California, Los Angeles, where Isherwood conducted a course in writing and gave public talks. Taping and transcribing appear to have been as ill-planned at UCLA as at Berkeley: the first two lectures in what was an eight-part series at UCLA were neither taped nor transcribed. Transcripts exist for what appear to be the final six lectures of the series. At least one lecture was promoted with the title "Writing As a Way of Life," but the series as a whole seems to follow the same concept as the three-part series in Berkeley. Both are organized in a strict chronology without the thematic arrangement of "A Writer and His World." This similarity in structure makes the two logical companions.

I have attempted to remedy the historical accidents of transcription and taping by combining the two series into one, giving them the title Isherwood used to describe his lectures in *Kathleen and Frank.* I added the titles of Isherwood's works as the titles for the lectures, to indicate the works discussed. The first two Berkeley lectures begin this section, and the final six UCLA lectures complete it. The first lecture opens with the composition at Cambridge of Isherwood's first unpublished novel, "Seascape with Figures." The content of the second Berkeley lecture overlaps with the third UCLA lecture (the first UCLA lecture printed here) as Isherwood describes his theater work with Auden in the 1930s. Although the UCLA lectures were given in 1965, the last lecture in this series ends with a discussion of *Down There on a Visit,* published in 1960; Isherwood does not talk about his final two novels, even though *A Single Man* had been published the year before the UCLA lectures.

Isherwood's Berkeley talks were polished public performances. The audiotape supports this impression and indicates that Isherwood received a warm response, including frequent laughter, from the audience. Isherwood's subjects in Berkeley ranged wide, from the "Freudian revolution" to the political engagement of the writers of his generation, which he says has been greatly exaggerated: "the kind of revolution which we were thinking about was a quite different sort of revolution. It was a highly individualistic poet's revolution."

The UCLA talks seem more detailed and less formal. These transcripts include a few of the questions from the audience (when they could be understood from tapes) as well as Isherwood's responses. (Although he asked for questions at the end of each session in Berkeley, few were posed.) UCLA audiences could be quite challenging, in fact, and Isherwood defends his work and artistic choices on more than one occasion. One gets the sense that the audience was not always sympathetic with his work and may have seen it as somewhat dated stylistically. Although other critical approaches were being developed in the early 1960s, the academy was still dominated by New Criticism, which had elevated the status of High Modernists. The May 4 session was particularly lively, and Isherwood responds to questions about other writers who were more experimental in their use of language, including Samuel Beckett and James Joyce: "I have to confess that I don't think primarily of form. What I'm concerned in doing is trying to communicate my experience of life. . . . when we get to *Finnegans Wake* I feel that the form, to put it very mildly, becomes a great deal more important than the experience." I have indicated the audience's questions with ellipses in the transcriptions when these are unclear from the tapes; one may reasonably surmise their content.

The lecture on May 11, 1965, is almost completely devoted to a description of the writing of Isherwood's novel *The World in the Evening* (1954). It may be that discussing a failure is more instructive for the audience than discussing a success, and it's no doubt that Isherwood felt *The World in the Evening* to be an artistic failure. Yet the minute dissection of the novel and its gestation seems excessive to the point that an audience member asks, "Aren't you being too hard on yourself?" To which Isherwood gives a self-deprecating reply: "Well, after all, this isn't the Nuremberg trials." He follows that joking response with an explanation of what he was trying to achieve artistically with the book and what it showed him about his own narrative technique. In addition to the aims and effects of *The World in the Evening,* Isherwood describes how his original intention for the novel went awry. He first thought the book would tell the story of his work with European refugees in Pennsylvania during the Second World War, but eventually the material about the refugees was omitted.

Isherwood excelled as a storyteller. Friends and contemporaries have told of his exciting table talk, and his interviews are distilled into enlightening conversations. In the relatively unrehearsed setting of his public lectures, Isherwood tended to get off track. Even after several years of public speaking, he acknowledged that he often talked more than he planned. "There's no sweeter music than the sound of one's own voice," he said toward the end of his second lecture at Berkeley. Notes for "The Autobiography of My Books" do not survive, so we do not know whether Isherwood used them as he did in Santa Barbara.

The chronological arrangement of "The Autobiography of My Books" suggests that he didn't cover as much as he had hoped. The final lecture ends abruptly, with a brief mention of the last section of *Down There on a Visit,* giving the entire series an unfinished feeling.

All the Conspirators, The Memorial

BERKELEY, APRIL 23, 1963

I'll start off with a reassurance: in order to follow my remarks it's quite unnecessary to have read any of my books. Furthermore, the whole question as to whether these books have any literary merit or not is entirely academic as far as this discussion is concerned. What I am going to talk to you about is simply this: as a child of my time, I have been concerned with certain themes which are typical themes of the different periods of my life and I have written about them. And by describing these themes, and so by indirection the books that I wrote with these themes, I shall in fact be referring to other books with the same themes and to many things in your own reading experience, I hope. So let's rather forget my personal involvement in this and just follow the productions of this writer, this alleged writer, Isherwood, and see where we get. I won't go through the nonsense of speaking of myself in the third person, but I almost feel like it to use that tone of voice to convey what I want to say.[1]

In 1928 I published my first published novel. I had, in fact, written a very long novel before that of a type which was usual in those days. It was the cradle-to-adolescence type novel, all about the interminable phases of growing up of a boy with deep feelings about Nature. Such novels were extremely usual at that time, and my models were, as a matter of fact, largely Compton Mackenzie's *Sinister Street* (1913–14) and the novels of Hugh Walpole. The novel was of immense length, longer than anything I've ever written or shall write again. And I remember reading it to my best friend at college [Edward Upward]. It took all night. We sat up with the marvelous enthusiasm of youth, drinking coffee. And the novel started at about 8:00 in the evening and went on until dawn, after which we were both absolutely exhausted. And in some very peaceful sort of way I'd realized that it was no good at all, without feeling very depressed. Somehow or other it was well worth doing just to have had the catharsis of reading it out loud. A few days later, my friend was able to admit to me that he too thought it was not altogether a masterpiece. And from then on in we had a lot of fun with it, reading bits out that we considered to be particularly awful. However, in due course, I pulled myself together and made a new approach.

What was I writing about when I planned and wrote and finally published the novel called *All the Conspirators*? I was writing fundamentally about the Freudian revolution which had just hit England with tremendous force. It was, of course, the greatest literary event of my time—and has been, I guess, in all countries where the Freudian ideas have had any acceptance whatsoever. For those of you who are younger, it's almost impossible to imagine the excitement with which we received the news that our parents were responsible for absolutely everything. It was all their fault, and we would never, never forgive. And what's more, all of the things that they said about morality and life were wrong and exploded and out of date.

It's worthwhile discussing in relation to *All the Conspirators* whether I and writers like me were premature Angry Young Men. No, I think there was a difference, a very clear difference. We were of course angry in that we were attacking and in an aggressive mood. But when you compare somebody like me with somebody like John Osborne, the author of *Look Back in Anger* (1956), you see that there is a different approach. What we were saying was that we attack the family. We attack the family because of its failure to recognize that a psychological revolution has taken place which has upset all of the values that it has been preaching and rendered them invalid. Mr. Osborne and his fellow writers, however, are attacking not the family so much as the establishment, the government, which, for the purposes of the attack, has to be regarded as a reactionary government.[2] And their approach is informing this government that a psycho-nuclear revolution has taken place, and this psycho-nuclear revolution, the invention of the atomic devices, has rendered their nationalism obsolete. In both cases, the angry young men are threatening their victims with destruction. We were threatening our people and saying, "Unless you revise all of your psychological ideas, you'll go mad." And nowadays the angry young men are saying, "Unless you revise all your political ideas and your ideas about nationalism, we'll all be blown to bits."

Nevertheless, there was a very clear relationship between these two phases. And this is all part of the tremendous transformation that we've seen taking place in the modern world on all fronts. This book, *All the Conspirators,* was in fact about a very half-hearted and weak revolt against the family, a revolt which fails. It's rather like an incident out on some frontier where a few shots are fired and somebody is done for, nobody cares, but the battle goes on someplace else.

I was once talking to Aldous Huxley—I'd recommended a typist to him, and he had a new novel. We were walking up the hill to see this lady to give her the manuscript, and I said, "What is your novel about?" It was the novel *Time Must Have a Stop* (1944). And Huxley said, after thinking very intently, the way he does, for a moment, he said that "it's a curiously *trivial* story told in considerable *detail* with a certain amount of *squalor.*" This would be quite a good description of *All the Conspirators.*

The general attitude with which I approached novel writing at that time was as a disciple of E. M. Forster. And by being a disciple of E. M. Forster, I meant, fundamentally, what has since been brilliantly pointed out by various critics of his work, that we were comic writers. We thought of ourselves as writers who, however much we were going to deal in tragic themes, rejected the idea of tragedy in the classical sense. There would always be a sort of farcical flash passing over the stage at the end of whatever we presented. We liked very much the phrase that comes somewhere in Henry James: "The whole thing was to be the death of the one or the other of them, but they never spoke of it at tea." And we had a phrase for the kind of way that we wanted to approach our material, which we called "tea-tabling." The idea was that the great scenes, scenes of violence or passion, should always take place offstage, and what you should see would be a curiously muted affect of these people afterwards or before. The violence should explode offstage, which of course it does to a large extent in Forster's novels. You recall the extraordinary surprise deaths, like when he casually says that one of the characters in *The Longest Journey* who is in the prime of health and a great athlete was "broken up" on the football field that afternoon. And that's all there is to it: he dies right away. Somebody else dies just in-between two chapters in *Howards End* and so on and so on. Very well.

What I wanted to present then was such a comedy, a tea-tabled version of life, which nevertheless took itself seriously and indeed with intense feeling, a feeling of a domestic struggle to the death—what Shelley calls the great war between the old and the young—in which the young are passionately fighting on the side of the Freudian revolution against their elders. There is actually in the book a sort of collaborator. One of the young men is more or less playing along with the old, but he meets with such scorn that he is treated really as one of the enemy.

The novel had a rather James Joycean texture to it. I'll read you a bit to show you what I mean. I don't mean by that that it was the obscure James Joyce—the James Joyce which is difficult to understand—but there is a certain use of the present tense which is very like that passage on the beach in *Ulysses* about "a porter bottle stogged to the waist, sentinel, isle of dreadful thirst" or however it goes, I've forgotten the passage. And here are two of the enemy in *All the Conspirators*: Colonel Page, who is an elderly sportsman and birdwatcher, and his nephew, Victor, who is a young university athlete but fundamentally a collaborationist who goes along with the enemy. And they are staying at a hotel and being observed by the two hostile young men. This is sort of through the eyes of the young men. This is described:

> Colonel Page was a very tall man. The sun had burnt his body sallow like pig-skin and his knees were covered with

> black freckles. His hands trembled. He used brilliantine for his thin, dark hair, and during the daytime wore a service wrist-watch, tweed jacket, brogues, stockings with tabs and khaki shorts. In a house built of plaster, tree branches and grass, at the edge of a bamboo forest, he had formed the habit of dressing regularly for dinner.
>
> "You cut in and feed, Victor, I won't be two shakes."
>
> "No sir, I'd rather wait."
>
> At their small corner table, watched by the eleven other visitors to the hotel, they conversed briefly, facing each other, in deep quiet tones. Victor wore a single knot bow-tie; his uncle the old straight kind. Both were washed like school-boys. Colonel Page's neck looked as though his collar hurt him. Whenever he had spoken, he touched his small mustache with a napkin.

And here we go off into a sort of Joycean vision:

> By the lake, Naivasha he has seen pin-tail, English garganey. And on Norfolk Broads, from a punt, late at dawn. Has woken to feel the weight across the blanket of heavy coils. Lies stone-still; then kick out and jump for your life. At Limerick, regimental cricket, bird-nesting in Shannon Woods; after Church Parade the band plays in the barrack square. Verdi, by request. Short-fused, at Hell Corner, a jam-pot grenade bursting too soon, crippled his well-known action, ugly, left handed.
>
> "Yes, my uncle's knocked about a good deal."
>
> Afterwards, in the lounge, they took out their pipes. Colonel Page's was short and heavy; Victor's, slender, with a flattened bowl. Colonel Page's tobacco pouch was made of cheap black rubber.
>
> "Have some of mine, sir?"
>
> "Thanks, I will. I get sickened to death of this stuff."
>
> Grateful, Victor gave his uncle a light, inhaled with a small, earnest frown. At something he uttered two laughs. Ha-ha. Ha-ha-ha. His glance crossed the room,

> met the eyes of a girl who listened. Back it telescoped. He flushed, myopic.
>
> But what did they talk about? Once, Allen had heard Colonel Page say: "The Hun did me a personal favour by mopping up the last two of 'em on the Somme."[3]

This curious tight style, bobbling with contractions so that part of it is really extremely difficult to understand—at the end of the book there's one chapter that I can't understand a single word of to this day—this style is obviously trembling with aggression. And you almost feel the clenched fists of the author as he approaches his material.

Another thing that I was tremendously concerned with at that time was that it seemed to me that the form of the novel should be exceedingly contrived. I thought of the novel as a contraption, and a contraption very much of the kind of the later manner of Ibsen's plays. You know in Ibsen's plays there are all kinds of wonderful springs, trapped doors, booby traps that have been set, waiting to go off. And they all do. Something dreadful that happened twenty years before suddenly rears its head and the whole machinery starts to work, and the woods "avenge themselves," as the old man says, in *The Wild Duck.* I thought that that's what the novel ought to be like. It was perpetually a trick played on the reader in a way. And every single word ideally ought to be a kind of clue, leading to a discovery of some sort. In fact, I thought of the novel very much in terms of the detective story. This attitude was completely changed later on.

The next novel that I wrote was called *The Memorial,* and that was in 1932. All novels have secret titles only known to the author, and the secret title of this novel was "War and Peace." I decided to write a tremendous family epic, but very short, because I dislike long books. In this epic I was going to describe the effect of the idea of war on a postwar generation. Now this again was a very real and contemporary theme at that time because, to a degree which is probably hard for the younger people here to understand, World War I was used in a way that World War II never has been: as a sort of stick to frighten the young. There was a tremendous feeling after World War I of the terrible authority of the War and the resulting feelings of inferiority which those people should have who hadn't been old enough to take part in it. It was one of the phenomena of World War I, from a literary point of view, that the front line soldiers who were writers formed in many cases an aggressive cult, as much as to say, "You didn't go through what I went through, and you never will understand it; and therefore, you never will be what I am." Which was very true, of course, up to a point, and was a great motivation to this day in the writings of Robert Graves, for instance, and in some of the more aggressive poems of Siegfried Sassoon. There's one in which he wishes how he could bring a tank back to London and drive it right through the stalls of a theater, shooting down all of the people that were sitting there, grinning.[4] And this hatred of the civilians was a very real psychological factor in World War I. Of course, the obvious reason why this no longer applied in World War II was that there weren't any civilians, not, anyway, on the European scene. Everybody got involved and bombed or threatened with bombs, and so it was a rather different situation. In fact, the paradox of modern military life is that it's possible in certain circumstances for the troops to be the only people who are in safety, while the civilians are dying by the millions.

But this is what I wanted to write about; I also wanted to write about my father. My father was killed in the First World War, and I was in a very ambivalent position towards him because he was not only a hero, but he was also an anti-hero. This is what I mean by that: my father was an officer in the regular army, the British army, which he'd been pushed into as people were in those days by the family. They said, "Well, the eldest son inherits all the money and the next one can either go into the army or the church or the law." And so he went into the army. And he was a very good officer and very efficient and had in fact been in two wars. He'd been in the war in South Africa, the Boer War—that infamous military exploit—and then, as I say, was killed in World War I. Now, on the one hand my father was conventionally a hero: he died in action. However, he died carrying nothing in his hand but a very small cane, what they call a swagger stick. And this was absolutely characteristic of him. He was always making anti-heroic remarks to me, young as I was. He said an officer's sword was only good for toasting bread and that he was frightened of his revolver, it made such a bang. He played Chopin extremely well and was quite a good watercolor painter and an energetic, if not subtle, character actor in regimental performances of *Charley's Aunt* and such things.

In fact, he was a very wonderful man. My very first literary memories are connected with his coming home from the barracks in the evening. After signing a lot of orders, he would take the duplicates, turn them over, and do comic-strip stories on the back. He told me all the stories of Sherlock Holmes, all kinds of adventure stories, anything that came into his head, and he thoroughly stimulated me. And what's more he made me see art in its aspect as play. Only in very dark moments in my life have I forgotten that and taken it seriously in the wrong way. Art is a function of play, and as long as you can remember that, you get the joy out of it which you are supposed to get.

What was bothering me you can, by this time, pretty much imagine. My father was dead and was a figure approved of by the establishment—by the staff of my first school, by everybody that I loathed, by all ministers of religion. I was passionately anti-religious at this time because I thought, and indeed was not far wrong, that religion was being used for absolutely improper patriotic purposes during World War I. We had to hear a great deal about God being on our side and about the angels flying over the battlefield at Mons and such phenomena. And I thought that the church was just about the lowest thing in existence. This in itself was a very formative factor in my life because I was for many years looking for an anti-religious religious attitude to take. I wanted passionately to be religious and later succeeded, but more of that later.

So I also wanted an anti-heroic father. And every time I tried to make my own father anti-heroic, much as I remember his wonderful characteristics, I was very much bothered by two things: first of all, that he was officially approved of as a hero; and secondly, that he had belonged to the British army, which during my young life was stationed in Ireland. Now of course my father had a perfectly good answer to the fact that he'd taken part in a repressive and completely unjust war against the Boers by saying it was his duty as a soldier to go; he had to go. And again, here we were in Ireland, and they used to shoot at the British on the way down to Church Parade. People would yell "Dirty Protestant" at me when I went out. And there were certain families that were allowed to play with us—just like collaborators with the Nazi occupying army in France during World War II. It became evident even to my youthful eyes that the Irish did not want us there, and that we had absolutely no reason—no *moral* reason—for staying and not very good political reasons.

And so I was deeply concerned, in a word, with the father figure as "hero," and this comes into *The Memorial* very much. There was another concept allied with it, which we called the "Truly Strong Man" and the "Truly Weak Man." I shall have to explain to you what I mean by that by reading to you from another of my books, the autobiographical book *Lions and Shadows,* which I wrote later (1938), but it has this passage in it explaining what I mean. Like all psychological literature I knew of in that period, this was something that Auden had dug up, a writer named Bleuler.[5] And Bleuler quotes in one of his case histories a statement made by a homicidal paranoiac:

> "The feeling of impotence brings forth the strong words, the bold sounds to battle are emitted by the trumpet called persecution insanity. The signs of truly strong are repose and good will . . . the strong individuals are those who without any fuss do their duty. These have neither the time nor the occasion to throw themselves into a pose and try to be something great." (207)

And then I continue in the book:

> "The truly strong man," calm, balanced, aware of his strength, sits drinking quietly in the bar; it is not necessary for him to try and prove to himself that he is not

> afraid, by joining the Foreign Legion, seeking out the most dangerous wild animals in the remotest tropical jungles, leaving his comfortable home in a snowstorm to climb the impossible glacier. In other words, the Test exists only for the Truly Weak Man: no matter whether he passes it or whether he fails, he cannot alter his essential nature. The Truly Strong Man travels straight across the broad America of normal life, taking always the direct, reasonable route. But "America" is just what the truly weak man, the neurotic hero, dreads. And so, with immense daring, with an infinitely greater expenditure of nervous energy, money, time, physical and mental resources, he prefers to attempt the huge northern circuit, the laborious, terrible north-west passage, avoiding life; and his end, if he does not turn back, is to be lost forever in the blizzard and the ice. (207–8)

There are a lot of phrases in here which I find deplorable, like "avoiding life." This is some nonsense that I have long since outgrown: there is no such thing as avoiding life. But the point I'm trying to make there, which will be very apparent to you, is that this Truly Weak Man—the man that has to prove his courage—is a great literary figure of our time. In a sense, a great number of the Hemingway figures are such people. And opposed to him is the Truly Strong Man who doesn't have to do any of this at all and sits at home. Auden summed it up in a typical piece of doggerel in his early manner:

> Pick a quarrel, go to war,
> Leave the hero in the bar;
> Hunt the lion, climb the peak;
> No one dreams that you are weak.[6]

So in this book, *The Memorial,* I was really taking a portrait of a family and using the family as itself a memorial, a war memorial, because this family represented the effects of the War in various aspects. And in this family there were the Truly Strong

Man, who had gotten killed in the War incidentally, and the Truly Weak Man, who had been a tremendous hero in the War and had emerged from it but was living a very wild and desperate kind of life. The book opens with an extremely clinical account of an attempted suicide which fails, something I was very proud of. I managed to find somebody who had done that and got him to tell me exactly what happened.

The other theme which is referred to a little in this novel is the theme of homosexuality. But, as this important theme occurs a great deal in my later work, I shall deal with it in the next talk. In fact, I see that we've run on so now that I really hardly know whether I can start on the next book, because what came after this were the two books about Germany, *Mr Norris Changes Trains* and *Goodbye to Berlin.* These books, of course, represented again an entirely different kind of involvement which the writer is apt to have. I became, as they say, socially conscious. I'm not saying this in a sneering manner, because as a matter of fact it was high time to be conscious of something when you got to Berlin, which was just about to blow up in any one of three or four different ways. For the first time I became aware that things like fighting in the streets and police brutality and murder and so on were not something that just happened in the newspapers, but which were something you might actually witness when you were out for a walk. And this began to alter my approach to my material very much, and this is one of the aspects of the books that follow.

However, I think I would rather invite any questions than go on to the rest of this, because it's opening too large a can of beans. Anybody got anything they want to ask me? *(silence)* Oh, come on now . . .

AUDIENCE: Why do certain memories of experience seem more meaningful than others?

My goodness, that is a question . . . I often think it's very much like sunspots. You know, why does this radiation come through suddenly at certain moments? It's all very well to say that certain phases of experience relate to your condition, but then of course the question arises: Why do you have the condition in the first place? I think every writer is puzzled enormously over this question, and I don't really see any answer to it. As far as I've been concerned, it's been something which just hits you one time and not another time. And you just hope to be hit as much as possible, because obviously that's when something happens to you.

Well, I think I'd better go on next time, because, as I say, if I once start talking about Berlin, that's a lot. And so we'll go on from there next time.

The Berlin Stories

BERKELEY, APRIL 30, 1963

Last time, for the benefit of those who weren't here, I explained that I was going through the autobiography of my novels. This does not mean, however, that you have to have read one single word that I ever wrote, because what I'm endeavoring to do is just to talk about the themes used by me and therefore by many others at different periods—what kind of themes were fashionable or in the social consciousness or zeitgeist—and also to dwell on certain technical problems, which again apply to many other writers besides myself.

I'm going to start today with the novels that I wrote about Germany. I went to Germany first on a brief visit in 1928, which is described in my most recent novel, *Down There on a Visit.* It was a visit to a man whom I describe in that novel as Mr. Lancaster. I then returned to Germany in 1929. I was under the impression at that time that I was preparing to be a medical student, and that this visit to Germany was in fact a weekend that I was going to spend with my old friend W. H. Auden, who had gone over to Berlin to study German in order to teach. But the part of one's will which runs one's life, often quite counter to one's plans, thought quite otherwise and was not impressed by the medical project at all, and got me out of it by the rather ingenious method of suggesting a new novel for me to write. And I found that, instead of studying the varieties of botany and physics, I was writing this novel the whole time, so I got the worst possible grades conceivable. And this was followed by a tremendous fit of recklessness in which I decided to make a complete break and go off to Germany and live for a while and see what would happen.

I suppose that this part of the will, which as I say runs one's life, had in fact decided that I needed a whole other kind of existence. And if somebody were writing a psychoanalytical treatise about me, much would be said at this point about the great importance of changing my surroundings and my language. The extraordinary charm of living in Germany came to be that I spoke often for days and even weeks on end nothing but German. However badly I did it, this provided a most marvelous kind of protection for the English part that was now only thinking in English, rather than speaking in English, and was almost entirely concerned with writing and the translation of experience. This came quite slowly at first; of course, I knew a great number of English people while I was in Germany. I went there and settled down in a room in a pension and started to earn my living by giving English lessons.

In due course, various things became apparent. First of all, I realized that living in Germany was entirely different from living in England. Not for my private psychological reasons of feeling protected by a foreign language—which meant that I could say anything I liked without being embarrassed (because it was in a foreign language it therefore didn't matter and didn't really mean what I said)—but also I became aware of the outside world in quite a new way. I became aware of what it was like to live in a city which was, in fact, already almost on the brink of civil war. There were a whole number of political factions which expressed themselves at the juvenile-delinquent level in gangs. These gangs all stood nominally for some political party or other, although the great fun of belonging to them was that you could beat somebody else up. Nevertheless, these gangs had an added sinister quality just because they were aided and abetted by the members of political parties who should have known better than to do such a thing and, by dabbling in violence in this utterly irresponsible manner, did in fact bring on the great wave of violence which was to follow. It was unspeakably strange to me to see a city in which you could actually witness tanks coming down the street in order to control the rioting and in which people would be assaulted and stabbed right in broad daylight sometimes in a crowded thoroughfare. This sense of tension and an impending disaster was, I regret to say, more stimulating than depressing to me personally because I was young and I found this feeling of something about to happen very, very exciting. And while not becoming greatly involved in any of it, I nevertheless was a sort of eager spectator.

At this time also came a gradual reorientation in the lives of myself and my friends—a political consciousness which had a sort of left-wing tinge. This is extremely misrepresented in most of the writings about the thirties, in general, and about us in particular, because people seemed to suggest that we were in some sense serious political participators, that we joined parties, specifically the Communist Party. More and more it seems to me that this was not only untrue but would have been impossible, because, psychologically, the kind of revolution which we were thinking about was a quite different sort of revolution. It was a highly individualistic poet's revolution. And the great spokesman of it, who was in fact Stephen Spender, has described in his remarkable autobiography, *World within World,* how he did in fact join the Communist Party for about ten minutes, and they couldn't wait to get rid of him. He was an absolute hot potato, because he was the most individualistic creature alive and an anticommunist in the deepest sense of the word for that very reason. Nevertheless, Stephen preached a sort of romantic, Whitmanesque, poetical kind of revolution, an implementation, if you like, of the Freudian revolution, by which everybody would be a great deal freer, particularly the young. This became romantically associated in our minds with the events that were shaping up in Europe. Of course the great, great event of the thirties around which all these groups constellated themselves was the civil war in Spain, about which I shall say more in a moment.

When I came later on to write about this period of my life in Germany, which was from 1929 to 1933, I found myself with an immense mass of characters and incidents and situations, and I wondered how in the world I should compose them. And I came to the conclusion that I would write a book that was called *The Lost.* As a matter of fact, I thought of the title in German, where it sounds much better: *Die Verlorenen.* "Die Verlorenen" was to mean, first of all, "the lost" in the sense of the entire German nation and indeed the world going astray into the paths of violence and destruction. This was the somber background of the material, but in the foreground and still faithful to the Forster slogan—we never cease to think of ourselves as comic writers essentially—in the foreground were to be figures that were amusing rather than somber and satiric rather than tragic. These figures were also to be "the lost" in another sense, that's to say people whom established society rejects in horror: a sort of bachelor girl, a boy of the underworld, an old crook, and so on and so forth. These people were to be my principal characters, and they were to play a butterfly dance against the approaching thunderstorm of violence which was the coming of the Nazi Party into power.

As soon as I left Germany in 1933, and Hitler was in fact in power, the Reichstag had been burned, and the Nazis had taken over after a mock election, I started to try to contrive this novel. It was enormously complex, which you may imagine, and full of the most extraordinary coincidences: the people met each other in the oddest ways, and everybody knew everybody, and it was quite impossible. It finally sank into a cat's cradle of strings and wires and connections and plots. And finally with a feeling of absolute despair, I thought well now, I must get some of this out and salvage it, and dragged out the figure who is called Mr. Norris, this curious elderly crook who makes his living in various countries. This is an account of the period that he spent in Germany before he was run out of there.

When I asked myself how I was going to tell the story of Mr. Norris—of course how you're going to tell the story is one of the most important of the two questions that you ask yourself when you write. (The other question is actually asked by the reader, "*Why* are you telling me this?" A very important question to be able to answer, incidentally. One has to know what the anecdote means: why am I telling you this? And then the question arises, Who is telling it?) I thought to myself, I only know Germany from the point of view of myself. I cannot pretend to be a German, and I can't identify myself with any of the other characters, particularly as they're presented as such freaks. So the only thing I can possibly do is to write in the first person. But I was nervous and had never heard of anybody writing in the first person and using their own name. So I took my two middle names and called myself William Bradshaw. Names I dropped when I became an American citizen, because to be called Christopher William Bradshaw Isherwood is too much for one man to bear. So William Bradshaw was the hero of this little novel I then proceeded to write.

I think that in writing this novel I made another absolutely fundamental mistake. That's to say that I didn't understand what I was trying to do and therefore attempted to tell a story. I was still under the spell of writing a contrived novel with a plot and all kinds of false direction. As magicians say, you hold the thing *there* and are really doing something *here*—all kinds of tricks and surprises and so forth. In my opinion this novel, *The Last of Mr. Norris,* is very much overcontrived.[1] I find myself in very great difficulties because I was lying about the very nature of my own experience, a thing that I have never done since then. I mean, I was making myself participate in the story of Mr. Norris in a way in which I in fact didn't participate. In order that I should assist at certain criminal proceedings which were going on in the story, I was made a great deal dumber than I ever have been, because I would have seen right through these people and had nothing to do with them. And so William Bradshaw turned out to be unsatisfactory as a vehicle for my perceptions. I was always worried about making him too smart and kept telling him to shut up. I fundamentally misunderstood the nature of what I was trying to do, which was to draw portraits.

I now see that I am really far more interested in portrait writing than I am in the novel per se, though I have written one novel since—that was rather a disaster, too. Somehow or other, plotting and construction, dearly as I love doing it as a kind of parlor game, or for somebody else's novel, always turns sour on me. And what I realized when I came to write the second book about Berlin, *Goodbye to Berlin,* was that what mattered to me primarily were the characters. And that the characters put forth the action, not vice versa. In other words, the action of the story was seen to be nothing else but a kind of exercise track with jumps to show off the paces of your horse. If the character has to be shown in certain circumstances that is only because he has certain characteristics that you want to bring out, and you can only bring them out by putting him under certain kinds of stress and strain, showing him in this kind of situation or that. This entirely revised my whole idea of how I should present fiction: I should present it, as far as I was concerned, in the form of a portrait. The only thing about this portrait that moves is this: that I try to start with a superficial false impression (how you would see somebody if you met them for the first time) and then, by means of the action, gradually go deeper and deeper into this person until you have seen him or her from a whole series of different angles and so gradually a portrait in depth is developed. And that is still my idea of how to spend my remaining years as a writer and, as I shall tell you next time, I've gone on beyond the question of using the first person at all. I think I see a way to do this even more intimately.

Because this character, this "I," is a real problem. I say that William Bradshaw was unsatisfactory: he seemed kind of dumb and strange, and I didn't altogether know him. So when I wrote the next book, *Goodbye to Berlin,* I decided to write with an "I" who would be as much me as possible. Why did I want to write with an "I" at all? There's a technique in Chinese medicine, or perhaps it isn't Chinese, but a technique of bringing the various poisons in the body to a head somewhere or other. They used to make a scar and keep it open, not let it heal, let it fester. The idea was that by doing this the whole thing became concentrated in this one spot and wasn't diffused over the whole body. What I'm trying to say is this—and here I'm really speaking very individually, I'm not laying down laws about the novelist's art—but it began to seem to me that the "I-ness" of oneself was like a poison that was apt to seep into everything else and confuse the clear lines of the character.

In fact, I revolted very much from the idea of writing in the third person because I felt this vitiates all of the characters: they'd all have a bit of me in them. After all, what do I know about the outside world? Only what I see, nothing else. I must not pretend to know anything else. I must only recognize exactly what I perceive. Of course in those days the word *existentialism,* if it had indeed been coined at all, was not in general currency. But this was a kind of existentialism. And what I began to feel then was: very well, I'll write entirely from the point of view of how I see events, how I see people, how I see characters. And in order to pin the "I" down, I will call it "Christopher Isherwood," and there it will be and it won't be allowed to interfere with anybody else.

This endeavor is not nearly so simple as it sounds because it's all very well saying, as I said on page 1 of *Goodbye to Berlin,* "I am a camera with its shutter open, quite passive, recording, not thinking, . . . recording the woman at the window doing her hair"—or something, I've forgotten. The point anyway was that I was sitting up at this window, and I was being like a camera. But of course you can't go right through a book being a camera. People started getting involved with the camera, talking to it, getting mad at it, even sometimes making passes at it, and the question was, how does the camera respond? The camera isn't allowed to respond very much, because if it responds then it will get out of hand and start bragging about how it fought some of the people and made love to others and did so and so. So it has to remain curiously detached in the middle of all of this turmoil. And indeed, one of my earliest reviewers referred to the "Christopher Isherwood" in *Goodbye to Berlin,* as I well remember, as "this sexless nitwit."

So the problem how "Christopher Isherwood" could be both observant and, to use another postwar word, engaged was a very difficult question indeed. I should say something at this point about what is, after all, in the great world, my only claim to fame: the play that my great, late friend John van Druten made out of certain parts of *Goodbye to Berlin,* which he called *I Am a Camera.* John van Druten, in fact, ran into exactly the same problem as I had run into, only onstage this problem was more brutally revealed, that's to say, Is this young man a camera, or what? Also a very interesting thing arose, which I had known instinctively but now observed for the first time: in the play as in the book, the "Christopher Isherwood" figure has a prolonged relationship with a girl named Sally Bowles, sort of a brother and sister relationship. Now we all know perfectly well that in life even the most impetuous of us have had such relationships with the opposite sex. It's entirely possible and casts no reflection on the attractiveness of either party. But on the stage, it's really terribly hard to do this. And when a good-looking romantic lead was cast in the part of "Christopher Isherwood," you could feel that the audience bitterly resented the fact that he never got seriously involved with Sally.

I always used to say that "Christopher" on the stage should be either very tall or very fat, because, owing to the mysterious cruelty of the laws of audience psychology, people figure that very tall and very fat people couldn't possibly expect to have a love affair, and therefore they are perfectly happy not to have one. It's amazing how we react in this way, but we do. Despite the very great talent shown by William Prince in the New York production, which of course contained the unforgettable performance by Julie Harris, I'm told that the London production was really more satisfactory because the actor who played "Christopher Isherwood" was kind of a bean pole and very amusing. He played the thing more as a comedy part and that's the only way it can be done.

John van Druten didn't very much interfere with the structure, except that it was much more tightened up into a sort of contraption, and the Jewish problem was brought more into the foreground. Here again great difficulties were experienced because the whole impending Nazi doom—which is terribly easy to do in a book, in which you can feed in a background throughout the whole thing and bring it up to the foreground when you feel like it—cannot be done on the stage unless you commit the crudities of having shots offstage or the "Horst Wessel Lied" being sung in the background, which of course he didn't do.[2] And so one difficulty was that it was a play about Germany in the early thirties without any Nazis. They were very much in the background, although they were spoken of; but they didn't really impose themselves. This is incidentally a problem which is going to arise again quite shortly, because we are going to attempt a musical of this thing.[3] It's interesting to follow these things through various art forms: this has a peculiar advantage denied to the stage play and, of course, was not possessed by the novel—you can do so much with the music itself. If the score is well done, I can imagine a very interesting mélange of Kurt Weill music of the period representing the Berlin that was swept away by the Nazis, also the kind of sentimental folk-song music that was extremely popular, including yodeling. (I had a character that was a yodeler in my story.) Also sinister military music, and there was a great deal of American jazz. All of these elements made up the musical background of the period.

When the play *I Am a Camera* was made into a film, the makers of it—with whom neither John van Druten nor I was concerned—completely lost their wigs and were so frightened about the relationship between Sally Bowles and "Christopher Isherwood" that they had him try to rape her at one point, after which they decided to be just friends. Which only shows you how conventional some people are.

There's no sweeter music than the sound of one's own voice, but I didn't realize it was this late. I must pass on quite rapidly because even with another hour I can only get up to the time when I left for America. I must mention another thing in which I was very much involved, and that was the three plays that I wrote together with W. H. Auden. These plays have really very little in them of value contributed by me, except probably the encouragement to write them at all. What happened originally was that Auden wrote a play by himself called *The Chase,* and out of this play was evolved the first of our plays that we called *The Dog Beneath the Skin* (1935–36). This play was written with all the wildness of something that you never expect to see performed and into it we put everything that we could think of, from the fairy tale quest of the hero who goes out to look for the missing prince, to all kinds of stealings from various authors, including a little bit of Brecht's *Stadt Mahagonny.*[4] This play, which if it were performed in its entirety would be longer than *Hamlet,* was very skillfully cut and presented and was quite a success, which encouraged us to write another one. In working on these plays, I always thought of Auden as the composer and myself as a librettist, as if this had been an opera. Indeed, these plays are valuable for the magnificent passages of poetry in them by Auden. Auden was once asked by some journalist, "How do you collaborate with Mr. Isherwood?" And Auden said, "Extreme politeness." And it's quite true: we really wrote these plays as though we were Quakers. That's to say, we never took a vote, there was none of this horrible majority, minority kind of thing. We simply went on and on praising everything until the other one said, "But I don't like that bit." And so by the most curious kind of attrition, we got them written. The first play was written chiefly by correspondence.

The next play, which was much more willed and designed, was called *The Ascent of F6* (1937). It was ostensibly about climbing a mountain, but was in fact about the figure I had occasion to speak of a good deal last time, the Truly Weak Man, the neurotic hero, as embodied in the figure of T. E. Lawrence, Colonel Lawrence of Arabia. We tried to convey the inner essence of this figure in the person of the leader of the expedition up a great mountain on which everybody is lost. The mountain was also a Freudian mountain and was haunted by a Freudian demon, who was the chief character's mother. She was waiting for him at the top. At least she was waiting for him at the top until Burgess Meredith, an old friend of mine and a very talented actor, was about to play the part in New York, and he said at once, with an actor's instinct, "I'm not going to have her up there. I have to be alone on the summit." But it worked just as well that way. He just surmounted her a little lower down and got up to the summit by himself.

The Ascent of F6 has been performed under all manner of circumstances, including a quite legendary performance, I think at Harvard, where they built a mountain about as high as this ceiling and the whole party fell—it was rather like the Matterhorn disaster—fell into the orchestra pit. There was another extraordinarily interesting performance, which I did see in a New York studio, where they had absolutely no scenery or props except that at one end of the studio there was a flight of stairs going up to a door. The climbers did nothing except mime climbing on the stairs and, by a stroke of real genius, they weren't even dressed as climbers, in fact. They wore blue jeans, were stripped to the waist, and climbed with electric flash lamps. At one moment, one of the characters is killed by an avalanche. Here again, the usual methods of producing an avalanche (which is to take a loudspeaker into a toilet and flush it—it's true, it's what we did in the London production)—these were abandoned. Instead of this, the producer had a truly astonishing effect, which I've never forgotten, which was that they are all leaning over yelling, "Look out! It's coming!" And then somebody backstage slammed a door as hard as he could, after which there was complete silence. I remember this really as one of the most remarkable theatrical effects I've ever seen on either the professional or the amateur stage.

Finally, we did a play called *On the Frontier,* which was a very much more overt comment on the existing world situation. It was performed in late 1938, but it was written a little earlier. This play was much better than the others technically but was rather a bore because it expressed the sort of suitable political sentiments so very patly—it was very much on the side of the angels. And the result was that the only really attractive character was a fascist tycoon named Mr. Valerian, who was much more fun than anybody else, because the theater is in this sense completely amoral. The first night was enlivened by a remarkable symbolic speech made by mistake by Auden, who had been told to appeal for funds—I guess for something having to do with the Spanish civil war. And what he wanted to say was that things were so bad in the world outside that anything that had happened on the stage that evening paled by comparison. What he actually said was: "As you all know, far worse things have been going on in the audience this evening."

Just to be very brief to round off this whole affair, I've really no time to refer at length to the significance of the Spanish civil war as a literary melting pot, which indeed it was. I had no direct involvement with it because just as we were all set to go off on one of those literary delegations to Madrid—which gravely impeded the military efforts—we got the chance of going to China. So instead Auden and I went to the war there and saw a great deal of the conditions, both in the cities behind the front line and also on two of the fronts, and also met an enormous variety of people. I think this was incomparably one of the most interesting experiences of my life, and we wrote a travel book about it called *Journey to a War* (1939). The further effects of this experience upon myself were to turn me quite definitely toward a realization that I really had always been and now more than ever was a pacifist, and that everything else was overlaid on that and must be removed. But of that more next time.

There's one other book that I haven't mentioned at all except that I read a little bit from it last time, and that was *Lions and Shadows.* This was an autobiographical book which covered my life up to the point of leaving for Germany in 1929. But here I shall stop. Does any question arise? Next time I'm going to speak about my last books; also, what I'm writing now and why.

The Dog Beneath the Skin, The Ascent of F6, On the Frontier

LOS ANGELES, APRIL 27, 1965

I am going to talk today about the three plays that I wrote with W. H. Auden and also about a travel book we wrote together later. These plays were all written during the 1930s, and our collaboration was really partially accidental. We had been close friends since our school days, and he used to show me everything he wrote. We had, at the beginning of the '30s, written a play which we did not at all expect to have produced and indeed was just a sort of parody or joke. It was called *The Enemies of a Bishop,* and it was somewhat inspired by a play we had both seen in Berlin by a very minor dramatist, Peter Martin Lampel, that was called *The Revolt in the Reformatory.*[1] I suppose partly because we did not understand German very well, this play seemed delightfully funny to us. It was a very usual kind of social document play showing how awful things were in reformatories, and for that time the action on the stage was rather daring. For instance, at one point in the play the front of a girl's dress was torn right off, but she had her back to the audience. And also there were complaints by one of the younger boys about the things that went on at night in the dormitories that he objected to. And so this play amused us because in the midst of all this realistic and rather rowdy action, people used to come down to the footlights and make corny political speeches, and we thought this was very amusing. I'm afraid that this extremely third-rate work was the real inspiration of our drama, much more than Brecht, who is always thought to have been our master in this field. As a matter of fact, we hadn't either of us seen any of his plays at that time, although the *Dreigroschenoper* had already been performed in 1928 or 1929 in Berlin.[2] In our play, two of the boys run away from the reformatory and land up in a luxury hotel, and the luxury hotel was really the only setting that was later used in *The Dog Beneath the Skin.*

Then about four years later, that would have been 1934, Auden wrote a play called *The Chase* in which the heir to the estate in a certain little English village has disappeared, and every year somebody is sent out to look for him. It's a sort of fairy tale situation, and none of the people who have been sent out to look for him have ever returned. The young hero, a sort of fortunate younger son of the regular fairy tale setup, whose name is Alan, sets out on this particular year and goes to look for the missing man, whose name is Francis. This was simply a mechanism to permit Alan to have all sorts of adventures in a kind of surrealist or parody version of contemporary Europe. He goes to different countries and encounters different situations. The countries all have imaginary names, and the situations are highly stylized, but a sort of crude political satire runs throughout the whole piece.

When Auden had finished writing *The Chase,* there was a definite possibility that it would be performed, because we were friends with a very enterprising and talented director named Rupert Doone, and he wanted to start what he later called The Group Theatre (quite distinct from the Group Theater in America) and put on plays by contemporary writers, and this was to be one of them. But when Auden sent me *The Chase,* I started to make certain suggestions about how I thought it could be elaborated and how the satirical part of it could be enlarged, and so we entered into a correspondence and then he came out to see me. At that time I happened to be living in Denmark. So we met in Copenhagen and revised this thing together, and it was performed finally in '36 in London. I never saw it performed myself.[3]

The play was very much elaborated in the course of our transformation of it from *The Chase* to *The Dog Beneath the Skin,* and one way we elaborated it was that the dog took on a great function. Auden had first of all approached the thing simply with the idea that it would be fun to have an actor in a dog suit on the stage. Of course, the classic situation for this is *Peter Pan,* and the big dog there looks after the children. But then we arrived at the idea that after all this dog ought to have a great significance, and we soon arrived at the idea that the dog was really Francis. In other words, Francis never had left the village at all, but he'd become so disgusted with the people in the village that he decided to dress up as a dog and live amongst them and observe them. This was a not very light-handed way of suggesting the action of the artist who retires into the kind of Proustian tower and observes society from behind some kind of barricade. What happens in this version is that the dog has remained all these years in the village, but when Alan goes off on his journey to look for Francis, the dog thinks it's about time he had some fun. So he jumps about and gets into Alan's good graces, and Alan takes him along, and they go everywhere together. Then in due course the dog reveals himself, steps out of the dog suit, and shows himself to be Francis.

The philosophy in back of all of this was one that I now somewhat repudiate. It was a very popular philosophy for that time: that the artist who shuts himself away in seclusion in an ivory tower is really frustrating himself and that he ought to enter into the broad stream of life—whatever the devil that means—and somehow or other be like other people. This now seems to me the most terrible nonsense because if there's one thing we need desperately in our culture it's as many outsiders as possible. The idea that we should all try to conform to a norm is very like the Freudian heresy. I say heresy because it was not held by Freud but is held by many analysts who, whether they admit it or not, secretly want to make everybody the same as everybody else, which is disastrous and quite contrary to the truths promulgated by Freud, who wanted people to adjust to their situation, which is something very different again. In both *The Dog Beneath the Skin* and *The Ascent of F6,* there was a great deal of the idea that these unfortunate outsiders should be brought back into the fold. *The Dog Beneath the Skin* ends with a rather ill-fitting kind of revolutionary theme that I have never liked and which indeed doesn't seem to lead anywhere. There were various versions of it. One was that Francis, having emerged from the skin, was immediately put to death by one of the ladies of the village and that then the journalists, who were a sort of Greek chorus throughout the play, come forward and say after all nothing has happened. A dog has simply been killed, all of which, of course, symbolizes the way the press hushes up inconvenient facts. And then Alan goes off on some kind of unspecified, vaguely revolutionary crusade. I find all this aspect of the play extremely unsatisfactory, and, of course, when you come down to it, the reason I'm standing here talking about this play or indeed any of our plays is simply that my collaborator was a great poet and that some of the passages in these plays are of incredible beauty and among the best things that Auden ever wrote.

In *The Dog Beneath the Skin,* I was in the position of a friend making suggestions, and I suggested several completely new scenes. Anything in verse was to be done by Auden, but that was by no means the whole extent of Auden's contribution, because anything that was heightened or poetic prose was also to be done by Auden. For instance, the big speech that opens *The Ascent of F6* was written by Auden. We were extraordinarily hard-boiled in our attitude to this collaboration, that is to say, the view was that there just had to be a speech at this point, and so Auden just wrote a speech. Often in discussions, it seems to me now that we took an attitude that I suppose would have shocked a lot of people if they could have heard us talk. We said, there had to be some farce here; there had to be a great speech where the actor would come downstage and address the audience directly; there had to be this; there had to be that. And the general overall feeling was to keep the whole thing alive and moving and changing tone and pace throughout. Auden went on record someplace saying that he liked *The Dog Beneath the Skin* the best of the three plays, and I think there's a great deal to be said for it simply in the sense that almost anything one does for the first time in a new art form is the best that you can do because you're so wild, you're so mad and fearless and irresponsible. We really didn't bother a bit about whether this play would ever be performed in its entirety, and indeed I doubt if it ever has been. It would take quite as long as *Hamlet*. . . .

The characters in *The Dog Beneath the Skin* are extremely crude. Regarded as characters, they don't have much subtlety; they're like the characters in a fairy story. Alan is just the hero. We just sort of hooked the scenes onto each other in the roughest possible way. . . . We allotted scenes to each other. We said, you do so-and-so and I'll do so-and-so. Auden was an incredibly fast worker, and we simply couldn't bear not to get anything finished once it was there on the drawing board. It was a marvelous stimulus because we had to keep pace with each other, and so we just wrote like mad. When we got to *The Ascent of F6,* it was even easier, and the entire play was written in a very, very short period. At that time, I was living in Portugal, and he came out there, and we worked on that together. . . .

As far as I can recall, I'd certainly not seen *Mahagonny* performed, but by this time I had read it. In *Mahagonny,* there's a scene of extreme gluttony in a restaurant. It was this idea that inspired me to have this scene in which the diner actually comes into the restaurant and there are a lot of chorus girls and a floor show going on, and he picks out one like you get a trout at the Sportsmen's Lodge, and she's going to be cooked to be eaten at the restaurant. Then this was followed by a floor show. I remember that was my idea, too. That was not out of Brecht. There's a comedian in the floor show called Destructive Desmond, and every evening Destructive Desmond destroys a real work of art of enormous value. It is a very crude sort of satire against the Philistinism of the capitalists, and the audience of the nightclub gets such kicks out of this that it is worthwhile doing onstage. In this particular case he had a Rembrandt, I think it was, and some kind of cheap lithograph, and he actually appealed to the audience and says, "Which one shall I destroy?" So there is a certain flavor of Jesus of Nazareth and Barabbas brought into the situation. There was a choice in which the audience all yells for the Rembrandt to be destroyed. This scene, I believe, is curiously effective on the stage. . . .

It's awfully difficult, if you haven't ever collaborated with somebody, to describe this process. It's very extraordinary, especially if you know somebody very intimately. There's a lot of telepathy taking place, and probably, in psychological terms, you actually create a sort of dual persona that does the work. The suggestions made by one or the other person are hardly verbalized very often. I mean, if you've got a tape of these people talking to each other, you would hear things like "and then he—," "the elevator," "yes, of course," "and afterwards, well they're waiting," this kind of thing. They're so quick with each other, and the slightest indication is picked up and developed. And just supposing somebody says, "no, *one* of them is waiting," you think, "Jesus, why didn't I think of that? That's terrific, you know!" That's because both people, like great chess masters, see miles of moves ahead right to the end of the game, so that every suggestion is immediately followed with its consequences to the end. However, having said all this, I suppose it is true that, particularly in the first play, since it was I who was making the suggestions, I was doing most of the new constructing. And probably as we went on this evened out much more in the other two plays.

Anyhow, *The Dog Beneath the Skin* was performed, and thanks to a really excellent cast and to the great skill of the director, Rupert Doone, the play was really quite a success. It was a kind of nine-day wonder in London. It had rather the status of an off-Broadway show—it was in a small theater but it did well, and there was a general consensus of opinion that we absolutely had to write another play. So we were now in the position of being, suddenly, dramatists. Up to this moment, although Auden had done things before on the stage, we really hadn't thought of ourselves as engaging in this activity very much except to amuse each other. But we then decided that we would next time do a play that had a lot more form and more consideration behind it. And this next play was *The Ascent of F6.*

One of the great figures of the 1930s was T. E. Lawrence, Lawrence of Arabia so-called, who represented a kind of neurotic hero in our view, a marvelous amateur who was supposed to be the greatest general of his time in small military engagements. But he could never receive any decorations because no senior officer had been present while he was doing these feats. This was a man who, one was given to understand from certain passages in *The Seven Pillars of Wisdom* (1926), had really fought the entire war for quite private reasons, and it was all a kind of projection of his neurosis. At least that's how we read his character, and we thought this was just marvelous, very exciting, and this is how Lawrence appealed to people at that time. The questions of was he a homosexual or did he enjoy dressing up in Arab clothes or was he a sadist or something simply didn't bother us one tiny bit. He seemed to be just the right kind of anti-heroic hero and, of course, he was also very exciting in that he was a writer. So we were very much drawn toward the idea of writing in some way about Lawrence, and while one can never actually explain how one gets the idea for anything, it was partly that and partly the fact that many of our close friends had been involved in mountaineering. Auden's brother, John, had actually gone quite a long way up Everest on one of the expeditions, and we were very much interested in reading accounts of the great climbers, of the satanic pride exhibited by some of them, the almost fiendish arrogance of Whymper in later life.[4] I've forgotten who it was, but one of the climbers is recorded as having reached the top of some mountain and shaking his fist at the valley below. In other words, this was a figure of incredible arrogance and near madness who at the same time achieved these heroic feats.

So with this basis in view, we imagined the character of a man we called Michael Ransom who was surrounded by a group of fellow climbers who in their different ways typified various attitudes to climbing—from the complete sanity of some to the most extreme forms of self-torture in others. There was one who would go absolutely anywhere and take the most appalling risks without even noticing it because he was a botanist, and all he cared about was some rare flora that had been blooming in exposed places. Then again, there was one who aspired to be a disciple of Ransom and to order others around, and there was another who was completely irresponsible and just did the whole thing for fun. There was a kind of sane middle-aged doctor who just climbed because he thought that they were all so crazy, and he wanted to keep an eye on them. However, we didn't just stick to this, perhaps many will say wrongly, but now the thing began to proliferate. In the first place, we dug up again the myth of brothers. There were two brothers: Michael Ransom was the climber, and the other brother was the absolute opposite. The other brother was worldly and was a politician and was in fact a member of the British Cabinet. His name was James. Both of these brothers had a kind of mother problem. The climber had rather rejected the mother, who adored him, and the politician, James, was terribly jealous because the mother preferred Michael. So there was a big Freudian thing, and, of course, the mountain itself assumed the proportions of a sort of mother figure. In order to tie James into the story, we had to make it a political climb as well as a psychological and physical climb. There had to be political reasons why the British party had to get to the top first. This is not nearly as silly as it sounds, because there has been considerable political friction about mountains, including the Chinese claim to have climbed Everest from the other side, and it's not at all unusual for a feat of this kind (going to the moon is another example) to acquire such prestige that it actually has political value. . . .

The similarity between the two characters in the novel I'm writing now[5] and the two brothers in *F6* struck me just when I was talking about it at this moment, which only shows you how blind you are towards your own mythmaking and how one always tends to do the same things over and over and over again. However, this is not to be deplored, because we go on doing them until we get them right—at least we hope so. And this structure in *F6* was, in all of our plays, a very crude kind of theater, a sort of political didacticism to some extent, and made memorable by Auden's poetry. There were further developments in the play. Watching all of this were the ordinary people, and they looked on this exploit as something designed primarily to amuse them but which nevertheless gave them a certain distaste and boredom with their own lives. When the play was performed recently—it's quite often performed in England, especially in schools and colleges, and it was done here on the air on KPFK[6] and I took a small part in it myself—what struck me was that the dialogues between these two ordinary people, who are simply called Mr. and Mrs. A, are in many respects the best thing in the play. These were entirely written by Auden. They're in verse and they represent interludes between the acts in which Mr. and Mrs. A talk to each other and discuss the events of the climb and how they feel about it. This gave the whole thing a strange sort of reality and, I think, much of its power.

The original performance of the play was quite extraordinarily successful. We were fortunate to have a young actor named William Devlin, who had just been playing Peer Gynt, and he played Ransom like Lear on the heath. There was no nonsense about it—he really roared. So it assumed a kind of expressionistic quality that was very satisfactory, and it carried everything else along with it. Since Auden had written him some rousing speeches, particularly toward the end, this was very effective. The end of the play was always a terrible mess, and we never really solved it. At a certain point on the mountain, Ransom has disposed of everybody, that is to say, they have all died, and Ransom goes on alone and enters into a realm of hallucination. He imagines a kind of tribunal in which he's on trial for his life, and his brother and all the other characters, including the climbers of whose death he accuses himself, appear against him. Here I must say I think we became extremely irresponsible and by dint of using lines out of earlier passages in the play and giving them to different characters produced an extraordinary sense of meaning without very much: the people would repeat something or other that was heard earlier in the play and this is always theatrically very effective. It doesn't matter what it means.

There was another memorable version of the play that was performed in 1939 or 1940 in New York. It was done in a studio, a long room with a staircase at one end. This performance was stimulated by the fact that Mr. Burgess Meredith, a good friend of ours, was seriously considering producing the play on Broadway (or anyway in a more elaborate form) and playing Ransom himself. And Mr. Meredith, with an unerring actor's instinct, said, "I don't want the mother at the top of the mountain.

I want to be there by myself." And he was quite right, I think. It sort of cleared the air. Instead of finding the mother seated on top of the mountain, as he does in the printed version, the mother is just the last of the phantoms that oppose his climbing the mountain, and finally he brushes her aside and reaches the summit alone. Mr. Meredith never did put on his production because then the war came, and it became impossible.

. . . . .

I've done a great deal of collaborating during my life and with a very wide variety of people. Under certain circumstances, particularly for the theater, it's stimulating, and, of course, as far as movies are concerned, there is no such thing as not collaborating because you must be collaborating at least with the director, unless you are the director. And even then, you are collaborating with the actors so that it is a group enterprise. . . .

I found working with most people that, almost without anybody saying anything, you tend to assume complementary roles. If one person is good at one thing, you kind of find it out, and the other person does the other thing. The one real rule for collaboration is not to strangle the embryo before it's born. And therefore a great deal of give and take has to go on in the early stages. A journalist once asked Auden, "How do you collaborate with Mr. Isherwood?" He said, "With extreme politeness." The point is that there is a time for politeness, if you call it that. It sounds an offensive word, but what I mean is that if you think that somebody is working on something, you must never, never, never smack it down in the beginning. If you start doing that with another person then you can never collaborate with them, and relations with them are quite hopeless in this respect. Later on you have to have the sense of getting the best out of this thing, and, of course, compromises are made. That's for sure. Whatever else our plays were, they did have the virtue of being very good vehicles for collaboration because Auden in his part of the work was functioning in a state of almost complete freedom. And the one thing he demanded was to know where we were going from there or what something was to be about. These conditions were supplied, and therefore it was a very good way for him to work. . . .

Our view of the actors was not very demanding. We demanded certain things from them, chiefly beautiful speech. One of the most commented-on speeches of *The Dog Beneath the Skin* was the performance of an actor named Robert Speaight, who later became noted in England for being the first person to take the part of Becket in T. S. Eliot's *Murder in the Cathedral* (1935) and also for a very remarkable performance in the original production of R. C. Sherriff's war play *Journey's End* (1929), when he played the coward. Speaight spoke very beautifully and all he had to do in *The Dog Beneath the Skin* was to speak the choruses, and I'm told this created a great impression and was one of the things the audience liked the most. . . .

To some degree at that particular time in our lives, we were accepting a rather superficial set of ideas. This going along with the United Front and the whole approach to the contemporary situation, while it was certainly perfectly good as far as it went and was nothing to be ashamed of, I don't feel that we drew very extended conclusions from this. I think the reason was that neither of us was really quite allowing ourselves to think certain thoughts that we thought later. Auden, although he had this very strong Anglo-Catholic upbringing, was rather choosing to ignore it (I won't say denying it) and choosing to ignore the hold it had over him. On my side, I was, as I very shortly afterwards discovered, internally turning very much toward the Quaker point of view, and this was something that I didn't choose to talk about. I wasn't aware of it, in fact. I don't mean that there was any kind of conscious suppression. It's just that sometimes you are thinking thoughts you're not aware that you're thinking, especially artistically speaking. . . .

Prater Violet

LOS ANGELES, MAY 4, 1965

. . . .

The last play we wrote was called *On the Frontier,* and Auden and I wrote that in 1938. As a matter of fact, we wrote it partly while we were traveling together to China. We wrote a travel book about that called *Journey to a War.* The play dealt more or less with the contemporary situation. That is to say, it was set in two imaginary countries that were on the verge of war. The only device of any particular interest in it was that on the stage simultaneously there were two families who were supposed to belong to the two different countries. The stage was divided in half, but with no wall: it was just two different kinds of furnishings on each half of the stage. These people ignored each other completely, but at the same time, because a lot of their talk was about the situation, it sort of dovetailed. You heard the point of view of the Ostnians contrasted with the point of view of the Westlanders who were on the other side of the stage. The only time the two sides of the stage had any kind of dealings with each other was in a dream sequence where the boy from one family met the girl from the other family; and right when they both die, again separately, but at the same time, they meet and say some lines at the end of the play. Otherwise, the play didn't contain anything except some rather usual kind of melodramatics based on the life of an armaments manufacturer, a super-tycoon type called Mr. Valerian who kind of ran the country and armed both sides and is finally murdered by a Hitler-type stormtrooper boy at the end.

One of the weaknesses of the play was that, although it was almost too conformingly correct in its antifascist views, the only sympathetic character was this fiend. One rather amusing thing happened during the rehearsals, I remember, which was that there was supposed to be a torchlight procession and the crew got very horsey about it. They said, "We can't do it. It's technically impossible." All that had to happen was that there was a torchlight procession passing backstage and you saw the flickering of the lights. There was an awful impasse. We all sat looking at each other, and then the foreman said, "Of course, we could do the burning of the reformatory from *Ghosts*." And we said, "That's splendid." But as far as I could make out, it was exactly the same, just some flickering lights appeared outside, but they had to think of it in that category. The opening night was distinguished by Auden's speech—on the opening night, we both had to say something. The play was produced under rather peculiar auspices. It was financed by Maynard Keynes, the economist, who was an enormous power in Cambridge because he had invested all of the money of King's College, his old college, and made it the richest college in Cambridge. There is a legend that he took all their money and disappeared into the financial district of London, and the dons of King's College went around saying, "In a week's time we shall either be the richest college in Cambridge or Maynard will be in prison for life." In actual fact, the investments were quite legitimate and it didn't take just a week. They did become immensely rich, and they had a playhouse there. Keynes had married one of the original Russian dancers of the Diaghilev troupe, Lopokova, and he wanted very much for her to be in the play, and she was. She played the lead. On opening night, Auden had to make a speech, and he wanted to say that it was all very well what we had shown on the stage in the way of fascism and approaching war, but really the actual situation in Europe was much worse. But he was a little distraught, as one is on opening night, and what he actually said when he came down to the footlights was, "As you all know, much worse things have been happening in the audience this evening than happened onstage." This caused an absolute riot.

However, the play was given a thorough burial by all concerned, and Professor Monroe Spears, in his book *The Poetry of W. H. Auden,* dismisses it firmly in the following terms: "The play marks in some respects an advance in technical skill, since it is far more like a conventional drama than either of its predecessors; unlike them, it has characters and a plot in the traditional fashion. But it is a propaganda work, against war and fascism, and utterly without permanent interest;"—it sounds as though it were utterly without permanent interest to be against war and fascism—"the characters are thin and conventional, indistinguishable from those of dozens of other anti-war, anti-fascism works; the ideas and references are dated, with the sentiments; the language is impoverished and near cliché. If the other plays are overly complex and tend to incoherence, this one is altogether too simple, in every respect."[1] It is significant that while Auden wrote a great deal of very beautiful poetry in the other plays, and printed much of it later, he himself never reprinted any of the verse in *On the Frontier* in his *Collected Works,* so that must be taken also into judgment against it.

As I said, this same year we also went to China, and we wrote a book about that. It was, as far as I was concerned, a perfectly conventional travel book, just describing what happened every day while we were in China, and the interesting part of the book is the series of sonnets by Auden, all of which have been printed separately. Just a word about travel books. I think the great difficulty about them is that they have to have a goal to be really good. It's like amateur detectives: there's something horrid about an amateur detective, because he's only doing it for fun. And somehow, traveling around and looking at things and saying, "How picturesque" and "How quaint" and "How interesting" becomes very irritating indeed, however cleverly you do it. I think most of the best travel books, perhaps all of them, are those in which the authors have a definite goal. They're looking for the buried ruins of the Aztec temple or they're trying to find what happened to Mr. So-and-so who disappeared in a neighborhood where there were cannibals, or what have you, and they arrive at some conclusions. The difficulty with this book was that there wasn't really any particular reason we were going to China. But at least it had the justification that my other travel book, *The Condor and the Cows* (1949), didn't have at all: we do tell people what the fighting in China was all about, which was at that time at least necessary. Everybody was very vague about it then and vague about the Japanese invasion of China, and I suppose from this point of view the book was sort of useful. *Journey to a War* marks the end of my period of being a kind of United Front leftist and turning back into a sort of liberal individualist again, and also discovering what I ought to have known all along, the fact that I was a pacifist. The war had a great personal effect on me in this manner, from the things I saw while I was there, because we saw a good deal of the effect on the civilian population. Anyhow, these two—the play and *Journey to a War*—were published in 1939. The result was that they were completely forgotten immediately because then the war began in Europe, and a whole new climate of literature set in.

During the war period, I really didn't write any fiction to speak of, except for a couple of short stories, which came out in *The New Yorker* and which were really exhibitions of sheer nervousness, nothing else.[2] One of them was about a man who has a psychic experience and goes into the future. The first time he goes into the future, he only goes a few hours, and then, I think, a few weeks, and nothing dramatic happens. But the next time, the last time (he has seizures, he never knows when it's going to happen), he's up in the attic of a house and he is looking through some old newspapers, and he suddenly becomes unconscious. He comes to himself, and he finds that the attic is completely empty, and he realizes that he is in the future. He can't see out, and when he goes to the door he finds it's locked. Then he finds in the corner a crumpled piece of newspaper on which there is a date that shows that he has gone five years into the future. He's terribly excited and eagerly starts to read the newspaper, but discovers that it is the gazette of a bird fanciers' society. The only thing he finds on the page of printed paper is instructions about how to treat slip claw in canaries ("narrow perches are the best"). He is absolutely unable to tell from this information whether there has been a World War or what has happened. And then, of course, he comes back into the present and is ready to do it again.

The only interesting thing about this business was that the

story was published in *The New Yorker,* and several people thought it was a perfectly genuine kind of extrasensory experience and wrote to me very seriously. One lady wrote to me and said that she had been casting my horoscope (I gave a fictitious birthdate and fictitious dates for all the occurrences to make them sound more convincing), and upon casting my horoscope she discovered that my psychic experiences were absolutely bound to have happened on those two particular dates. So I had to write to her and break the news that I was actually thirty-two years younger than my character, and that I was a Virgo (not a Leo), and that altogether the whole thing was loused up. Somebody else wrote, which was really marvelous, and said, Mr. Isherwood, don't fear your great gift because there is a gentleman in our town who passes into the future every week without any ill effects. Idiotically, I didn't follow it up, which I should have done. It would have been very interesting. That's something Huxley would have done. He always followed up those things, and really he met with some very extraordinary people as a consequence.

The other story is even more trivial. It's a story about how a husband and wife are not getting along well, and she starts keeping a diary in which she accuses him. Then one day by accident she discovers that he is keeping a diary, too. She starts to read the diary, and she begins to realize that, as a matter of fact, he is reading her diary, although he never says so right out. Then they begin to communicate by means of the diaries, and everything is set for a reconciliation until one day, just before it seems evident that one of them is going to speak up and say why don't we make up again?, she comes in and catches him reading her diary. She's so outraged and startled that she goes into a scene before she can stop herself, and this breaks up the marriage finally.

Aside from these pursuits and all the other things that were happening at the time, I became deeply interested in and involved with Vedanta philosophy, in general, and this Hindu monk, Swami Prabhavananda, in particular. I did a good deal of work for him, doing translations with him of various Sanskrit classics—he supplying the Sanskrit and I supplying a rephrasing of the material.[3] That was really all I did until 1944 or '45, when

I wrote a short novel called *Prater Violet.* It's an account of an experience that I had a great deal earlier, to be exact in 1934, my first job in the movies. I got this movie job in a rather peculiar manner, through one of my characters, the girl who is called Sally Bowles in *I Am a Camera.* Sally Bowles was always meeting extraordinary people. On this occasion, she met this remarkable Viennese, Berthold Viertel, who was not only a good poet and writer but he was also a film director. He and his wife, Salka Viertel, had been out in Hollywood for some time already. They were later to be one of the great centers of help for the Jewish refugees who came from Europe. They themselves were both Jews, but they left before Hitler came to power. He had already made several movies in Hollywood, and he was offered by Gaumont British, the studios in London, to come to England and make pictures there. He made three pictures in all in London. The first, the only one I worked on, had the very off-putting title of *Little Friend* and was based on a novel called *Kleine Freundin,* a German title, by Ernst Lothar.[4] It was a story of a little girl who brings her parents back together after they have quarreled by attempting to commit suicide. It was made rather more sophisticated by bringing in a lot of Freudianism and dreams, and was really quite an elegant production in certain respects. I think that Viertel's other two pictures were far more interesting. He made a picture based on *The Passing of the Third Floor Back* (1935) by Jerome K. Jerome. After that he did an extremely interesting and indeed politically quite daring picture on the noted colonial British hero Cecil Rhodes, called *Rhodes of Africa* (1936). It was customary at that time to admire Rhodes rather uncritically, and Viertel did an extremely frank account of his life, showing that he was, shall we say, not an unmixed blessing to the native population and indeed was responsible for slaughtering thousands of them indirectly. Rhodes was played brilliantly by Walter Huston. They had a very strong cast altogether. It is probably Viertel's best picture, in many respects. It was also the last he made, but after the War he went back to Vienna, where he established quite a big reputation again as a theater director and was the first man not only to direct but to translate *Death of a Salesman, A Streetcar Named Desire,* and *The Glass Menagerie.*

The original of Sally Bowles had met Berthold Viertel and had become his secretary in the kind of mad way that she did. She was always becoming people's secretary for about a week. The person who was working with Viertel on the screenplay was a writer named Margaret Kennedy, who was very well known at that time for her novel *The Constant Nymph* (1924), which was later made into a play (1926) and film. Elisabeth Bergner, the brilliant German actress, who also had to leave Nazi Germany, was preparing her debut in English in London in Margaret Kennedy's play *Escape Me Never* (1934).[5] They got so excited about this play that Kennedy just suddenly walked out on the film project because she wanted to be around when the play was being performed.

So suddenly the film job was vacant, and Viertel didn't know any English writers. And here was Sally Bowles to whisper in his ear that she knew, of course, the greatest living genius, etc., etc., the way she talked about all her friends, which was me on that particular occasion. So Viertel said, "Show me something that he has written." She called me up on the phone and said, "Would you please send me one of your books?" And I said, "No." She said, "Why not?" I said, "Well, it's a waste of a perfectly good book." This kind of thing is always happening: they ask to read something. You never hear any more from them, and what's more, you don't get the book back. She said, "If I go out and buy a copy, will you pay half?" I said, "No." She said, "If I go out and buy a copy with my own money and you get the job, will you give me half of your first week's salary?" I said, "Certainly, of course," and dismissed the whole matter from my mind. And the next morning, or whenever it was, she called up in an awed voice and said, "Darling, he thinks it's good!" What Viertel had done was to read the scene in *The Memorial* where one of the characters, named Edward Blake, attempted to commit suicide. This scene was very solid because I got it from somebody who had attempted to commit suicide, so at least it was all quite correct in its details. So Viertel, who was a man of quick decisions, read whatever it was, a page and a half, then shut the book exclaiming, "This is clearly genial." He meant *genial* in German, which means gifted with genius. I was hired immediately.[6]

I knew absolutely nothing whatever about movie writing, but we had a ball. It was absolutely wonderful, and every day was like a mad session with, well, he used to speak of himself as an old Jewish Socrates. This wasn't a bad description of him. He was full of wit and Viennese jokes, and all kinds of stuff. I did, of course, speak German, which helped; he liked that. So we got along like a house on fire, and he's really very much one of the reasons that I am standing here right now, because he was eternally talking to me about his life in California and about Santa Monica Canyon, where he lived, and about all the people he knew. I got a tremendous yen to come out here and visit it at least to see what it was like. And we lived under the shadow of these improbable people who seemed so remote from London, like, for instance, Garbo, who was a great friend of his wife's. I remember that we went to get a present for Garbo, and when Viertel had to tell the clerk in the bookstore the name and address, he just laughed. He couldn't believe it was being sent to her. She was such a legendary figure in those days it seemed to be ridiculous that somebody would be actually sending something to her.

Prater Violet simply tells the story (really, correctly in most of its details) of working together and of the making of the film. Its adverse critics said it was nothing but elegant journalism. But many people like it very much. It was very successful, in fact. Of course, the character of Viertel, whom I called Bergmann, came out very strongly and was very easy to describe. It was done on radio later, and I guess someday it will be an awful musical or something of this kind when I am short of money next.

In *Prater Violet* I again employed the method of narration of calling myself "Christopher Isherwood," and he has all the experiences. I have talked to you before about the difficulties of this method, because you try to say, "Well, look, I'm Christopher Isherwood, but never mind me. This is not about me. Just watch the birdie, and let's get on with things." Whereas, as a matter of fact, you cannot help, if you put yourself in a book, starting to get really into the book and get involved and caught in the book, and your reactions to the other characters begin to make you increasingly humanoid, and finally you're in the book. *Prater Violet* was probably the most successful use of the "Christopher Isherwood" method (which I have now abandoned forever), because Viertel (Bergmann) talked so much that really nobody else got a word in edgewise. Therefore it didn't matter very much about who was telling the story; I was just nothing but a kind of straight man for all the anecdotes, jokes, carryings-on of Viertel himself. All the more so when we got to the part where he was directing the film, because there I just had to stand in the corner and watch. So from that point of view, the method was very successful, I think. It worked quite well in this particular book, and as a sort of added little joke at the end I suddenly reveal that I have a whole private life of my own which Viertel doesn't know about because he's never bothered to ask me. The book ends in a soliloquy in which the "I" character reflects on what his life is really like, which is of course immensely far from the way he is viewed by Bergmann. This was unfair to Berthold Viertel, who took almost too much interest in my life and in the lives of almost everyone he knew. He nevertheless quite enjoyed the book, and he used to talk about it a great deal. He soon revealed that he was in fact the original of it. So I am not breaking any confidences in saying this. He's dead now, he died some time after the war.

.....

This was really a very formative experience in one peculiar way. I'd written two other novels as one writes novels, shut up in a room, and now suddenly I'd had the experience of writing for a medium that was audible. It's really very odd the first time you do this, the first time you realize that the words are actually going to be spoken. Especially when shooting the film, because there are always rewrites to be done, and you find yourself working right there on the floor and writing things that are then immediately given to the actors, and maybe ten minutes later they are actually spoken and recorded. You have suddenly the most tremendous sense of immediacy, from being a kind of introvert—shut up in this room—you're terrifically extraverted, your voice is echoing out over the countryside, as it were. I think this had a lasting effect on me, starting with *Mr. Norris,* which was the first book I wrote after having worked on this film. A whole new element, part of which was good, I guess, and part of it bad, came into my work. One of the good things was that I took to hearing much more clearly what the speeches would sound like. Once you get into that habit, you don't lose it.

Working with Viertel was totally unlike any other movie work I've done since. In fact, I can't remember the physical act of writing at all, because it seemed to me that we talked the whole film into existence. He never stopped talking for a single instant, and he never let me alone for very long. I guess I just wrote things down in the midst of the conversation somehow or other. We walked about all over London together, and although he had only just arrived he was one of those people who knew all about the town, at least from his point of view. Just as they say that D. H. Lawrence would arrive at a place and start writing a novel about it before he had even unpacked because he used to get these terrific intuitions right from the start about what it was really like, and that was his genius.

Viertel would lecture on the people and on the buildings and the way of life of the English and everything else in an absolutely unceasing flow of inspiration. Somebody was asking me, did I take notes at the time. I find that the only thing that I really took (I was aware that I would write about this in some form—it was far too good not to write about) were some strictly technical notes about what happens when you shoot a scene: what the sound recorder says, what the director says, what the makeup man says, what the electrician says, and the technical names for lights and everything.

.....

There are obviously two completely different kinds—two whole families—of dialogue: dialogue that is to some extent naturalistic or realistic, and dialogue that does not attempt to be, and should not be, realistic. Such nonrealistic dialogue you will find in the later novels of Henry James, which fits perfectly into the structure of the prose, but if you try to make the characters talk like that and leave out the prose you are in grave difficulties (in other words, if you try to turn Henry James's novels into plays). I saw an interesting example of that, incidentally. Stephen Spender had been asked by somebody or other to dramatize a rather late James book called *The Golden Bowl* (1904), and he had enormous difficulties because of the dialogue. When isolated from the undergrowth of prose out of which it grew (the descriptive prose), it seemed so wildly mannered and artificial and strange, and yet the story itself is not, after all, a fairy tale or a legend or something that will sustain poetical speech. It is not as if he were writing *Pelleas and Melisande* or something. It is fundamentally a drawing room comedy-tragedy of the period, and it is supposed to be realistic, and the thing just doesn't work. Now this is an example of writing to be read: if you speak it you're getting into trouble. But again, if you read the whole book aloud, it's true you wouldn't be bothered by it.

.....

D. H. Lawrence varies wildly. I think that sometimes he is extraordinarily realistic and knows very well how the north of England people talk and so on. But when the people start to lecture, as they sometimes do in his books, we get into a kind of language that is weird and not at all naturalistic.

.....

If one is not to abandon the realistic method, then the only alternative I can think of is that the observation has to be awfully good. Everything you notice, everything you describe must be described with a peculiar kind of sharpness and relevance. Bad writing is bad not just because the language is humdrum, but the quality of the observation is so poor.

.....

.....

I don't believe (if we can make a distinction here) that it's more novelty that we need; I think it's more probing. I always liked it when my friend Francis Bacon, the painter, says, "I want to get down to the nerve." It seems to me that's what really produces originality—going down to the nerve. It's exposing the simplest things. So many of the writers who do that use very conventional material. Lawrence is a very striking example of that. You think it's about nothing in particular, just about some animals he saw, or some people staring at each other, but somehow he gets down to the nerve and makes it really quite shocking.

.....

I shall finish my life doing what I do, you know. I don't foresee any great branchings off. I have a tremendous lot of stuff that I want to tell still, and I will just go ahead and do that the best way I can.

.....

With every possible respect for the authors concerned, I cannot regard either *Finnegans Wake* (1939) or Samuel Beckett's novels as entirely satisfactory. I must say that. I really find *Finnegans Wake* impenetrable. And Beckett, not that this is an absolutely annihilating criticism, but he bores me terribly. I must say that I find some of Beckett, for example *End Game* (1958), bores me but moves me at the same time, rather like Antonioni does.[7] Sometimes I feel that I can't stay in the theater another moment, but I know that if I do stay I shall be glad, and next morning you wake up with the curious feeling that you've had an experience. I've had great difficulty with the novels, I must say.

.....

They are talking about the question of form a great deal. You see, I have to confess that I don't think primarily of form. What I'm concerned in doing is trying to communicate my experience of life. I'm probably barking up another tree in that respect. Of course I know that you'll say that these people are also certainly communicating their experience of life, but when we get to *Finnegans Wake* I feel that the form, to put it very mildly, becomes a great deal more important than the experience.

. . . . .

The minute I start boring myself, I shall stop. That's the fairest I can say. I sometimes think, Oh, Jesus, must we go through with this. But there's usually something you can *do* about it. I was explaining about this novel I'm writing now where I had become disgusted, temporarily anyway, with describing scenes between people. So I'm writing the entire thing in the form of letters and a diary. And the scenes are only referred to very obliquely, and you find out only in a very oblique manner what's happening. So I suppose I'm up to something as far as that's concerned.[8]

. . . . .

The great objection to most letter-form work is that they far too obviously tell the plot, whereas letters should be intensely subjective and allusive, and should only glance over the surface of the thing. Never say, "As you may recall, you are my wife, and we have two children, and need I remind you of the early days of our courtship," and that sort of thing. That's what most letter-novels are like fundamentally. I think in my way I'm improving on that quite a bit. But it's a real problem, and I have just to keep on doing it, and we'll see what happens.

. . . . .

The language itself is changing, and always will be. We shall go on—the language will probably change right in our hands, as we are doing things to it; the language will change and that in itself will introduce new problems. But I don't think there's the least bit of alarm to be felt about anything because the whole conditions of life are going to change, and there are going to be so many entirely new fields to discuss and write about. I don't know whether there has been a literature that has really dealt at all yet with the conditions under which we will be living in twenty years. . . .

One thing we are very apt to forget in our provincialism is that nobody really elected us to be the standard-bearers of the arts. It may be entirely new things will evolve in Asia, for instance, as changing conditions impinge on the classical cultures there, and there will be a whole period where there will be a complete artistic takeover by other portions of the globe. One can't be sure of that.

. . . . .

Some people do like to dictate into a tape recorder. My great endeavor in writing is to get away from the personalized feel of the words. That's why I always work on a typewriter because my handwriting is too intimate. I can hardly see something that I have written by hand. It's all tangled with me, but by writing it on a typewriter I can stand away from it. In the same way, if I were to use a tape recorder, I would be bothered by the fact that it was my voice speaking, and this would give it all sorts of illegitimate overtones and so forth. It might be that if you were bursting with some idea or other and wanted to get all your thoughts down quick like a bunny, and simply couldn't face the idea of writing it down, it might be good to turn the thing on. But as far as I am concerned, I would never want to use it any other way. Lots of people do use it for that very purpose—in order to hear the thing spoken. But me talking aloud is not speech, as far as I am concerned. I mean, I have to hear somebody else talking aloud. I haven't any idea what things sound like otherwise.

Writing for the films has all sorts of other aspects to it. In the first place, the use of the words has to get further and further and further away from what we ordinarily think of as dialogue. The words really should form a kind of patter of their own because too often in the conventional film they simply serve as captions for the action, and the more you see foreign films, the more you don't miss the words, and you begin to think that maybe they really aren't necessary at all. But that again is heresy, I think. Words have a very important function, but it should be as something quite separate from the image. Otherwise you just

. . . . .

have that awful kind of narration where somebody not only does something but what they're doing is described. You see it even in the best circles quite often: I was worried, I lit a cigarette, I couldn't sleep, I got out of bed. And the man is playing all this while he's telling you.

. . . . .

There's a generalization I make, and I'm not at all sure that it will hold water, but it occurs to me again and again, and so it has some value. I always feel that the film has a sort of anonymous and saga-like quality about it. I'm speaking now of the very early silent films as well as works by some of the very latest people. There's a curious thing that comes again and again in the film, be it in Chaplin, be it in Antonioni, of saying, "There was a boy, there was a girl," rather than saying, "I'm now introducing you to Mr. and Mrs. So-and-so." There's a generalized poetic, saga quality about films, and the characters, while they can be perfectly well defined as characters, nevertheless in films that seem really good always seem to have an eternal aspect, very much more than characters on the stage, for example.

The World in the Evening

LOS ANGELES, MAY 11, 1965

In 1941–42 I was working with the American Friends Service Committee at a Quaker hostel in Haverford, which is outside Philadelphia and is in some respects the center of Quakerdom in the East.[1] I found myself very sympathetic to the life led by the Quakers in general and also to the humors of life in the hostel. The hostel consisted of a whole group of refugees from central Europe, all of whom were professional people, the great majority of them schoolteachers who had left because of the Nazis and had been lucky enough to find their way to this country, usually by very indirect means. Some of them had got what was then relatively easy to acquire: passports to various South American countries. There were passports that you could buy but they were very expensive, and people landed up in Ecuador, Panama, and such places, and then managed to get a visa to the United States. Others had gone down to Lisbon, and a great many crossed from there. In Spain the position was very ambiguous; the Gestapo was active. It was very dangerous, but you never quite knew what was dangerous and what wasn't. One man I know got through and was therefore not sent back to a concentration camp, because, with great presence of mind, he pretended to be a Jew. He discovered right at the last moment by a sort of sixth sense that on that particular day or week the Gestapo from some idiosyncrasy or other had decided that the Jews could all go to the United States but no other kind of anti-Nazi could go. The refugees had extraordinary stories to tell, including, of course, stories that one must never forget. I never told about Nazi officials who helped them, but that happened sometimes, too. There were cases where the official knew he wouldn't get caught doing it and would sometimes let people through.

When they got to the United States, they formed a somewhat confused and in general middle-aged group of people who were extremely intellectual but in a way that made it hard for them at first to teach in America. What they needed chiefly was not so much to learn English (they had a certain amount of English, most of them quite a lot), but to learn the ways of teaching and the much greater informality that exists in American classrooms. So they lived at this hostel at the expense of the American Friends Service Committee and whatever funds could be raised, and they used to go out every day and sit in on classes at Haverford College and places around Bryn Mawr to find out how things are done in this country. Sure enough, within about a year most of them had academic jobs that, I guess, many kept to this day. My job and the job of the other people there was to help them along with their English in their spare time and to organize the circumstances of their lives all the way from washing up dishes to seeing them into Philadelphia, seeing they got on the right train. It was a very absorbing and amusing job.

There was undoubtedly a whole book to be written about these people and their various attitudes, and I even had a title for it. There was a very remarkable man in the group: he was an Austrian poet named Stern (he wrote under the name of Josef Luitpold), and he was very critical of the group because he thought they weren't, shall we say, rising to meet their opportunities with sufficient energy. On one occasion, a couple, who had been, I must say, quite tiresome and had finally gone off to some job, had left their room in a terrible mess, and Mr. Stern came in, looked around the room with disgust, and said, "Such people are not fit for the school of tragedy."[2] I thought this a marvelous remark. I took it in its widest implications to mean that tragedy happens not only to heroes and to cowards but also to people who are quite neutral and in fact are not fit for tragedy—you would never cast them in the role. But that's the way life differs from art. Nevertheless, they have to face up to these appalling situations, too, and some of them, as Mr. Stern put it, were not fit for the school of tragedy, which they demonstrated by not making their beds before leaving and not sweeping the floor. Anyway, I thought this was a good title for a book, and I wanted to call it *The School of Tragedy*.

But then the old, old question set in: just exactly who is telling you all this? My answer up to that point had been "Christopher Isherwood is telling you and don't mind him, he's just someone who works here, and he'll tell you all about this." But the trouble was that working in a Quaker hostel in Haverford was—anyway, for somebody like me—such an exotic occupation, probably the most exotic occupation I've ever taken part in, that I felt more explanation was necessary. It wasn't enough just to have an "I" who had somehow or other got himself in there, especially as this "I" started behaving in a way that was again unpredictable. He didn't stand apart from the thing at all. He was getting very involved in it, and in fact had all the makings of becoming a Quaker. He was very soon saying "Thee is," and so forth, and was attending Meeting and even "speaking," which, I must say, to him, being a professional, was an extraordinarily disconcerting experience because there was no applause afterwards. A Quaker meeting is the only place where you can stand up and absolutely dazzle everybody and sit down again, and all you get is, as you leave, somebody comes up to you and says, "Thank thee for thy testimony." As they say that to everybody who spoke, you don't feel much sense of achievement, and you have to learn not to mind that at all. The point I'm trying to make is that the problem of who is the narrator, and why, began to bother me very, very much, and I began to conceive of a person who might have come to this place for very special reasons. And that, as people who dislike *The World in the Evening* say, was the beginning of my downfall, because it produced a completely different novel. Perhaps the story of how it was produced is the most interesting thing about the book anyway.

The plan for a book of amusing memoirs—the amusing, touching, sometimes tragic memoirs of the members of this group—was gradually abandoned in favor of a story about somebody who comes to such a group and what makes him do it. I began to conceive of a character who had led a very different life and who makes this switch as the result of some kind of crisis. Then I began to feel, well, if he makes this switch, this must be a contrast between the two halves of his own personality. If the life that he has been leading represents one side of him, then the fact that he comes to this Quaker establishment, rather than somewhere else, must prove the existence of another side of his character. So here I was, getting further and further away from good old "Christopher Isherwood," whom I knew and trusted and loved, to this synthetic person who was going to figure as the chief character in *The School of Tragedy*. Gradually, gradually, gradually, the character or rather the implications of the character took over by mathematics; that is to say, as I got more and more interested in why this person would ever have come anywhere near any Quakers at all, I began to get further and further away from the Quakers themselves and from their keeping a hostel, because, I said to myself, this is wrong because it's doubly exotic. It's quite enough that somebody who is leading some other kind of life suddenly goes to work for the Quakers. That's all right, but now to find out that he is also going to work for a whole lot of German refugees—why should he? How do you explain this? In my case, it was the most natural thing in the world for me to go to work with German refugees because I'd been spending my time with German refugees in many countries in Europe ever since Hitler came into power, and I spoke adequate, rather inaccurate German. I really joined the outfit not because the people were Quakers but on account of the refugees. But now my character didn't have this side to his experience, and I somehow couldn't fit it in—it was too much to swallow. And so was finally evolved this character I called Stephen in *The World in the Evening*.

The next thing is, what is this tremendous climax that makes Stephen get mixed up with the Quakers? One day I was down on the beach with the son of Norma Shearer; he was a young man then. We were down in one of those old, large mansions that stand right on the beach in Santa Monica, and there was a swimming pool, and by the side of the swimming pool there was a large doll's house, but it was such a large doll's house that children could actually get into it. It was a playhouse for very small children. I suppose it was partly because young Mr. Shearer, or rather Mr. Thalberg, was telling me about his girlfriends at the time that put the idea into my head, and I suddenly thought how amusing if two adults had an affair in this doll's house. Picturing the idea of this encounter in the doll's house, I then came to the further idea that somebody or other had to interrupt them, because otherwise where's the action? From this I deduced that it must be Stephen who interrupts these two, from which it follows that the girl is his wife and that the shock of discovering these two people might be just the last straw that would make him take off and go back East to see somebody who is a Quaker.[3]

So now things are beginning to tie together slowly, and I figured out, as follows, that this Stephen had an old aunt who was actually British. (The Quakers are very international.) In order to give Stephen some early background that I knew personally, I thought I would have him raised by the aunt, both his parents being dead. The father was a Philadelphian American, but the mother was English, and he spent some time in England but then came back to this country and had a considerable amount of money through the father. And here was the aunt who was a Quaker and she, too, comes to America and settles there. All right, now we have some machinery going, and now we have Stephen, who has an unhappy marriage. I can't remember at what point in the midst of all this something else started to work, anyway I next deduced that this was Stephen's second marriage. As this second marriage was with a young and very sporty American girl, the first marriage, by mathematics, must have been with an older woman who turns out to be English. So now a curious figure began to emerge who had the rather beautiful name of Elizabeth Rydal. She was a novelist, and one of her books was called *The World in the Evening.* I fell in love with this title a very long time ago in a sort of illicit way, because *Die Welt am Abend* (which doesn't actually mean "the world in the evening" but *The Evening World*) was the name of the communist newspaper in Berlin in the days before Hitler. But I've always loved the word *evening*, which neither the British nor the Americans pronounce properly. We all say "ev'ning," but when you say it with all its syllables out as it is in poetry it becomes very beautiful. There was a line from John Donne, something about "the great world to his aged evening" that kept haunting me.[4] So I thought I would call the book *The World in the Evening*, and since it was the title of somebody else's novel I didn't have to explain why it was called that, which was, of course, an advantage.

Now I got the idea that Stephen has his break with his second wife and goes off in a sort of flap, leaves the house, leaves everything, goes across country to stay with his aunt. What does he take with him but a thing that he's been working on for a long time, and that is a file full of Elizabeth Rydal's letters. He always takes this with him. He somewhat uneasily has always felt he ought to do something, he ought to write something about her. He ought to edit her letters. But he never quite gets down to it because he has a feeling of guilt about her. He hasn't behaved well to her, and she's dead. But he takes them with him.

I wrote the first chapter of this book: it was all about the party up at this house where there was a pool and how Stephen comes out in the middle of the party and hears his wife and this young movie actor together inside the doll's house. He bangs on the roof and then rushes off. He's terribly drunk and drives away from the party, goes straight home, rips all of her clothes to pieces with a razor blade (one of my friends did that), and then gets on a plane and goes East to see his aunt. This part of the novel was very rousing and was published separately and excited the brightest hopes about what the rest of the novel was going to be like.[5] But as a matter of fact it proved something that I learned later: it was too exciting. Beware of very exciting first chapters. It left you thoroughly bored; there was no place to go. There was a terrible letdown after this thrilling scene in Hollywood. You didn't exactly want to stay in Hollywood, but you most certainly didn't want to go to Philadelphia. You didn't quite know which of the characters, if any, you wanted to have anything to do with because you hadn't really met any of them up to this point. Stephen just narrated what he did, and all this took a tremendous amount of time and torture and false drafts and all kinds of effort.

Then I had the idea that Stephen, having arrived in Haverford, would be confronted with his Quaker background and it would fill him with horror. I have a scene that I think is really quite good and is in a way the last good thing in the book: in the third chapter, where he goes to Meeting, he realizes the tremendous power of the Quaker Meeting and yet he feels somehow terribly alienated from it. He feels he has no business coming here at all with his neurosis and being so tiresome. And here's his aunt who thinks about nothing but helping various lame ducks and working on all kinds of projects from morning to night, and who has an absurdly exaggerated opinion of him that doesn't correspond to reality. He begins to feel very ashamed of himself, and he decides to walk out again, to leave, to do anything, to get out, to go to New York. He doesn't think what he'll do: he's got money, and so he's very irresponsible. He starts to walk down to the station, and he has—what I thought was an amusing idea at the time—he has a psychosomatic accident. That is to say, he wants to be detained in this place; he wants to be forced to stop running away and so he gets knocked down by a truck right in the middle of the day, and he's not drunk or anything, and the truck is not going very fast. He's crossing the road with plenty of time, and he suddenly falls down right in the middle of the road, and the truck breaks his leg.

So now here he is in a cast, stuck in bed at his aunt's with nothing to do except read Elizabeth Rydal's letters. This is what he ought to do anyway, so he's forced to do it, to read them through and sort them and think about the question of editing them, making them into a book. In other words, this novel has turned into one enormous flashback in which you explain all the reasons why Stephen left his second wife. This is really what the whole thing amounted to. By the time I'd finished, we'd got right away from the refugees. It's true there was a German girl who was staying there and who flirted a bit with Stephen and nursed him while he had a broken leg. But, actually, the refugees had otherwise completely disappeared from the novel, and everything had become dominated by this mechanism of explaining why Stephen broke with his second wife. The Quakers were sort of vestigial, too. They only appear offstage or in this one scene in the meetinghouse, and there is the study of the aunt, who is maybe not bad. He starts to read these letters and he begins to relive the whole past and how he lived with this woman. Finally she died, and then he married this girl whom he'd already been having an affair with, and then in due course split up with her. Right at the very end of the book he's going off to join some kind of ambulance outfit. He's going to North Africa—the war is on. It was set around 1940, 1941.

The book was received with storms of dislike, chiefly because of the lack of real richness in the characters, which I think is quite justified. I'm not here concerned with questions of value, nor am I really concerned with plot, but I just want to discuss certain things in connection with this whole business that I think are of general interest. I have already discussed to some extent what happens with the problem of the "I," when you try to transfer the "I" onto somebody else without really thinking the matter through. In this case, what I had in effect done was to say, "Oh, Stephen, he's me except that he's tall and he's good looking and he's rich, very rich, and he's been married twice, and so on." And I went on like this until, of course, a completely unreal person who is just a dead limb grafted onto a live tree appeared. I had a feeling that I had to make Stephen what's called "bad," and so I got on to this topic of the bisexual. Since I really want to go into this all in its sociological aspects and, particularly, its artistic aspects at a little more length, I'll veer away from that for the moment and just observe that the first of the things that went wrong was to write a novel with the "I" and yet not really know who the "I" is and not be able to share in his deepest reactions to things; this always shows. The novel should undoubtedly have been written in the third person. Secondly, the character of Elizabeth Rydal, for the same reason, is very ambiguous. I was much complimented on the letters that I wrote for this woman, but there was something extremely sinister in the fact that I could write them so easily. I realized that they were a sort of pastiche of the letters of Katherine Mansfield and that they don't consist of any real emotion or artistic insights but only a kind of clever little monkey-like sensibility. (I'm not saying that this characterizes Katherine Mansfield's letters, because she was a woman who was suffering deeply and in many ways had a very rich, powerful, emotional nature underneath a great deal of surface artificiality, I'm told by people who knew her.) Anyhow you feel that in this character and the attitude of Stephen toward this fallen idol is something very ambiguous. I was far too smart to make her a good writer because I knew how fatal that is when you do it in books and somebody is supposed to be a great writer. But then the question arose: if she isn't good, how bad is she? And this, of course, presupposes an absolute world of subtlety. In fact, to write a novel about a second-rate writer is so difficult that I'm not sure it's ever been done; I mean, where it's really explained why she's second rate, what is the flaw in her, because, artistically speaking, you must engage to explain that. In real life it's just a sort of mystery, but it's something you must explain if you're characterizing people. And so we had great difficulty there. I think the device of the flashback did work. It satisfied the *Wuthering Heights* test; that is to say, if you can get the readers sufficiently interested in the characters before the flashback, then it's all right to have the flashback.

.....

Many writers say that you should never write about a writer, and I thought I could get away with it by giving her the polarity of being a woman and also rather hushing up the writing part. But even so, I think that in itself was a mistake, bringing in a writer in this way. If you have a character like "Christopher Isherwood" who writes, this is all right because what he's doing is telling you the story. He's giving a specimen of his writing all the time so you never have to discuss it. You never have to say, is it good or is it bad or anything about it because you're reading the book or you aren't, and if you're reading the book that means that he's, at least to some extent, cutting the mustard, and if you throw the book away then automatically he's off the air so that's all right. The minute you get a writer as a separate character, I think you're in a very great difficulty. I know that Somerset Maugham did it again and again. He did it in *Cakes and Ale* (1930), where he took these two characters who were popularly supposed to be a novelist like Thomas Hardy and a younger novelist like Hugh Walpole (although this was denied later). But it was really very, very unsatisfactory. There were all kinds of other things in the book that worked very well, but it's difficult.

.....

On the surface of life, motivation seems very vague. I quite admit that this is a psychological peculiarity of mine, but in writing I have to have absolute motivation. In fact, I very often have motivations that I never mention to the reader directly. I like motivations for money, for sex, for power, or as a reaction against something else that I can understand. Then I feel safe, and then that can all be covered with sugar and/or ashes, as the case may be.

.....

Stephen is a person who behaves quite badly quite often, but when you're inside the skin of such a person you're always in danger of either excusing yourself too completely or of condemning yourself too much, whereas with other people we find it very easy to find them simply interesting or amusing. You're mad at them sometimes, then again you forgive them and, in short, treat them as human beings. Artistically speaking, it's very hard to treat yourself as a human being. It's terribly easy for me to pretend, at least, that I think you're all separate individuals, but when I turn to myself I know that this is of course absolutely not true. I'm such a constellation of things and often so loosely held together that to regard myself artistically as a single individual is exceedingly difficult. This is at the root of all the difficulties of using the "I" in fiction, because you have to have a sort of shop front, you have to have a party line, you have to have a philosophy. There has to be a code of some kind, or else there has to be the code of not having a code. There may be a code of irresponsibility, madness, anarchy, but there has to be something and all this has to be somehow displayed, and it's frightfully difficult. It's much easier in the third person. I should have taken this character Stephen and had him tell the entire story as a minor character, but then I don't quite see how I would have done it, because great difficulties arose when it came to the question of the letters and the reminiscences about Elizabeth.

To get back to Stephen and his sexual life: Stephen was a bisexual. As we all keep hearing nowadays from psychologists, this is in fact the normal state of human beings. The abnormal person is somebody who is exclusively and aggressively hetero- or homosexual. The really normal person fluctuates in a situation in which it's not absolutely out of the question under certain circumstances that he or she might not prefer his or her own sex. Very good. But now, in our particular culture we run up against this difficulty, which is from the artist's point of view a great attraction and a great reason to write about such people, and that is that their life—if they practice both hetero- and homosexuality—becomes departmentalized very much. On the one hand, there is respectability, and I don't just say this in a pejorative sense, but I mean the whole sanction of society and the fact that what you do you do, as it were, in the open and in the daylight and with social approval. On the other hand, there's the nocturnal and, at least to some extent, concealed activities of the other, homosexual half of the person's life. This leads to wickednesses because the practicing bisexual sallies forth from his fort, which is the marriage and all its security, toys with the feelings of people who are perhaps much more homosexual than he is, and makes them thoroughly miserable. Then he says, I can never leave my wife, and he goes back into the fort and leaves this person out on a limb. This kind of thing one observes a great deal in the world. There's the somewhat amusing and exciting and dangerous jungle of extramarital relationships made all the more jungly by the fact that they are actually forbidden by the police. You go to prison. Yet, there's the whole business of the marriage, which now has reached a point where a certain amount of adultery is perfectly respectable and can be included in fiction, so that the spectrum becomes very large indeed. What I'm getting at in this, from the point of view of the novels, is that this encourages an extraordinarily deep-seated deception and fission in the character of people who practice such a life, so that in the end they hardly ever speak the truth about anything because the lie involved infects both the marriage and the relations with people of their own sex. That much is quite obvious.

From that point of view, it has a good deal of the psychological danger implicit in what with Negroes is called "passing." That is to say, there's nothing in the world against it in itself, but in our present culture it tends to be an act of betrayal. You understand, I say all these things very much for the individual and as a novelist—I'm not generalizing at this point. Passing can be a form of treason of a very undermining sort for the individual, and in exactly the same way, as long as homosexuals are exposed to the persecution of the law, this type of homosexual passing is also something exceedingly suspect and is apt to undermine the character of the individual. For this reason, it is marvelous material for the novelist because one of the most interesting things a novelist can do is to explore the various layers of truth and deceit. So, very good, I thought, that's my boy. That's what Stephen must be. He must cheat in every possible way on everybody. As far as it went, that was all right, but there I fell into a trap that was waiting on the other side, which was that his victims, or rather the one victim, became altogether just too nice for words. This was Michael Drummond, whom Stephen seduces, who then became a sort of saint just by counterbalance—the scales tipped over before I could stop them—and, as Mr. V. S. Pritchett said in a review, "Here we see homosexuality in its Sunday suit."[6]

.....

Very often you can see far more, as it were, by not pretending to get inside another character, by writing about him from the standpoint of yourself observing him. You pick out a few very interesting things that you notice, and this brings him to life.

Well, that was the end of the affair with *The World in the*

Evening. It was all tied up quite neatly but somehow the parcel had leaked and an enormous mass of the original material had excluded itself from it. I don't know whether I shall ever write about those refugees. I kind of think I won't now, but there were some quite marvelous scenes in connection with them. I always remember two of them were arguing about the philosophical nature of pleasure during a football game at Haverford, and one of the faculty members was outraged because they hadn't the slightest idea who was winning. They were staring at the game and discussing the nature of pleasure. . . .

Somebody was asking the question whether one mulls things over a lot before starting to write. It depends very much on what kind of book you're going to write. In this particular case, one reason I was led astray was that I started out thinking that I was going to write a very different sort of open novel of episodic structure, rather like *Goodbye to Berlin* or *Down There on a Visit.* Instead of that, I got involved in a tremendously structured book. There may be some absolute difficulty I have with very, very structured things—I'm very much drawn to them. Theoretically I love the idea of writing something with a really very intricately structured plot, but, on the other hand, whenever I do I'm awfully apt to spend so much time on the wiring that there's nothing else. What you're left with is simply a great big blueprint that looks like something for electronics. I think that was a great difficulty, but I know there's a way to do everything, and there would have been a way to write this book. Perhaps there was too much plot, or perhaps the fuss with the second marriage was a mistake—perhaps I should have thrown all that out. Just because you can do something, it's a terrible mistake to think that it belongs where you've done it. You may have written what in fact was a bit of some other novel, but then there you have it and it seems so appealing to you, having written it, that you can't bear to part with it. My advice there always is don't destroy it, whatever you do. If you throw it out of one book, you'll be amazed—it will turn up and fit into something else just like it was made for that.

. . . . .

AUDIENCE: Aren't you being too hard on yourself?

Well, after all, this isn't the Nuremberg trials. It doesn't much matter; I'm not concerned with the extraordinary virtues of my work.

. . . . .

With this method I'm attempting here in these meetings it really is quite irrelevant whether I'm right or wrong about the book. The point is, I'm making certain generalizations about writing, and even if these generalizations are not true about my book, they're certainly true about a lot of other books so that whether I'm being unduly severe or not is really not the point. Otherwise this whole thing would become a most distasteful display of masochistic coquetry, but I don't mean it like that at all.

. . . . .

As I have tried to suggest in this whole description of *The World in the Evening,* the plot was in each case a projection of the character. If you want to move a character from point A to point B, the plot is how you do it. The whole thing grows by what I like to call mathematics, a sort of logical argument, rather than by flashes of intuition. The intuition is applied much more to the characterization itself, and the moving of the characters is a more intellectual function, if you can make these distinctions, something more akin to chess.

Down There on a Visit

LOS ANGELES, MAY 18, 1965

In the winter of 1954–55, I made a trip to Mexico, and I got interested in the idea of what it means to cross a frontier, going from one country to another. I superimposed on that the idea that a country can be both itself, a perfectly ordinary country with inhabitants, and, at the same time, it can be a sort of limbo or purgatory for all sorts of people who are living there not necessarily connected very closely with the country at all, that is to say, various kinds of expatriates who are living in the place. I began to construct the idea of a graduated purgatory going all the way down to the center, which was Mexico City. This book was to be an episodic journey through this place by a man who comes from outside, and it was called *Down There on a Visit.* After I finished it, I realized that it just didn't work. It was two things at once, and the two things were inhibiting each other. In the first place, it was a sort of satire, a form in which I have never been really interested as such, and the satiric aspect of it was kind of killing the realistic drawing of the characters, which was what really interested me. All I wanted to do was to take some people and write about them, and try to see them in all of their aspects as people, and nothing more.

So I abandoned the entire scheme of this book, the Mexican *Down There on a Visit,* extracted two characters from it, and wrote some other character sketches. It was an extremely loose form, and the only connecting link in the whole book is the "I." This "I" is studied for the first time as a creature that is growing and getting older in the different episodes—it's still called "Christopher Isherwood." It starts as a young man and is therefore regarded by the author as somebody other than himself. In other words, I'm writing about myself now as I was as a young man, which means practically as a stranger. In the later episodes, the two Christophers come more and more into focus and finally I'm writing about myself more or less as I am now. This book consisted of a number of characters who are alienated in one way or another from their society, but they are a great deal more aggressive than the characters who appear in *Goodbye to Berlin.*

The first episode is about a British consul in a German seaport ("Mr. Lancaster"). It's pretty obviously Bremen, but it isn't actually called that, and he isn't actually called the consul. I had a cousin who was the British consul in Bremen, and I went to visit him there once. I turned this into a study of the hopeless misunderstanding between a young man and an older man when the older man has invited the younger man in order to lecture him about life and to acquire a sort of disciple or nephew to whom he can tell all the things he would have told to a son. Instead of which he gets an extremely aggressive, though mild and meek-mannered, creature who is watching him like a lynx and judging him, and he has no idea how grotesque he seems to this young man, who describes him as a completely bizarre figure. Right at the end of this character study, you realize that as a matter of fact the older man is a human being. He's very lonely and very unhappy indeed, and he shoots himself. That's the first episode of the book.

The next episode is a visit to an island in Greece on which there is a wildly eccentric Englishman named Ambrose who is rather in the manner of the kind of Englishman who used to go to Greece and all around the Levant in the nineteenth century. He has a whole establishment of people around him, and he's a sort of exiled king in his own estimation and almost prey to hallucinations. There's a suggestion that the various people on this island may be projections of the imagination of the writer, and you don't quite know how many people there are on the island or what it all consists of. I was haunted while I was writing it by that line out of *The Tempest*: "the isle is full of noises."[1] The theme of Ambrose's delusions of grandeur is that he is an exiled homosexual dictator, and he envisages the world as it would be if he ran it. It's a theme that is handled much more brilliantly and at great length in Calder Willingham's novel *End As a Man* (1947).[2] I always seem to neglect, with a characteristic lack of generosity, to remark my great admiration for Calder Willingham, who, to me, is really in some ways the most interesting young American writer, and by all odds the least recognized. His books are quite extraordinary, particularly *Eternal Fire* (1963) and *Geraldine Bradshaw* (1950), which is about a girl who is a psychopathic liar, and it is really quite well worked out. It's like an interminable fugue: she lies herself out of every conceivable kind of situation, including a love scene in which the boy nearly goes out of his mind, and they get right into bed almost, and then she makes the most marvelous excuses and tells five or six more stories, and by the end of it everybody's got their clothes on again and they leave. It's really the most extraordinary tour de force. It's one of the great comic novels of this century in my opinion, but *Geraldine Bradshaw* is not a very alluring name for a novel, and I think this is one of the reasons more people haven't read it. But I'm digressing from speaking about "Ambrose." Toward the end of the visit to the island, a woman appears and a lot of events that were purely fictitious take place. The woman, Maria, pleased many people, and there was quite a movement to dramatize this story, but unfortunately it didn't get off the ground. With the aid of a whole lot of fishermen, she kidnaps one of the young men from the island. It's the kind of thing that makes an attractive farce.

The third episode, "Waldemar," is something I'd thought of working on much earlier. While I was in Berlin I knew a girl who had come to Berlin and got communism, very bad indeed, in the form of a craze for the workers as such. They were completely holy, and she asked for nothing better than to associate with them in every possible manner, and she took it for granted that being workers they too were all communists. (One of the first things you discover when you get to know workers is that this is not true.) She used to work in a very passionate and severe manner at the Communist headquarters in Berlin. She was rather like an adherent of one of the grimmer Protestant sects. I was fond of her, and then she took up with a young German carpenter, and they left Germany and traveled around together. I had always wanted to write a book about these two, and so, in *Down There on a Visit,* I did write about a somewhat similar affair, in which a German boy is brought to England and there is terrible friction with the girl's parents, ending in the ultimate betrayal of the boy, who is left to go back to Germany again.[3]

The last and longest episode of the book, which most people (including myself) think is the best, is called "Paul."[4]

Part III

Lecture Notes

. . . .

Lecture Eight (notes) A LAST LECTURE (Lobero Theater) 1
UCSB 60-1961

Explain the idea of a 'last lecture'. Not a farewell performance but a summing-up and report on experience.

I am also tidying up. Want to deal with certain points which got left out when I scrapped the talk called A Writer and Politics or A Writer and the Others.

I believe that the function of a writer is to be, first and foremost, an individual. He writes, ultimately, out of his experience. And ~~maybe~~ he should think of himself as addressing a number of other individuals --- not a mass.

Isn't this one of the differences between art and propaganda ? P's for the mass.

The writer may belong to a majority political party, but as an individual. He must always reserve the right to dissent. If, in a crisis, he decides to merge his individuality in mass-opinion and write for the mass, then he has become a propagandist. And lost some of his value.

It follows that a writer should always be an outsider, to some extent.

Function of outsider, already described. It is cooperative. What matters is not so much the dissent but the clarification of the issues caused by the dissent.

Occasionally, the dissent must be absolute. If this leads to persecution, this is just when he must avoid pride and holier-than-thou. If it is wrong to persecute him, he must be the first to try to dissuade his fellow-citizens from commiting such a crime. Don't be aggressive or bait them into it.

The man who can dissent with the least aggression I call my anti-heroic hero. Anti-heroic in contradistinction to the tragic hero. The tragic hero doesn't bother about avoiding aggression. And he is tragic. The anti-heroic hero is never tragic in this sense, even when he dies. Socrates and various saints. More about tragedy later.

I myself am more than usually an outsider. A foreigner by temperament. I like my surroundings to have a touch of strangeness --- if only to remind me not to takeLife for granted.
The State exists for the individual & must win his loyalty.

But I must state my own dissenting beliefs. I don't believe in recourse to war, international or civil, under any circumstances. I don't believe in the rightness or utility of capital punishment. I don't believe that the Law should interefere with the individual adult, as long as he is doing no harm to another individual. I am therefore opposed to its interference in his sex-life, in his choice of reading matter, or in any other occupations or acts which concern only himself.

You may say I have no right to state such controversial opinions and run away from them. I reply that this talk is descriptive, not argumentative. Besides, if this were really my last lecture, it would be too late for argument All that's left of you in the end is an example. We say of someone, he was suchandsuch a kind of person. His opinions are of interest, that's all. The most admirable opinions can be held by a skunk and vice versa. If a bad persor holds a good opinion, it's for the wrong reason.

About writing, here are some of my beliefs :
By Jingo if we do. GET SOMETHING DOWN. About collegues
Don't shoot the pianist. The effort ~~man~~ is always worth respect. Only the boosters and bandwagon ~~riders and critics~~ riders are vile.
The green baytree. The Nobel Prize

A manuscript page, typed by Isherwood, of his final lecture in the series "A Writer and His World" at the University of California, Santa Barbara.

Editor's Note

Lecture Notes

The following notes are an integral part of this collection. They are significant for what they are not as well as for what they are. They are not fully developed lectures that were meant to be read at a podium. Rather, they are prompts for a speaker who mixed together some of his best anecdotes about himself and others with thoughtful commentary on many topics. They are the "funny stories" he told to his students (as he reported in his diary on May 18, 1960; *Diaries* 1: 856) inserted into a thematic discussion of his own life and work.

The first set of notes were prepared for "A Writer and His World," Isherwood's lectures at the University of California, Santa Barbara in 1960. Since the transcripts largely follow the notes, presumably Isherwood delivered the Santa Barbara lectures using these notes. Most pages are marked with the author's own handwriting (signaled by the annotation **AN**, for "author's notes"), which supports this supposition. The typed notes are in no particular format but rather combine different types of prompts for the speaker. Each contains mere phrases from which a complete anecdote will be constructed; compare, for example, the note Isherwood wrote himself for "A Writer and the Films" ("Conrad Veidt in Jew Suss; the candy") to the nearly two-page anecdote that appears in this lecture in Part I. The notes also include more fully conceived sentences that might appear in the transcripts largely intact. Not surprisingly, sometimes these sentiments are stated more concisely in the notes than in the lecture transcripts. Indeed, the notes to "A Last Lecture" read almost as a set of aphorisms: "Don't shoot the pianist. The effort is always worth respect" and "Don't be a megalomaniac about results."

The Isherwood archive preserves several pages of notes relating to the lectures. In the case of the first lecture, "Influences," there are multiple sets of notes, suggesting that Isherwood spent considerable time refining his thinking on this all-important first appearance. Two sets are presented here. It's not clear which set was composed first, or even if one set were written after the lecture was given, but both correspond to the substance of the actual lecture with interesting variations.

Part III also prints notes for lectures for which no transcript survives. For example, the reader will have to imagine the lecture on "Writers of the Thirties" given at the Monterey Park (California) Library on March 31, 1962. Although Isherwood dismisses the grouping ("the W of the T") as a "journalistic concept," he was, no doubt, highly qualified to deliver remarks on the topic. One suspects the topic was requested by the librarians rather than suggested by the speaker. Also included here is "A Personal Statement," delivered as part of a panel at the University of California, Berkeley, on August 30, 1962. This statement might have been written by Isherwood as a parallel to E. M. Forster's "What I Believe," a type of credo for himself as a writer. It features statements found elsewhere in the lectures, such as "the writer should always write as an individual," as well as discussion of the role of the writer in politics ("the writer's only policy is to try to tell the truth"). It is easy to imagine Isherwood using this page of notes on subsequent occasions when asked to serve on a panel to discuss general topics.

The notes resemble Isherwood's diaries, in which the happenings of the day are distilled into a few lines of precisely chosen words. The same day Isherwood described telling his students funny stories, he wrote: "On Sunday, we went to the Selznicks' and I got drunk and hugged Marilyn Monroe a lot, and then banged with my fist on the piano, saying, 'That's how I feel.'" Isherwood also wrote occasionally in his diary about what he wanted to accomplish in his writing. In March 1952, after a visit to England, he was optimistic about his life and work: "there is no reason to despair, no cause not to rejoice . . . there is still some love and joy somewhere in this old pincushion of a heart. And something I still want to say in my writing—oh, I haven't even started. Fear not. Cling to what you know is real" (1: 442). In the diary, Isherwood followed this bit of advice with an ego-deflating scolding: "Okay—now you've had your customary spiritual douche." In the lectures, too, he refused to take himself too seriously: "after all, this isn't the Nuremberg trials."

The lecture notes are presented here as closely as possible to the way they exist in the archive, as shown by this reproduction of the first page of notes for "A Last Lecture." I did not try to correct or regularize Isherwood's typing, spelling, capitalization, or punctuation; I occasionally added *[sic]* to indicate original text that might be confusing or interpreted as an error of this publication. I left in strikeouts, typed and handwritten, and I included handwritten notations that I could decipher.

A Writer and His World

. . . .

A Writer and His World: Lecture 1: Influences

AN: *1960*

Lecture Notes. University of Calif, Sta Barabara *[sic]*.
First lecture.

INFLUENCES

First of all, this series is called A Writer and His World. A, not The. In this first lecture, I'll deal with influences on a writer; next the nerve of interest in a novel; next a writer and the theater; next, a writer and the films, next a writer and politics, next a writer and his Religion, and then a Last Lecture.

Like the lady from Forest Lawn, I shall speak from experience.

When the 19 century people spoke of Influences, they usually meant books. But books don't change you unless you're ready for a change. It wasn't really T.S. Eliot who changed Auden from writing like Frost and Hardy, although Auden did read Eliot in early youth and was extremely turned on by him.

To go back to the beginning, one of the early influences-figures on me was Judge Bradshaw. The mystery of Bradshaw—how he rose to the occasion of his great office ~~and~~ although people had thought him quite unworthy of it, and defied Cromwell and helped the Quakers. Some members of my family tried to atone for Bradshaw's crime—like my Great-Aunt. Others, like myself, honored him.

Our family background. The old House. The paradox of that part of England—landed gentry pretensions, and the rough democracy of Manchester. The Squire confronted the mill-hands. The peculiar snobbery of the landed gentry, thinking themselves superior to the aristocracy.

Wyberslegh Hall, the atmosphere of the Peak, the mystique of Wuthering Heights romanticism. Ruskin denounced its ruination by the railways.

Also the romanticism of Beatrix Potter, connected with old Marple Hall, the hollow walls, the rats, feeling that by opening some little door you will find yourself in another world, 'there's a hell of a good universe next door.'

And this brings us to animal totemism, a device by which humans sometimes sublimate their relationships. (See 'Look Back in Anger') Let no one underestimate the power of the nursery fantasy.

And then again, when one is in the London *[sic]*, there is the poetry of departure, Joseph Conrad expresses it best.

The position of my Father—a paradox. Here is the man I love and admire associating himself with militarism, an unjust war against the Boers, the putting down of a strike, the garrisoning of a captive province, Ireland. When he was killed in the 1914–18 war, I was told he was a hero. The people who told me so were swine, in my opinion. So in order to go on admiring my Father I had to make him into an anti-heroic hero, and stress his knitting, his drag comedy acting, his Chopin-playing, his watercolours.

My life has been mainly occupied in writing about people who don't fit into the social pattern. They may defy society or be terrified of it, or they may lead lives of scandal and alienate everybody, or they may be the gadflies of society, like Socrates, or they may be true Outsiders.

The voices of outsiders, confronting Society—Timon (may you a better feast), Lawrence (Mr Meade, that old old lily) Dickens (Dead, Your Majesty) Tolstoy (I knew that it was unnecessary and wrong) Best of all, What I Believe by Forster—'I hope I should have the guts to betray my Country'.

Forster points out that what is shocking is that nowadays are personal relationships. You are supposed to sacrifice them to a Cause. But, he points out, Dante condemned Brutus and Cassius to the lowest circle of Hell because they betrayed Caesar, their friend.

The Outsider should be one of the most socially valuable people in the community, precisely because he doesn't always agree and always reserves the right to disagree. BUT the Outsider's disagreement must not harden into defiance. He must go along with the Others as far as he can manage to, and when he is forced to disagree he must still not blackmail the Others into making a martyr of him, if that can be humanly and honorably avoided.

A propos of Outsiders, the remark made by Estelle Winwood, 'we are no more they than you are'.

A Writer and His World: Lecture 1: Influences

LECTURE ONE **AN:** *(notes)*

Originally advertised as The Writer and his World—a title I'd never presume to use. It's A Writer—and the writer is me.

I speak from experience. (Forrest Lawn). I have no other authority. If my experience is shared by you, good. I am not anti-academic, but I refuse to play the amateur scholar. I present myself as a guinea-pig.

The lectures: Influences

Why Write at All?
The nerve of the interest (the novel)
A writer and the Theater
A writer and the Films
A writer and Society (politics)
A writer and Religion
A last lecture

I'll answer written-in questions; no matter how irrelevant.

Influences. I don't mean Plato, etc. This will involve autobiography.

Influences are what speaks to your condition—so which comes first, the influence or the predisposition to be influenced in a certain way? Example: Auden's switch from Hardy-Thomas-Frost poetry to Eliot poetry.

Pre-natal, family influences: Judge Bradshaw. Family guilt about Charles. Catholicism. The enigma of Bradshaw's character.

Marple. The last Miss Bradshaw and the first Mr Isherwood. Shipbuilding. The American Isherwoods. Annapolis.

My Grandfather as 'The Old Squire' contrasted with Manchester democracy. 'Where there's muck there's money'. The peculiar snobbism of the upper middle class. I still think of myself as an aristocrat, maybe? Also describe the Manchester cultural snobbery. The Monkhouses.

The scenery of Wyberslegh: the industrial desert and the moorland.

Baetrix *[sic]* Potter—leading to back-door worlds, worlds within the wainscoat. Mortmere. The totemism or second-life as animals led by many lovers. Look Back in Anger.

Emily Bronte: romantic love in the home setting.

But this leads to the longing for London. (And my Mother was a southerner) The romance of London: Dickens, Stevenson, Chesterton.

And the Thames leads to the romance of the sea: Conrad, Masefield.

My life as an Army child. My Father—his talents, his attitude to his caste-duty. Ireland, where they didn't like us. His death, as an anti-heroic hero—contrasted with the phoney interpretation of the War at my first school.

Edward Upward. The kind of education you can only get from people of your own age. An Enemy of the People. Life at Cambridge. Mortmere. The Conspiracy against the College. (See Lions and Shadows).

Adoption of Forster as our father-hero. (More about this later: we are comic writers)

My theme as a writer has always been The Outsider—the Lost—the Enemy. Now, the Outsider may speak with many different voices—ranging from the silence of the insane sulker in the madhouse—

—the rage of Timon—live loathed and long, most smiling smooth . . . etc

—Tolstoy's 'superstitious belief in progress'. It's *[sic]* instability revealed to him when he witnessed an execution in Paris. 'When I saw the head part from the body, and how they thumped separately into the box, I understood—not with my mind but with my whole being—that no theory of the reasonableness of our present progress could justify this deed; and that though everybody from the creation of the world had held it to be necessary, on whatever theory, I knew it to be unnecessary and bad; and that therefore the arbiter of what is good and evil is not what people say or do, nor is it progress, but it is my heart and I.

—Dickens, on the death of Jo: 'Dead, Your Majesty. Dead, my lords and gentelmen *[sic]*. Dead, right reverends and wrong reverends of every order. Dead, men and women, born with heavenly compassion in your hearts. And dying thus around us every day.'

—Lawrence's 'And Mr Meade, that old old lily

—Forster's 'I hope I should have the guts to betray my country' from "What I Believe"

—story about Estelle Winwood, Sybil Thorndyke—'they're really quite charming, aren't they?'

The function of the cooperative outsider.

Don't bait the opposition into crime. Socrates. The objectors in World War Two.

A Writer and His World: Lecture 2: Why Write at All (Lecture notes)

U.C. S.B. Lecture Notes. LECTURE TWO.

Spender says that he thinks autobiography is the characteristic art-form of our time. All my life I have kept diaries. The moral of a diary is always the same, 'cheer up, you got through it somehow so you probably will again'. For me art always begins with my own experience. What does it mean? Does the external world mean anything, and if not what shall I make it mean?

But diary-material is so untidy. So one develops it into structured forms.

I have been concerned with two kinds of fiction; a contrived novel-form, and a portrait form.

My life at Cambridge with Upward. Our drastic attitude toward everybody. But Forster was on the whole the writer we most wanted to be like.

From Forster we learned two things—the ambition to be comic writers, because tragedy had become impossible; and the idea of toning down melodrama 'tea-tabling' it, as we called it.

How do I start to write? What turns me on? I get interested in a person or a situation. For example, the situation of the movie-studio in Prater Violet, the oil=camp in the jungle, in Ecuador. Or you meet a character who seems so marvelous that he needs raising above the sphere of mortals, being seen sub specie aeternitatis.

As for the action of the story, that simply evolves. If you have the character, you want to display him, put him through his paces, and so you create the kind of action for him which will do this. If, on the other hand, you have a situation, a place, then you create characters who will demonstrate the potentialities of this place or situation.

So there are two aspects of a work of fiction. One is to bring the people and the place to life. The other is to say what it means, to say why the author is telling you all this.

The use of symbols. The symbol is really a kind of rivet. It is a tree, let's say, and as such part of the scenery; but it is also the symbol of Life enduring against Death, perhaps, or of England. (Howards End)

Writer's block. It is connected with a terror of the formal act of writing. You don't want to sit down at a table. So you trick it by writing standing up, like Scott. Or again you can turn the whole thing into a lecture, work your way into the material while dictating to a secretary, as James did; thinking aloud in fact.

A Writer and His World: Lecture 3: What is the Nerve of the Interest in a Novel (Lecture notes)

U.C.S.B. Lecture Notes. LECTURE THREE.

What is it that makes a novel vital alive good great? What is the nerve of the Novel?

James says 'here are the circumstances of the interest but where is the interest itself?'

Stevenson: to find where the joy resides and to give it a voice, for to miss the joy is to miss all.

No great writer misses the joy, the exhilaration. But this is the very opposite of Disneyism, meliroism *[sic]*. It is what the Hindu scripture means by saying, In joy the universe was created, in joy it is sustained, in joy it dissolves. This is a very hard saying. But how can the novelist experience joy in the midst of human suffering?

Because the great novelist works at two levels. If he succeeds on both levels he produces a masterpiece.

On the level of human suffering he has to be involved, he has to mind that people suffer, condemn the bad, rejoice in the good. On this level he can feel passionately, get angry, weep, have a system of ethics. (What the writer's moral code is, is immaterial almost; so long as he really believes in it)

But also the novelist must look down, like God. He is at one and the same time down there in the battle, covered with blood, angry, moved, involved; and also looking down, loving everybody, all of this battle and all its protagonists, enjoying artisically the tortures along with the joys. The novelist as he looks down is not unfeeling however; he has to have compassion. But he delights in every character and he cares nothing for their righteousness or unrighteousness.

Therefore a book can fail on two levels: it can fail in involvement, or it can fail in compassion.

By compassion I do not mean sentiment, emotional pity, at

least not necessarily. What is necessary is that the compassion shall be true not false. The compassion of Flaubert is qute *[sic]* unsentimental. The compassion of Dickens is noisy and emotional. But both are genuine. Read from The Tale of Two Cities, where the child is killed by the Marquis's coach (Book 2 chapter 7) ending with 'all things ran their course'.

In great writing there is a constant reference back and forth, between the individual incident which is being described and the general predicament of Man.

As a contrast to Dickens's method, read a pasaage *[sic]* about the jealousy between Swan and Odette, in Proust. Or the death of the Grandmother.

A Writer and His World: Lecture 4: What is the Nerve of the Interest in a Novel, continued

AN: *U.C. Sta Barbara 1960 Lecture Four (notes)*

Recapitulation: we were looking for the nerve of the novel. Stevenson's 'where the joy resides'. *The novel has two levels: the level of moral values, opposed forces and the level of acceptance, of compassion. When these two levels are brought into focus, we get the flash.

Now this flash can occur under all sorts of circumstances. It is no use trying to limit it and say, these are the circumstances of great art.

Realism is not the point: look at Virginia Woolf, Melville, James.

Style is not the point: look at Dreiser, and James succeeds in spite of it.

Scope is not the point: look at Dostoevsky, Forster, Proust

Restraint is not the point: look at Dickens

Emotional heat is not the point: look at Flaubert, Moore (Read)

However, people seem to think that scope is important: it can be awful, as in the 'great' epics; but scope is also found in War and Peace. Parallel between Petya Rostov and Paco in Hemingway's story (read)

The greatness of Lawrence. He re-educated our perceptions. The tactile values. The Blind Man. St Mawr (read)

Repeat: Realism is not the point. Melville. An outstanding example of 'where joy resides'. He derives from Shakespeare. Everybody is having a ball. (read)

AN: **great art is never depressing: Ivan Ilytch.*

A Writer and His World: Lecture 5: A Writer and the Theater (Lecture notes)

AN: *U.C. Sta. Barbara 1960 Lecture Five (notes)*

My first attempts at Theater. La Lettre (influence of Grandmother) and my toy theater (influence of Father) Out, out, spot

Auden's plays:

Paid on Both Sides	1933
Dance of Death	1933
Enemies of a Bishop	1934
The Chase	1934
Dogskin	1935
Ascent	1937
Frontier	1938
van Druten dramatizes Sally Bowles	1951
Laughton?	

The Theater is a box; the cinema is a window. The point of the theater is that the players and the audience are confined together, and among other things the play is about how they escape from this confinement.

In the conventional theater, the play works out like a sum, and the danger is tidiness. But I learned, from seeing I Am a Camera, that what really matters in such plays is character, not plot. Great impression made on van Druten by Member of the Wedding.

When Auden and I wrote the plays, we said we wanted to open up the theater by showing the cyclorama, and having people jump from the audience on to the stage and vice versa. (This was at least as old as Galsworthy) But in fact the more you open up the theater, the more you involve the audience. Olsen and Johnson (the gorilla). Samuel Beckett (slowing down) The Connection (the actors accost the audience during the intermission) Read end of Godot?

The Theater is for great speech. We had an inability to take the Theater seriously, but maybe so do lots of others. The danger of the poetical theater is double-talk. "No, Prince, it is not the birds that fear the sea . . ."

What stays with you in the Theater is character and utterance. What stays with you in the cinema is image and movement.

Read Auden's The Two from Dogskin.

A Writer and His World: Lecture 6: A Writer and the Films

AN: *U.C.S.B. 1960 Lecture Six (notes)*

Recapitulate: the stage is a box containing live actors. It exists to create claustrophobia. The drama is in the confinement of the actors with the audience. The theater is for utterance and character.

The film is a window. The actors are not live. You look out, are not confined. You can go out when you please; this isn't fatal. The film is a sort of tight-rope; if movement is lost, it falls. The cinema is for movement and image. Not sound. The proof of this is in the memorableness of image: the stained glass window in Dark at the Top.

The silent film was poetic; characters in relation to their environment. Cowboys, for instance—so Westerns are relatively pure cinema. The environment was more important than the particular situation and characters. The situation was generalized: A city like all others. . . . The film says Once upon a time there was a boy—any boy— The film looks deeply into the poetry of nature. The closeness of the film-eye.

The intrusion of the sound-film. It ran away with the screen. The Talking Dog.

Meanwhile, the cinema has always also been a convenience, for showing canned plays.

The classic cinema exalted the director. This is right. The Writer is representing sound; therefore minor, the producer is only a back-seat driver; the camera-man is too much within the image.

How Eisenstein and DW Griffith used actors: the closet-scene. Here you have something new. Not that the actor is mistrusted to be able to give a performance; the director doesn't want him to give a performance. He photographs him as one would photograph an animal. The Russian idea of using identical shots for various emotions.

The star-system abolished the poetry of the cinema but created its own poetry. Now this too is being lost because the stars have no mystery. Sarah Bernhardt, the first movie star. Conrad Veidt in Jew Suss; the candy.

What we have today is a hybrid. We try to pack epics into two hours or at most three. Robert Flaherty said that the film is the longest possible distance between two points.

The unsolved problem of sound: it should go against image. Methods of writing films; dictation. What is important in film-writing is sequence (making the links between scenes) and telescoping (hitting the scene in the middle) But the film still exists to produce stretches of pure soundless movement.

Work in the studio: the vices of bigness. Nothing so cowardly as a million bucks. The disruption of the creative unit because of contract obligations; the director arrives too late. Independent units better.

Cinema is the art which functions under the greatest difficulties; constant interruption. Disagreeable domination of technicians. Even worse before sound.

A Writer and His World: Lecture 7: A Writer and Religion

AN: *Lecture Seven (notes) U.C.S.B. 1960* *8.30 5th*

A WRITER AND RELIGION

Define what I mean by religion. I don't mean literature dealing with religious organizations. I am referring to the problem of portraying saints in literature

So I must define a saint. A saint is a man of enlightenment; a man who has made some contact with God. A saint is also a good man, but not primarily a good man. The right relations between prayer and conduct is. . . . etc

Why should one want to write about saints? Because the saint is the most elastic of all possible characters. Not bound by fear and desire and so he may do anything.

But it's different because the saint, as an end-product, is so strange. You can't identify with him.

Yet—Smith Jones and Brown are all potentially saints. This has to be proved. Every saint has a past . . . etc

One difficulty is that the public thinks of the saint as a sweet dreary bore. So you start by showing the saint as reassuringly ordinary. Zossima the young army officer, Larry the all-American boy.

The moment of vocation or engagement. Maugham vague: Larry's army experiences. Huxley in Time Must Have a Stop jumps from Sebastian the boy to Sebastian the mature man. The duel scene in the Brothers K. Read.

Visions are a form of cheating, unless you're writing historical fiction.

But what is this conversion? How can you prove the man hasn't merely gone insane? He turns his back on the pleasures of Smith-Jones-Brown. But S-J-B are also searching; they doubt their pleasures. Getting drunk and money-making are misguided forms of searching for peace and happiness.

Struggles toward sainthood should be funny. The Garden of

Allah is no tragedy unless it's a tragedy of weakness. We can never be sorry for the spiritual aspirant or the boxer. Gaily the boxer, the boxer. . . . etc Moore's Sister Teresa too gloomy. Maugham's Larry too lighthearted about the whole thing; no trouble. Father Sergei. Read.

AN: *Stephen Kasatsky. Pashinka.*

My own effort—Sarah.

But the best is to keep to biography: Ramakrishna.

A Writer and His World: Lecture 8: A Last Lecture

AN: *Lecture Eight (notes) A LAST LECTURE (Lobero Theater) UCSB 60–1961*

Explain the idea of a 'last lecture'. Not a farewell performance but a summing-up and report on experience.

I am also tidying up. Want to deal with certain points which got left out when I scrapped the talk called A Writer and Politics or A Writer and the Others.

I believe that the function of a writer is to be, first and foremost, an individual. He writes, ultimately, out of his experience. And XXXXXX he should think of himself as addressing a number of other individuals—not a mass.

Isn't this one of the differences between art and propaganda? P's for the mass.

The writer may belong to a majority political party, but as an individual. He must always reserve the right to dissent. If, in a crisis, he decides to merge his individuality in mass-opinion and write for the mass, then he has become a propagandist. And lost some of his value.

It follows that a writer should always be an outsider, to some extent.

Function of outsider, already described. It is cooperative. What matters is not so much the dissent but the clarification of the issues caused by the dissent.

Occasionally, the dissent must be absolute. If this leads to persecution, this is just when he must avoid pride and holier-than-thou. If it is wrong to persecute him, he must be the first to try to dissuade his fellow-citizens from commiting *[sic]* such a crime. Don't be aggressive or bait them into it.

The man who can dissent with the least aggression I call my anti-heroic hero. Anti-heroic in contradistinction to the tragic hero. The tragic hero doesn't bother about avoiding aggression. And he is tragic. The anti-heroic hero is never tragic in this sense, even when he dies. Socrates and various saints. More about tragedy later.

I myself am more than usually an outsider. A foreigner by temperament. I like my surroundings to have a touch of strangeness—if only to remind me not to take Life for granted.

AN: *The State exists for the individual & must win his loyalty.*

But I must state my own dissenting beliefs. I don't believe in recourse to war, international or civil, under any circumstances. I don't believe in the rightness or utility of capital punishment. I don't believe that the Law should interefere *[sic]* with the individual adult, as long as he is doing no harm to another individual. I am therefore opposed to its interference in his sex-life, in his choice of reading matter, or in any other occupations or acts which concern only himself.

You may say I have no right to state such controversial opinions and run away from them. I reply that this talk is descriptive, not argumentative. Besides, if this were really my last lecture, it would be too late for argument All that's left of you in the end is an example. We say of someone, he was suchandsuch a kind of person. His opinions are of interest, that's all. The most admirable opinions can be held by a skunk and vice versa. If a bad person holds a good opinion, it's for the wrong reason.

About writing, here are some of my beliefs:

AN: *By Jingo if we do. GET SOMETHING DOWN.*

Don't shoot the pianist. *About coleagues. [sic]* The effort XXX is always worth respect. Only the boosters and bandwagon ~~riders and critics~~ **AN:** *riders* are vile.

AN: *The green baytree. The Nobel Prize.*

Don't tell the young that 'fame is nothing'. The experience of celebrity has a great deal to teach, and the young have the right to demand it.

Don't be a megalomaniac about results. Lawrence opened a little window for the bourgeoisie. Not bad!

But in the largest sense, you have no right to the fruits of work. The reward is in the writing itself. That means that art—and all other honorable activities—should be symbolic activities, *as far as you yourself are concerned.* The results may be most important, but that's beyond your control.

Why should you do your best? Because, by doing it, you fulfil the law of your own nature—your dharma. Your dharma is right livelihood—*for you.* Don't play around with somebody else's dharma.

It's evident I have started talking about Life now, rather than Art. So I'll say a few things about Life.

Don't worry too much about 'sins'. The Hindu idea of 'obstacles' is more helpful.

The main obstacle is untruth. Slyness and all lying is bad; indirect lying is the worst.

Cruelty. Heaven arms with pity. . . . Cruelty destroys *you*—never mind the others. It is dwelling too much on the effects of cruelty on others that we run the risk of practising cruelty ourselves without realizing it.

The mystery of sloth; tamas. An objective attitude to the gunas is necessary.

The weakness of the flesh must be judged from the point of view of your dharma. The writer must ask himself: do they interfere with my writing?

The over-advertized vice of cowardice. It's only dangerous when not admitted to; then it leads to greed and fear and cruelty. You must at least be brave enough to say, 'I'm afraid, dont rely on me' Otherwise you may let others down.

The meaning of Life? If you think it has none, remember that Art has meaning. So begin with that. For the rest, be an existentialist. Never try to censor your own experience or disguise its meaning from yourself. Don't take refuge in other people's dogmas, except as a working hypothesis.

Anything beyond this is a grace. If you have the grace to meet someone and believe in his belief and make that experience your own; that's grace.

Two mysteries—the mystery of Death and the mystery of Joy.

Death is made cheap and vulgar nowadays. Because we're afraid of atomic war. It should be an experience and an art. Frankly, I don't know about this. I just hope I'll get by. I believe in continued life—but this is hardly the point anyway. For me, religion is something to do with this life.

The mystery of Joy. Joy, like Death has been cheapened. We no longer understand the mystery of meta-comedy, super-farce. The cult of tragedy has obscured this great truth. Joy is not cheap optimism and it's not fatalism. It aint no use to grumble and complain. . . . contrasted with, in his will is our peace.

The above are the reflections of an individualist and a liberal who has found liberalism crumbling beneath him and at first felt ashamed. Then, looking around, he decided there was no special reason for shame, since other people, whatever they felt, were equally insecure. And as for individualism—there seems no way of getting off this, even if one wanted to. The dictator-hero can grind down his citizens until they are all alike, but he canot *[sic]* melt them into a single man. That is beyond his power. He can order them to merge, he can incite them to mass-antics, but they are obliged to be born separately and to die separately, and, owing to these unavoidable termini, will always be running off the totalitarian rails. The memory of birth and the expectation of death always lurk within the human being, making him separate from his fellows and consequently capable of intercourse with them. Naked I came into the world, naked I shall go out of it! And a very good thing too, for it reminds me that I am naked under my shirt, whatever its color. What I Believe 1939

Writers of the Thirties

. . . .

Writers of the Thirties

Notes for lecture, Monterey Park Library, March 31 '62

The Writers of the Thirties—a journalistic concept. And "The Thirties" really started with the stock market crash in 1929.

The W. of the T., according to journalists, were Auden, Spender, Day Lewis, MacNeice, Rex Warner, Upward, Lehmann.

Orwell was opposed to them. (Homage to Catalonia); Graham Greene was labeled a Catholic, but not really opposed. (The Confidential Agent) However, he had denounced the persecution of the Church in Mexico. Henry Green belongs later, despite Blindness and Living. Evelyn Waugh belongs both earlier and later.

Characteristics of the W of the T: Romantic-political (c.f. Wordsworth, Shelly *[sic]*, Byron), Anxious sense of doom (Kafka), a different kind of expatriate; more directly involved with the foreign countries they lived in. Germany rather than France.

The Writers of the Thirties—the Lost Generation—looked back to a War—1914–18 gave them their motive for despair; their youth had been taken away. Now they are unsocial. They had hated all non-frontline-soldiers and all civilians during the War. The W of the T looked forward to a War. (Read Spender's "Who live under the shadow of a war") And compare Auden's attitude in "oh what is that sound" and "certainly our city". And Day Lewis's first Overture to Death and MacNeice's Eclogue for Xmas.

Characteristics of the Thirties, the Stalin-Trotsky schism. The W of the T were probably temperamentally drawn to Trotsky. (Spender's socialism romantic, Whitmanesque and universalist: read "oh young men" and "after they have tired")

Then why did they feel they ought to join the Stalinists? Guilt and the attraction of dogma and the exhausting effort of standing alone. Every writer is by nature a non-joiner, and a totalitarian government of any kind must be against his interests. That is exactly what made the totalitarians so appealing; intellectual suicide, and an end to the agony of doubt. This often led to a stern no-time-for-culture attitude. **AN:** *Having betrayed Art, they pretended to despise it—said it was selfish, ivory-tower, useless.*

The Moscow Trials—severely ignored by leftists. "The intellectual life of the thirties turned into a debate on ends and means."

Spanish Civil War breaks out, July 1936.

The serious communists, Sommerfield, Cornfield. The possessive commissars, Bates. The International Brigade fighters. The political tourists. Mrs Haldane distributes white feathers.

Auden leaves for Spain. "Its *[sic]* farewell to the drawing-room's civilised cry." His "Spain"—c.f. Picasso's Guernica. (Neither of them really understood but respectfully received by the faithful.)

Spender joins the communist party. (See The God that Failed, 229; and World Within World 210) Spender in Spain. The Writers' Congress (W.W.W. 238) "Ultima Ratio Regum"; Spender faces the reality of War. Returns to England (WWW 249) His "Trial of the Judge". The Group Theater. The Auden-Isherwood plays.

Auden and Isherwood in China. Decide to go to America. Pacifism. Anglo-Catholicism (Auden's Mother and T.S. Eliot) Vedanta.

The Writers of the Thirties are now blamed for having been irresponsible, cliquish, makers of private jokes. They are regarded as not having been political enough.

Epitaph on the Thirties: William Plomer's "Father and Son 1939"

The Novel As Experience

The Novel as Experience

Los Angeles City College: May 2nd 1962

What does this title mean?

I take it to mean—how far and in what manner does the novel grow out of the novelist's personal experience of life?

There are writers who claim they invent everything. And the laws of libel anyhow encourage us to be dishonest about this. But I admit that my work is always founded on direct experience. If you compare me with an artist, I'm like one whose work is representational. I seldom abstract much. Many writers abstract a great deal. For example: historical novelists, writers of science fiction, writers of fantasy.

But we all have the impulse to examine our experience—what is happening to us, and, hence, what we are. Because what is happening to us is what we are. The psychologist's saying I used to have above my des[k]: what am I that they can do this to me?

D.H. Lawrence: "I am a man and alive. For this reason I am a novelist."

Gerald Heard: "We are each of us novels written in protoplasm." Something—the submerged part of the iceberg of consciousness—is writing us. If we believe this, we musts believe that our experience has meaning. And we must want to discover that meaning.

Also, there's Goethe's Verweile doch—To catch something from the flying moment, we collect the heads of big game, stuff fish, keep bits of bombs, locks of hair, snapshots, sound-tapes, etc. And we keep diaries.

Never underestimate the diary. Even when very little is recorded, that little recalls much, because the entry was made at another time, with other ink, another eye, voice. And at least the diary reassures you: this too will pass.

Why go beyond the diary? To impose philosophic and artistic form on life. Philosophic form is difficult in a day-to-day narrative. Artistic form is impossible without lying.

I don't start with stories, as some writers do. I start with a character or a situation-place, e.g., Bergmann—Imperial Bulldog Studios. The story is formed to present the characters and situation, to show them off, put them through their paces. An inspiration is a flash of understanding how to transform material into artistic and philosophic form.

Philosophic form. I am trying to evoke a place: Berlin. But I must also say what 'Berlin' means to me as a concept. This is the answer to your question, 'what's your novel *about*?' Illustrate this—showing the difference between the events of the story and its meaning. The symbols are bolts joining the story to the philosophical form: the tree in *Howards End*, the forest in *Heart of Darkness*. When symbols join nothing, they are bad and arty.

Choice of the tone of voice and viewpoint. A wrong choice will commit you to insincerity. The boyish, the manly, the sincere, the injured. 'Most of the time, thank goodness, we suffer quite stupidly and unreflectingly . . .'

The problem of writing in the first person. How far are you allowed to lie, when you do? My rule: never to say I did or said or felt anything which I couldn't possibly have done, felt, said. I dislike using my own name, but the alternative is unsatisfactory for me because I simply cannot believe that I know how other people feel.

The novel should be beyond comedy *and* tragedy.

A Personal Statement

. . . .

A Personal Statement

AN: *U.C. Berkeley. The Writer in Mid-Century—the Moral Crisis. August 30, 1962*

Define dharma. What is the dharma of the writer?

The writer should always write as an individual, writing for other individuals. Writing for other people as a mass, rather than a collection of individuals, is one of the differences between art and propaganda.

The writer is necessarily an outsider. **AN:** *This is not the same as being a rebel.* Even when he's in full agreement with the majority, this is a temporary agreement. He always reserves the right to dissent. This is not the same thing as belonging to the so-called loyal opposition, because the opposition has a policy. The writer's only policy is to try to tell the truth and to examine whatever seems interesting to him.

Therefore the writer can never be really happy in a totalitarian state, even if he agrees with the way that state is run. And the totalitarian state has no use for the kind of outsider-writer I am describing.

If he participates in politics, the writer must keep art and propaganda apart. Propaganda is concerned with righting wrongs. But art is always apt to interest itself in the nature of the bad and the wrong and subversively find them more fascinating than the good and the right. Art is only interested in understanding. Therefore, if the wrong is mysteriously awful, it must be interested. Example of the concentration-camp.

Writers make bad totalitarians, because they feel guilty. So they are apt to cover their guilt by attacking art itself, calling it formalism or decadence or escapist, and extolling in its place what is in fact propaganda.

If a writer is persecuted, he must still endeavor, as long as he can, to dissuade the state from commiting this crime against him and itself. As soon as he becomes merely defiant and tragically heroic he has lost his usefulness.

The vice of our society is blandness. We rub off the corners. 'Not doing too well'. The kind of trash we produce is nicey-niceness. The function of art is to restore feeling to this semi-anaesthetised body politic.

In this connection, I should say that I don't think the writer's function is necessarily didactic. Most of us are ignorant and silly. But we can impart enthusiasm. The enthusiasm of the elderly is reassuring to the young.

If art is to restore feeling to the unfeeling, what about pornography?

The only satisfactory definition of pornography is four-letter words. If you get into the question of what is sexually exciting you become lost. If you try to distinguish between pornography and art you can't, because pornography is always fantasy at least, and fantasy is a mode of art.

The writer must demand freedom to be pornographic. He will be restrained by artistic considerations; too much pornography weakens its own effect. The only allowable censorship is the public's refusal to read.

The writer should be as much of an outsider as he can bear to be. But his dissent, like his assent, must be sincere.

My ways of being an outsider: I put the individual before the state, pacifist, anti-capital punishment, opposed to laws which interfere with the private life. But what matters is our examples rather than our opinions.

Some points for the writer. Attitude toward colleagues. Attitude toward celebrity. Attitude toward 'the fruits of work'. Vices. Sloth. Non-attachment: 'I am the vessel through which the Sacre passed'.

Voices of Novelists and Dramatists: Modern

....

Voices of Novelists and Dramatists: Modern

Garden Grove, October 21 1962

This is not a lecture and not a recital. The usually accepted way of dealing with a book is to read it through from beginning to end, and that's that.

I suggest to you that the 'story' of a book is no more revealing, superficially, than an entry against a name in Who's Who—where was he born, whom did he marry—at the end of which we ask, 'yes, but what was he like?'

I am asking you to get into the habit of considering books in this way—of listening to the voice of the author, his tone of voice, and thus getting to know his literary personality—

Which is different from his actual personality. Sometimes there is a big difference. Some authors come to us ornately masked. Others more or less without makeup, even.

Two kinds of voices are to be heard, right through literature: the special writing-voice and the voice which resembles, or seems to resemble, natural speech.

Moll Flanders. Les Liasons Dangereuses. Our Mutual Friend—three characteristics of the modern age appear long before it: the informal voice, the shockingness, the savage satire of social conditions.

What is really characteristic of our age? The concept of relativity—i.e., the destruction of certainty; and the Freudian revolution. We are still mopping up.

About the material: I don't apologize for it. I don't even speculate as to why it is like it is. I reject utterly the suggestion that the

United States and England 'deserve' a better kind of literature. Literature is not a burnt offering to some heathen idol. I suggest that those who want such a literature should go to Russia.

The function of Art is always to challenge accepted values. And this never does any harm, because all values are relative anyhow.

Read: Beginning of Styron's The Long March: an example of nice solid good writing, in the Conrad tradition.

End of Waiting for Godot* and Pinter's The Caretaker* (Act Two, 44–45)

Mailer's Advertisements for Myself, parts of the first advertisement: 15 & 19. Osborne's They call it Cricket: 64–66.

Kerouac's The Subteraneans: 1–3

Salinger: most of A Perfect Day for Banana Fish. The sane are the mad and the mad are the sane. The sane are people like people in advertisements.

Henry Green, Living 245–6; Pack My Bag 241 to end.*

Amis: Extract on babies from Take A Girl Like You.

Williams: the cannibalism speech from Suddenly Last Summer, and maybe the introduction to Cat on a Hot Tin Roof

McCullers: Most of A Tree, A Rock, A Cloud*

AN: ** had to be cut for lack of time*

What Is a Novel?

What Is a Novel?

UCLA May 17, 1965

The Novel tells a story. "A fiction in prose of a certain extent."

That is as far as you can define it. The only other definition is by negatives. The novel, we agree, is not journalism, is not a political pamphlet, is not a religious sermon, is not a historical essay, is not a sociological treatise, is not an essay in one of the natural sciences. Yet you have journalism in the USA trilogy of dos Passos, political pamphleteering in Steinbeck's The Grapes of Wrath, sermonizing in Huysmans La-Bas, history in War and Peace, sociology in Brave New World, natural history in Hemingway. And there is Biography, which is also a sort of novel. And memoirs.

Then there is the question of form. Everybody agrees that the novel is not a short story, but when you start to ask what the difference is, we can only speak of length. For the short story may be a novel in capsule. And even if it is just a sketch, we find that a book of such sketches becomes a kind of novel. And what about the so-called picaresque novel of the eighteenth century? Isn't it really a bundle of short stories in the form of encounters, loosely tied together by the thread of the hero's personality?

(An analogy to pornography. As soon as you abandon the proscription of certain words, you are lost. The distinction between pornography and art won't hold, because then pornography simply has to be admitted as bad art.)

As for form, a novel can be in verse, or in various kinds of prose which border very closely on poetry, Joyce, Melville, Stein and all their descendants. It can have no descriptions, or no psychology, it can be all in dialogue, it can theoretically include music, illustrations, exhibits, the paper can be of different colors with trick type, it can be written entirely in one sentence.

There is talk about the anti-novel, but this is rather meaningless. How can you be anti anything so amorphous?

So we come back to 'it tells a story'. We can think about the novel more conveniently if we stop visualizing books and think about people sitting around a fire, telling each other things. Now, there is nothing to stop the teller singing, or speaking in dialect, or illustrating his narrative with photos and keepsakes he takes out of his pockets—all that corresponds to the question of form. He can tell his story in a minute or an hour, badly or well. But the questions which really arise, as we listen to him, are Who is telling this story? Why is he telling me this? And (related to that question) what is this story really about? Around the campfire, people tell things in order to make a point, or support or contradict someone else. And this is true also in the novelist's art, however much it may be disguised.

The question Who is telling this story also applies to the novelist. For the teller can be of many kinds—the wry observer, the kook, the prophet, the accuser, the hard-boiled, the old hand—Maugham, Kerouac, Lawrence, James Baldwin, Mailer, Hemingway. He is always judged on his own terms. We ask, by what authority do you tell this, who are you, what is your attitude. And he answers, because I'm disgusted, because I love everybody, because I'm too cute for words, because I'm indignant, because I've been through it all and I want to warn you. If we decide that he is lying, then so much the worse for him. That is one of the most important ways in which a novel can be bad.

Another way is lack of vitality, lack of vividness, lack of authority.

Why are you telling me this?

All such story-telling, no matter how simple and epic or how complex or how indirect, has for its conscious or unconscious aim the making of a statement about Life. If the statement is made with sufficient vitality, it will be worthwhile.

Wilde said that All Art is quite useless. But I believe that these statements, when well-made, actually make life more bearable. This is equally true if the statements are intensely what we call pessimistic. Fitzgerald's if you didn't want it to be snow, you just paid some money. Tolstoy's Ivan Ilytch's life had been most simple and most ordinary and therefore most terrible. Yeats's translation from the Antigone of Sophocles, Never to have lived is best.

Greatness in the novel. No themes are necessarily great or petty. That is a heresy of current fashion. Greatness is achieved when the novelist expresses the double nature of man—the god-like and the human, the passion of man and the compassion of God. We must be involved, we must care, we must be passionate. And also we must stand aside and look down with compassion on the struggle.

Metacomedy. The heartlessness of the 'comic' novel, the superficiality of the 'tragic view of life.'

It is asked, will the novel survive? I think it will just because it isn't specifically anything. It most certainly isn't a matter of form. As long as individuals seek to communicate with each other, they will probably make use of some sort of storytelling.

It follows that statements which lack these qualities make Life less bearable. We all know the days when the triviality of advertisements, and usually their meliorism, is almost too much to take. It's the heartlessness. We live in the age of merchants. But I believe that their culture is about to be shattered, for reasons which I referred to in my last lecture. They advertise the goods of life, but the goods they advertise are not the Good of Life and this we shall begin to discover, the more the affluent society is established.

The Novel and the Novelist

. . . .

The Novel and the Novelist

AN: *U.C.R. March 22 1966*

What is a novel? Forster, it tells a story. James, the most prodigious of literary forms, is better.

Other definition by negatives: not journalism, not a political pamphlet, not a sermon, not an historical essay, not a sociological treatise, not a scientific work **AN:** *not poetry*—<u>but</u> Dos Passos USA, Grapes of Wrath, La-Bas, War & Peace, Brave New World, Hemingway-Kipling-Mann. Biography and Memoirs also have the nature of the novel. And the psychiatrist's case-history.

And what about form? What's the difference between it and a short story? Length, but what about books of stories and picaresque novels? The novel can be in verse, poetic prose, entirely dialogue. It could include music, illustrations, exhibits, colored paper, trick type. It can have no descriptions, no psychology. It can be all in one sentence.

What is a novelist? Somebody rambunctious, like Hemingway or Mailer. **AN:** *Too tough to be a poet.* He should have marital difficulties, drink, maybe turn on with pot or acid. **AN:** *He should suffer.* At the very least he should have a past. He is often employed by universities, those patrons so much preferable to the nobles of the 16th, 17th, 18th centuries, to talk about himself. He is in some ways among the freest members of our (great) society because we don't object to his scandals.

AN: *Qualities of the Novelist—not ideas, he can be stupid. He takes the trouble to explain—a poet doesn't—he sees things in terms of people and their interplay—he says by showing—*

Auden on the Novelist's dharma:

> he
> must struggle out of his boyish gift and learn
> how to be plain and awkward, how to be
> one after whom none think it worth to turn.
> For, to achieve his lightest wish, he must
> become the whole of boredom, subject to
> vulgar complaints like love, among the Just
> be just, among the Filthy filthy too,
> and in his own weak person, if he can,
> must suffer dully all the wrongs of Man.

In other words, Auden sees the poet as a star, and the novelist as a sort of underground worker, in contact with the human condition. This seems to put much emphasis on experience, but I feel that everyone after a comparatively early age has enough experience. I don't believe in bullying young writers by telling them that they must, for example, experience combat or love or fatherhood before they can write. In any case, a very little of these things goes a very long way.

It is agreed that the novelist is expected to tell the truth, but that doesn't mean journalistic truth. Writing down 'what actually happened' is an excellent journalistic discipline but it doesn't necessarily produce art.

The truth means *my* truth. Jung says at the beginning of his Autobiography, my life is the story of an act of self-realization by the unconscious, everything contained within it seeks outward manifestation. He says all that matters is to tell 'my fable, my truth'.

In fact, we *are* novels, all of us, the novel written in protoplasm. Some of us feel the urge to express it in terms of literary art, some in other ways. Most of us probably try, at one time or another.

What we actually write down may not be autobiography in the strict sense. It may even be utterly fantastic. (Dickens' 'don't you wish you *had*' met people like my characters?) He may write about what he has never actually experienced. His facts may be inaccurate but still true. All that matters is that the reader shall feel they are true in terms of what the writer is.

So it follows that we ask the writer 'who are you? What sort of a person are you, who is telling me this?' And again, 'why are you telling me this?'

This question of the personal truth of the storyteller is answered if in fact you are with him—all telling each other stories around the fire. A storyteller can tell a story which is quite obviously untrue, because there is a certain sort of truth in a liar, if he is honestly a liar, that is, if his lying is part of himself.

The problem of the choice of subject matter, what interests you personally? The story of the volcano and the saucer illustrates the difference between what is merely extraordinary (and therefore only interesting if true) and what is really interesting as an idea, true or not. The saucer is not suggestive, the couple are.

So much of the art of fiction consists not in what to tell but how to tell it, one has to find the tone of voice which suits what one is. This kind of a collaboration is very strange, because your collaborator, the unconscious, wears a mask. Young writers often lose their nerve because they are suddenly appalled by the sheer indiscretion of writing.

Types of literary personality—the wry observer, the amused spectator, the kook, the prophet, the accuser, the old hand, the grim pessimist, the irrepressible optimist—Maugham, James, Kerouac, Lawrence, Baldwin, Hemingway, Samuel Beckett, Saroyan. Each is judged on his own terms—by his answer to 'why are you telling me this?' But all of them really amount to the qualities of being in control of the medium and being seriously involved in the circumstances of the tale.

Poe on My Heart Laid Bare, and Baudelaire. But Wilde was wiser when he said "not everyone who says I, I, can enter into the kingdom of the ego." And in fact, telling one's truth is not necessarily a sort of stripping. One may obey the contemporary command to take it off and find oneself, in the end, merely denuded.

Editor's Notes

....

Introduction: The American Isherwood

1. Christopher Isherwood, *Lost Years: A Memoir, 1945–51* (New York: HarperCollins, 2000). According to my interview with Don Bachardy (December 3, 2002), the publisher chose this title for the second volume of Isherwood's diaries, but this characterization is used not least by its editor. Katherine Bucknell says in the first volume that Isherwood's life in 1950 was "out of control" and had reached a "new-low of dissipation" due to excessive drinking and sexual activity. See Christopher Isherwood, *Diaries, Volume 1, 1939–1960,* ed. Katherine Bucknell (New York: HarperCollins, 1997), xxvii.

2. Chris Freeman, "'Making Fun out of It': Rethinking *The World in the Evening* and Isherwood's 'Lost Years,'" "Isherwood in America" panel, American Literature Association convention, Long Beach, California, June 1, 2002.

3. Isherwood continued to give lectures, either singly or as a series, throughout the 1960s. He had visiting appointments at several universities in California, including the University of California campuses at Berkeley, Los Angeles, and Riverside.

4. Christopher Isherwood, *Kathleen and Frank* (New York: Simon and Schuster, 1972), 509.

5. George Wickes, "An Interview with Christopher Isherwood," in *Conversations with Christopher Isherwood,* ed. James J. Berg and Chris Freeman (Jackson: University Press of Mississippi, 2001), 28.

6. Dan Luckenbill, "Isherwood in Los Angeles," in *The Isherwood Century: Essays on the Life and Work of Christopher Isherwood,* ed. James J. Berg and Chris Freeman (Madison: University of Wisconsin Press, 2000), 32.

7. Albert Gordon, "Christopher Isherwood: A Faithful Performance," *UCLAN Review Magazine* (Summer 1959): 28–32.

8. Christopher Isherwood, *A Single Man* (New York: Simon and Schuster, 1964), 79.

9. Winston Leyland, "Christopher Isherwood Interview," in *Conversations with Christopher Isherwood,* 100.

10. David Garnes, "*A Single Man*: Then and Now," in *The Isherwood Century,* 198.

11. Claude J. Summers, personal correspondence to editor, November 20, 2002.

12. Wilde inscribed a copy of the article he sent to Isherwood: "For Chris, All good wishes. As ever, Alan (This grows out of the talk at the MLA Seminar last year. I hope the Autobiography goes well.)"

13. Christopher Isherwood, *Christopher and His Kind* (New York: Farrar, Straus and Giroux, 1976), 248.

14. Tony Russo, "Interview with Christopher Isherwood," in *Conversations with Christopher Isherwood,* 162.

15. Peter Parker, *Isherwood: A Life Revealed* (New York: HarperCollins, 2004), 835. Published in the U.K. as *Isherwood: A Life* (London: Picador, 2004).

16. Peter Edgerly Firchow, "The American Auden: A Poet Reborn?" in *W. H. Auden: Contexts for Poetry* (Newark: University of Delaware Press, 2002), 170.

17. Both Auden and Isherwood became "certifiably" American when they received citizenship after the war.

18. Stanley Poss, "A Conversation on Tape," in *Conversations with Christopher Isherwood,* 20.

19. Alan Wilde, *Christopher Isherwood* (New York: Twayne, 1971), 4.

20. See Malcolm Bradbury, *The Modern British Novel* (London: Penguin, 1994/1993), and Richard Jacobs, "The Novel in the 1930s and 1940s," in *The Penguin History of Literature: The Twentieth Century,* ed. Martin Dodsworth (London: Penguin, 1994).

21. See, for example, Robert Caserio, *The Novel in England, 1900–1950: History and Theory* (New York: Twayne, 1999). Caserio, an American, refers to *Prater Violet* as "post-modern."

22. Isherwood read and was a fan of Salinger, which suggests that the influence might have been conscious or even intended.

23. This essay was reprinted in Bradbury's *No, Not Bloomsbury* (New York: Columbia University Press, 1988).

24. Bradbury was one of Britain's most distinguished Americanists. See his *Modern American Novel* (New York: Viking, 1993) and "The American Risorgimento," in *Contemporary American Fiction,* ed. Malcolm Bradbury and Sigmund Ro (London: Edward Arnold, 1987), neither of which mentions Isherwood in the context of American writing.

25. Asked in 1971 by Len Webster what he thought he would be remembered for, Isherwood replied, "Oh, that old Berlin stuff, I suppose. It's always the way" (*Conversations with Christopher Isherwood,* 71).

26. Randall Stevenson, *The British Novel since the Thirties: An Introduction* (Athens: University of Georgia Press, 1986), 41. Caserio is an exception among American critics in that his study of Isherwood's writing ends with 1950.

27. Frederick R. Karl, *American Fictions, 1940–1980* (New York: Harper and Row, 1983), xiii.

28. Such studies include Robert F. Kiernan, *American Writing since 1945: A Critical Survey* (New York: Frederick Ungar, 1983); Karl, *American Fictions*; and Marcus Cunliffe, ed., *American Literature since 1900* (New York: Peter Bedrick Books, 1987), the ninth volume in the series that became *The Penguin History of Literature.*

29. Morris Dickstein, *Leopards in the Temple: The Transformation of American Fiction, 1945–1970* (Cambridge: Harvard University Press, 2002), xi. Parts of this book were previously published in *The Cambridge History of American Literature, Volume 7, 1940–1990,* ed. Sacvan Bercovitch (Cambridge: Cambridge University Press, 1999).

30. Dickstein's examination of James Baldwin places him squarely in the East Coast, African American, and Jewish American traditions, aligning him with Richard Wright, Ralph Ellison, and Norman Mailer rather than Vidal, Williams, or Capote.

31. Isherwood had met Vidal and Bowles previously in Europe.

32. The comparison is made offhandedly in a review of the reissue of the film *Breakfast at Tiffany's,* by Philip French in the *Guardian* (February 18, 2001), http://film.guardian.co.uk.

33. Claude J. Summers, *Gay Fictions* (New York: Continuum, 1990); David Bergman, *Gaiety Transfigured: Gay Self-Representation in American Literature* (Madison: University of Wisconsin Press, 1991); Gregory Woods, *A History of Gay Literature: The Male Tradition* (New Haven: Yale University Press, 1998); and Reed Woodhouse, *Unlimited Embrace: A Canon of Gay Fiction, 1945–1995* (Amherst: University of Massachusetts Press, 1998).

34. Woods is not alone in finding this lack troubling in the novel; see Garnes, "*A Single Man,*" 199. Claude Summers stresses that the need for community is paramount and is seen through its absence.

35. "Isherwood's titles increasingly show his commitment to people—*Christopher and His Kind, My Guru and His Disciple*—rather than to place. In some ways *Mr Norris Changes Trains* suggests the mobility of the

gay man, and it is important that the book starts off as they are crossing a border" (Bergman, personal correspondence to the editor, December 10, 2002).

36. David Bergman, *The Violet Hour: The Violet Quill and the Making of Gay Culture* (New York: Columbia University Press, 2004).

37. David Bergman, "Isherwood and the Violet Quill," in *The Isherwood Century,* 203.

38. Edmund White, "Tale of Two Kitties" (review of Parker), *TLS* (London), June 4, 2004.

39. *Los Angeles Times,* January 8, 1986; reprinted in *The Wishing Tree: Christopher Isherwood on Mystical Religion,* ed. Robert Adjemian (San Francisco: Harper and Row, 1987).

40. Gore Vidal, Preface to *Where Joy Resides: A Christopher Isherwood Reader,* ed. Don Bachardy and James P. White (New York: Farrar, Straus and Giroux, 1989; reprinted, Minneapolis: University of Minnesota Press, 2003), ix.

41. Lisa Colletta, "Exile in Paradise: Christopher Isherwood in Los Angeles," "Isherwood in America" panel, American Literature Association convention, Long Beach, California, June 1, 2002.

42. The first edition of Lionel Rolfe's *Literary L.A.* (San Francisco: Chronicle Books, 1981), for example, features Huxley on the cover and mentions Mann, Lowry, Upton Sinclair, Robinson Jeffers, Theodore Dreiser, Henry Miller, and Jack London, among others. Isherwood is discussed in relation to Huxley in this edition, but he is left out of a later edition (*In Search of Literary L.A.* [Los Angeles: California Classics Books, 1991]), which still discusses Huxley but puts Charles Bukowski on the cover.

43. William Alexander McClung, *Landscapes of Desire: Anglo Mythologies of Los Angeles* (Berkeley and Los Angeles: University of California Press, 2000).

44. The superficiality of McClung's reading of this passage is illustrated by his description of Stephen: "As it happens, the narrator of *The World in the Evening* is, in his own words, 'floundering stupidly in the mud of my own jealous misery'; he is also scathing about homosexuals, using language like 'pansy bastard.' Perhaps he does not speak for the author" (60). I think not.

45. "The Shore" was originally titled "California Story." Both "Los Angeles" and "The Shore" are reprinted in *Exhumations* (New York: Simon and Schuster, 1966).

46. There is an echo of this idea in an anecdote Peter Bogdanovich

tells about Orson Welles. Welles said, "The terrible thing about L.A. . . . is that you sit down, you're twenty-five, and when you get up you're sixty-two" (quoted in Paul Vangelisti, *L.A. Exiles: A Guide to Los Angeles Writing, 1932–1998* [New York: Marsilio Publishers, 1999], 17). Vangelisti's book is a collection of writings about Los Angeles by some of these "exiles," and it includes passages from *A Single Man.*

47. *Conversations with Christopher Isherwood,* 32.

48. Vangelisti, *L.A. Exiles,* 13.

49. *Conversations with Christopher Isherwood,* 22–23, 59.

Part I. A Writer and His World

1. These lectures by Auden have been reconstructed by Arthur Kirsch in *W. H. Auden: Lectures on Shakespeare* (Princeton: Princeton University Press, 2001).

2. Wickes, "An Interview with Christopher Isherwood," 36–37.

3. Carola Kaplan, "The Wandering Stopped: An Interview with Christopher Isherwood," in *The Isherwood Century,* 271.

Influences

1. The trial of Charles I is dramatically told in C. V. Wedgwood, *A Coffin for King Charles: The Trial and Execution of Charles I* (New York: Macmillan, 1964). Isherwood's depiction of Bradshaw's conduct of the trial is substantiated by Wedgwood, with, perhaps, more sympathy from the historian than the descendant. Isherwood may have relied on his mother's reconstruction of the family history for the lectures, but he used Wedgwood when writing of Bradshaw in *Kathleen and Frank* (see chapter 13).

2. William Penn wrote in his Preface to the original edition of Fox's journal (1694): "And through the tender and singular indulgence of Judge Bradshaw and Judge Fell . . . the priests were never able to gain the point they laboured for, which was to have proceeded to blood, and, if possible, Herod-like, by a cruel exercise of the civil power, to have cut them off and rooted them out of the country" (George Fox, *The Journal of George Fox,* ed. Norman Penney [New York: E. P. Dutton, 1924], xvii). Isherwood owned a 1944 reprint of the Penney edition of the journals, with an Introduction by Rufus Jones. He wrote an Introduction to the journals in 1947, in which he discusses Fox as a mystic in terms that he also uses when writing about Vedanta: "God is precisely this awareness

that we are not merely ourselves, that our life has a larger reference and a larger responsibility" ("The Journal of George Fox: Introduction," Huntington Library Catalogue No. CI 1073, 3).

3. John Ruskin, *Fors Clavigera* (Letter 5): "There was a rocky valley between Buxton and Bakewell, once upon a time, divine as the Vale of Tempe; you might have seen the Gods there morning and evening—Apollo and all the sweet Muses of the light—walking in fair process on the lawns of it, and to and fro among the pinnacles of its crags. You cared neither for Gods nor grass, but for cash . . . The valley is gone, and the Gods with it; and now, every fool in Buxton can be at Bakewell in half an hour, and every fool in Bakewell at Buxton; which you think a lucrative process of exchange—you Fools Everywhere." Quoted in Isherwood's unpublished Commonplace Book, 123.

4. Isherwood kept in his personal library in Santa Monica a copy of *The Roly-Poly Pudding* from 1908 (London: Frederick Warne and Company). The book had been given to him on his sixth birthday with an inscription: "Christopher from Arthur Forbes / August 26, 1910."

5. The story of Frank Bradshaw Isherwood (1869–1915) is told in *Kathleen and Frank.*

6. Shakespeare, *Timon of Athens,* 3.6.93–99.

7. D. H. Lawrence, "Innocent England," in *Complete Poems* (New York: Penguin, 1993), 579.

8. Leo Tolstoy, "My Confession," in *A Confession, the Gospel in Brief, and What I Believe,* trans. Aylmer Maude (London: Oxford University Press, 1940), 12–13.

9. E. M. Forster, "What I Believe," in *Two Cheers for Democracy,* Abinger Edition (London: Edward Arnold, 1972), 66.

10. Tallulah Bankhead, *Tallulah: My Autobiography* (New York: Harper and Brothers, 1952), 315. Isherwood was fond of this anecdote, which he first recorded in his diary in 1951 after being told of Bankhead using the line in a different context (*Diaries* I: 436). Bankhead's text reads: "Estelle's eyebrows shot up as she turned to the errant ogress: 'Look here! We're no more "they" than you.'"

Why Write at All?

1. Stephen Spender, *World within World* (New York: Harcourt, Brace, 1951).

2. Edward Upward, coauthor with Isherwood of *The Mortmere*

Stories (London: Enitharmon Press, 1994). He eventually published a trilogy of novels called *The Spiral Ascent,* incorporating *In the Thirties* (1962), *The Rotten Elements* (1969), and *No Home but the Struggle* (1977).

3. Written by André Gide in 1926 and translated as *The Counterfeiters.*

4. Lionel Trilling, *E. M. Forster* (Norfolk, Conn.: New Directions, 1943).

5. E. M. Forster, *The Longest Journey* (1907). The character is Gerald.

6. See Christopher Isherwood, *Lions and Shadows* (London: Hogarth Press, 1938), 173–74.

7. Isherwood was working on *Down There on a Visit,* published in 1962.

8. W. Somerset Maugham, "The Kite," in *Quartet* (1948). The film, directed by Arthur Crabtree, was one of four short films released as *Quartet* in 1949.

9. Isherwood describes this experience in his South American travel diary, *The Condor and the Cows* (1949).

10. This is one of Isherwood's favorite Latin phrases. It roughly translates to "under the eye of the eternal" or "from the point of view of the eternal."

11. Theodora Bosanquet, *Henry James at Work* (London: Hogarth Press, 1924). An annotated edition of this book was published by the University of Michigan Press in 2006.

What Is the Nerve of Interest in the Novel?

1. Henry James, "The New Novel" (1914) in *The Art of Fiction and Other Essays,* ed. Morris Roberts (New York: Oxford University Press, 1948), 189. This essay concerns mostly Arnold Bennett and H. G. Wells but also discusses Joseph Conrad, John Galsworthy, Horace Walpole, and Compton Mackenzie.

2. See Robert Louis Stevenson, *The Lantern Bearers and Other Essays,* ed. Jeremy Treglown (London: Chatto and Windus, 1988), 234. Quoted in Commonplace Book, 81. Don Bachardy and James P. White used this quotation for the epigraph of *Where Joy Resides: A Christopher Isherwood Reader.*

3. Christopher Isherwood, *Ramakrishna and His Disciples* (Los Angeles: Vedanta Press, 1965), 103.

4. Ibid.

5. Isherwood is paraphrasing the Bhagavad Gita. See page 59 of

his translation with Swami Prabhavananda (New York: Penguin, 1972 [1944]).

6. Charles Dickens, *A Tale of Two Cities,* centenary ed. (London: Chapman and Hall, 1911 [1859]), 2–3.

7. Isherwood copied long passages of Proust into his Commonplace Book from the Modern Library's two-volume edition of *Remembrance of Things Past* (New York: Random House, 1934); this quotation is on page 13 of his Commonplace Book, and the second quotation in text is on pages 21–22. While most of Isherwood's books do not contain any notes in his own hand, each volume of Proust has a list of page numbers and brief descriptions of the passages. For example, in the back of volume 1: "62 The face of true goodness. 88 The longing for something to happen. . . . 442 No peace of mind in love." The first passage quoted in the text is from *Within a Budding Grove* (442), and the second is from *Cities of the Plain* (116–17).

What Is the Nerve of Interest in the Novel? (continued)

1. Leo Tolstoy, "The Death of Ivan Ilych," in *Twenty-three Tales,* trans. Aylmer Maude (Oxford: Oxford University Press, 1930). Quoted in Commonplace Book, 99.

2. George Moore (1852–1933), Anglo-Irish novelist and playwright, was influenced by Zola, and his novels dealt with themes that put him at odds with conventional Victorian morals.

3. George Moore, *Sister Teresa* (London: Unwin, 1901), 234–36. Quoted in Commonplace Book, 37–38.

4. Originally published in 1936 as "The Horns of the Bull"; reprinted in *The Fifth Column and the First Forty-Nine Stories* (New York: Charles Scribner's Sons, 1938).

5. *The First Lady Chatterley* was published in 1944; the censored versions of *Lady Chatterley's Lover* were published in the United States and the United Kingdom in 1932. Another version of the novel was published as *John Thomas and Lady Jane* in 1972. "The Blind Man" was published in 1918 and reprinted in *England, My England and Other Stories* (1922 in the United States; 1924 in the United Kingdom).

6. D. H. Lawrence, *St. Mawr and Other Stories* (Cambridge: Cambridge University Press, 1983), 144. Quoted in Commonplace Book, 93.

7. Isherwood saw an essential theatricality in *Moby-Dick.* A handwritten note inserted in his copy of the novel reads: "Moby Dick is something between a play and a novel. Although its accounts of the

whaler's life are accurate and realistic, its story has a larger than life quality which relates it to the Elizabethan stage. It is partly a realistic novel, partly a poetic drama, with something of Shakespeare in it, and something of Goethe's *Faust.* It is more philosophical than Shakespeare, more melodramatic than Goethe."

8. Herman Melville, *Moby-Dick, or The Whale* (New York: Random House [Modern Library], 1930), 820.

A Writer and the Theater

1. In the late 1960s Isherwood with Don Bachardy adapted his novel *A Meeting by the River* and Bernard Shaw's *The Adventures of the Black Girl in Her Search for God* for the stage.

2. See *Kathleen and Frank,* 373.

3. The text of Isherwood's collaborations with Auden, as well as Auden's other theatrical work, can be found in *W. H. Auden and Christopher Isherwood: Plays and Other Dramatic Writing by W. H. Auden, 1928–1938,* ed. Edward Mendelson (Princeton: Princeton University Press, 1988).

4. The archaic name for the Icelandic parliament, now called the Alping.

5. Rupert Doone (1903–1966). The final Group Theatre production was a revival of *The Ascent of F6* in 1939. See Jean Seay Haspel, "W. H. Auden," in William W. Demasters and Katherine E. Kelly, *British Playwrights, 1880–1956: A Research and Production Sourcebook* (Westport, Conn.: Greenwood Press, 1996), 15–24.

6. *The Dog Beneath the Skin* has rarely been revived.

7. This production is noted in Isherwood's diary for April 1939, soon after his arrival in New York (*Diaries* 1: 13).

8. *I Am a Camera* was subsequently made into the musical *Cabaret.*

9. Ole Olsen and Chic Johnson were vaudeville comedians and producers. *Hellzapoppin'* is described in *The Best Plays of 1938–39* as a "resounding hit . . . which the experts found a little on the loud and common side, but which the laugh-starved crowd literally gobbled" (ed. Burns Mantle [New York: Dodd, Mead, and Company, 1940], 407). *Hellzapoppin'* was still running a year later.

10. Isherwood's appreciation for *Waiting for Godot* seems to have developed after reading it. He saw the first London production in January 1956, which he describes in his diary as "Franco-Irish ugliness and stupidity" (*Diaries* 1: 570). He owned a paperback copy of the play (New York: Grove Press, 1954).

11. W. H. Auden and Christopher Isherwood, *The Dog Beneath the Skin, or Where Is Francis?* (London: Faber and Faber, 1935), 13–15.

12. The play, written for Bernhardt, was first performed in 1900, when the actress was fifty-six. She performed the second act in London in 1910 on a bill with acrobats and jugglers at the Coliseum. See Arthur Gold and Robert Fizdale, *The Divine Sarah: A Life of Sarah Bernhardt* (New York: Knopf, 1991), part VIII.

A Writer and the Films

1. *The Connection,* by Jack Gelber, was produced by the Living Theatre in 1959.

2. *Jew Suss,* directed by Lothar Mendes, was produced by the Gaumont British studio the same year Isherwood was working on *The Little Friend.*

3. Isherwood's screenplay is called *The Wayfarer* and was written for producer Edwin Knopf. Two copies of the script, dated October 3, 1955, are in the Huntington Library archive. The palace is described "with a view to dramatic effect rather than historical accuracy": "King Suddhodana sits on a golden throne, under a canopy of obsidian, which is carved to represent a gigantic black cobra, erect to strike, with hood extended" (7).

4. The sequence Isherwood describes is from the middle of his 178-page screenplay, the first draft of which is dated June 10, 1957. Despite his optimism here, the film was never made. Isherwood's screenplay of *Jean-Christophe* is based on the Modern Library edition of the book (trans. Gilbert Cannan [New York: Random House, 1938]), originally published in ten volumes in France between 1904 and 1912. Romain Rolland was widely acclaimed during his lifetime and won the Nobel Prize for Literature in 1915. He was a pacifist during the First World War and left France to live in Switzerland.

A Writer and Religion

1. Oscar Wilde, *A Woman of No Importance* (1903), in *The Importance of Being Earnest and Other Plays* (Oxford: Oxford University Press, 1995), 135.

2. This passage is marked in Isherwood's copy of *The Brothers Karamazov,* trans. Constance Garnett (New York: Random House [The Modern Library], 1929), 311.

3. Leo Tolstoy, *Father Sergius and Other Stories* (New York: Dodd, Mead, and Company, 1912).

A Last Lecture

1. Douwe Stuurman is identified in *Diaries* (1: 855–56) as the professor at Santa Barbara through whom Isherwood's appointment was channeled in May 1960. The chancellor was at first opposed, then relented.

2. In *A Single Man,* Isherwood has George give a similar message to his student Kenny: "'You asked me about experience. So I told you. Experience isn't any *use.* And yet, in quite another way, it *might* be. . . . You want me to tell you *what I know*—Oh, Kenneth, Kenneth, believe me—there's nothing I'd rather do! I want *like hell* to tell you. But I can't. I quite literally can't. Because, don't you see, *what I know is what I am*? And I can't tell you that,' says George, as he sums up the dilemma for teachers and students as well as gurus and disciples" (148–49).

3. The issue of loyalty oaths was an important one at California universities and would still have been fresh in the minds of any faculty in Isherwood's audience. The Regents of the University of California required its employees to sign an oath, beginning in 1949, which was vociferously opposed by the faculty. The controversy was integrally related to other anticommunist practices in the 1950s, and it raged for three years, providing some of the background for the Free Speech Movement of 1964. "The issues which constituted the conflict remain essentially unresolved and promise . . . to erupt again into public debate," wrote David P. Gardner in 1967 (*The California Oath Controversy* [Berkeley and Los Angeles: University of California Press, 1967], xviii–xix).

4. Norman Douglas (1868–1952), *Looking Back* (London: Chatto and Windus, 1933), 351. This quotation is from Commonplace Book, 128.

5. This line does not appear in many translations of *Tao Te Ching,* including the edition in Isherwood's library at the time of his death, Witter Bynner, trans., *The Way of Life according to Laotzu: An American Version* (New York: John Day Company, 1944). This quotation is very close to Stan Rosenthal's translation: "heaven arms with compassion those / whom it would not see destroyed" (http://www.clas.ufl.edu/users/gthursby/taoism/ttcstran3.htm; accessed December 30, 2002).

All the Conspirators, The Memorial

1. Isherwood refers here to his practice of giving characters in his novels his own name, which he stopped after *Down There on a Visit* (1962) but adopted again in his later memoirs, *Kathleen and Frank* (1971) and *Christopher and His Kind* (1976).

2. British writers from the mid- and late 1950s usually considered part

of the group called Angry Young Men include John Osborne (1929–1994), Kingsley Amis (1922–1995), and Alan Sillitoe (born 1928).

3. This passage is from the opening of chapter 2.

4. This poem is "Blighters" from Siegfried Sassoon, *The Old Huntsman and Other Poems* (London: E. P. Dutton, 1918).

5. Eugen Bleuler (1857–1939), a Swiss psychiatrist who introduced the term *schizophrenia,* was an early follower of Freud and believer in the unconscious. Auden may have read Bleuler's *Textbook of Psychiatry* (1916) [trans. Abraham Arden Brill (London: Macmillan, 1924), 531]. Bleuler was a mentor to Carl Jung and Hermann Rorschach, among others.

6. This verse is the first of the "Shorts" presented in W. H. Auden, *Collected Shorter Poems, 1927–1957* (New York: Random House, 1966), 42, which is dedicated to Christopher Isherwood and Chester Kallman.

The Berlin Stories

1. Isherwood refers to the novel here by its American title. The British title was *Mr Norris Changes Trains.*

2. "Horst Wessel Lied" was the official song of the Nazi Party and became one of two songs used as a national anthem in Germany when the Nazis came to power.

3. Isherwood's attempt to collaborate with Auden to adapt the Berlin material for a musical came to nothing. The musical *Cabaret,* by John Kander and Fred Ebb, debuted on Broadway in 1966.

4. Brecht's play *Mahagonny* was performed in Berlin in July 1927. Brecht and Weill collaborated on the opera *Aufsteig und Fall der Stadt Mahagonny,* which was published in 1929 and performed in March 1930. It was translated as *Rise and Fall of the City of Mahagonny* by Guy Stern (1959) and by Auden and Chester Kallman (1976).

The Dog Beneath the Skin, The Ascent of F6, On the Frontier

1. Peter Martin Lampel (1894–1965) was known as a socially engaged writer. He was arrested by the Nazis in 1936 and later emigrated to Switzerland, Australia, and the United States. He returned to West Germany in 1949 and died in Hamburg. *The Revolt in the Reformatory* was made into a film in 1929 by director Georg Asagaroff (www.cinegraph.de; accessed January 7, 2003).

2. The first performance of *Die Dreigroschenoper* (in English, *The Threepenny Opera*) was in August 1928 in Berlin, with book and lyrics by Brecht and music by Weill. Brecht also published the story as a novel,

Dreigroschenroman (1934), which was translated by Desmond Vesey (with verses translated by Isherwood) as *A Penny for the Poor* (1937). See *Kathleen and Christopher* for a sample of Isherwood's verse translation (89–90).

3. Much of Isherwood's work with Auden is described in *Christopher and His Kind,* chapters 11–12, 14, and 16.

4. Edward Whymper (1840–1911), English artist and mountaineer, was the first to attain the summit of the Matterhorn, in 1865. Several of his party plunged to their deaths on the descent.

5. Isherwood was working on his final novel, *A Meeting by the River.*

6. This was recorded on October 5, 1962, and broadcast on November 7, 1962 (and repeated on March 22, 1964). KPFK is an affiliate of the Pacifica Radio Network, and the audiotape of the play is in the Pacifica Archive.

Prater Violet

1. Monroe K. Spears, *The Poetry of W. H. Auden: The Disenchanted Island* (New York: Oxford University Press, 1963), 102.

2. The stories are "I Am Waiting" (1939) and "Take It or Leave It" (1942); both are reprinted in *Exhumations.*

3. Isherwood's work with Prabhavananda includes the Bhagavad Gita (1944) and *How to Know God* (1953).

4. Isherwood shared the writing credit for the film with Margaret Kennedy and two others. Berthold Viertel was born in 1885 and died in 1953.

5. *The Constant Nymph* was filmed three times: 1928 and 1934 in the U.K., and 1943 in the United States. *Escape Me Never* was filmed in 1935 with Elizabeth Bergner and in 1946 with Ida Lupino.

6. See *Christopher and His Kind,* 149–50ff.

7. Michelangelo Antonioni (1912–2007), Italian film director. Isherwood was impressed by *La Notte* (1961), which influenced the writing of *A Single Man.*

8. The novel he was writing became *A Meeting by the River* (1967).

The World in the Evening

1. The American Friends Service Committee is the social agency of the American Society of Friends (the Quakers). The hostel was known as the Cooperative College Workshop.

2. Josef Luitpold Stern is described in *Diaries* (1: 192); this remark can be found there (1: 229).

3. Norma Shearer later thanked Isherwood for the honor of using her pool house in his novel (see *Diaries* 1: 877).

4. John Donne, First Song in *The Progress of the Soule,* I: 5.

5. The early publication was "The World in the Evening," *New World Writing* (New York: New American Library, 1952), 9–18.

6. This review of *The World in the Evening* was published in *The New Statesman and Nation* 47 (June 19, 1954): 803.

Down There on a Visit

1. The speech is Caliban's: "Be not afeard. The isle is full of noises, / Sounds, and sweet airs, that give delight and hurt not" (*The Tempest,* 3.2.138–39).

2. Calder Willingham (1922–1995) turned *End As a Man* into a successful and controversial stage play (1953) and film, called *The Strange One* (1954). He wrote the screenplay for *The Graduate* (1967), with Buck Henry, and *Little Big Man* (1970).

3. The character of Waldemar is described by Isherwood as "a mere second edition of Otto Nowack" (*Christopher and His Kind,* 138). The story of his "betrayal" in England is clearly based on Isherwood's attempt to bring his lover, Heinz Neddermeyer, to London and on Heinz's expulsion from England (ibid., 159–62).

4. The length of this lecture and its sudden ending suggest that pages are missing from the archive.

Index

. . . .

Christopher Isherwood (1904–1986) is a major figure in twentieth-century fiction and the gay rights movement.

James J. Berg lives in Palm Springs, California, and is dean of social sciences and arts at the College of the Desert. He is editor, with Chris Freeman, of *The Isherwood Century: Essays on the Life and Work of Christopher Isherwood* (winner of a Lambda Literary Award for gay studies) and *Conversations with Christopher Isherwood.* He holds a PhD from the University of Minnesota.

Claude J. Summers is William E. Stirton Professor Emeritus in the Humanities and professor emeritus of English at the University of Michigan, Dearborn. He has published widely on twentieth-century English literature and is general editor of www.glbtq.com, an encyclopedia of gay, lesbian, bisexual, transgender, and queer culture.